TERESA WOODS-CZISCH M. A.
UNIVERSITÄTS-LEKTORIN
IM WINKELRAIN 16
72076 TÜBINGEN

PENGUIN BOOKS

A Woman's Life

Anne Else is a freelance writer, editor, reviewer and lecturer; she is currently working on a book about adoption in New Zealand.

Heather Roberts, a policy adviser in the Department of Social Welfare, is the author of a book on New Zealand women novelists from 1864 to 1987.

A Woman's Life

Writing by women
about female experience
in New Zealand

Edited by
Anne Else and Heather Roberts

PENGUIN BOOKS

PENGUIN BOOKS

Penguin Books (NZ) Ltd, 182–190 Wairau Road, Auckland 10, New Zealand
Penguin Books Ltd, 27 Wrights Lane, London W8 5TZ, England
Viking Penguin Inc., 40 West 23rd Street, New York, New York 10010, USA
Penguin Books Australia Ltd, 487 Maroondah Highway, Ringwood, Australia 3134
Penguin Books Canada Ltd, 2801 John Street, Markham, Ontario, Canada L3R 1B4

Penguin Books Ltd, Registered Offices: Harmondsworth, Middlesex, England

First published 1989
1 3 5 7 9 10 8 6 4 2
Copyright © Introduction and this selection, Anne Else
and Heather Roberts, 1989
All rights reserved

Designed by Richard King
Typeset in Goudy by Typocrafters Ltd, Auckland
Printed in Hong Kong

Except in the United States of America, this book is sold subject to the condition that it shall not, by way of trade or otherwise, be lent, re-sold, hired out or otherwise circulated without the publisher's prior consent in any form of binding or cover other than that in which it is published and without a similar condition including this condition being imposed on the subsequent purchaser.

CONTENTS

Introduction	9
Acknowledgements	13
PATRICIA GRACE: Taranga	15
from *Wahine Toa* (1984)	

Childhood

JANET FRAME: The Reservoir	19
(1963)	
JOY COWLEY: The Woman Next Door	30
(1985)	
ROBIN HYDE: The glory hole	33
from *The Godwits Fly* (1938)	
YVONNE DU FRESNE: Coronation Day	38
(1985)	
KATHERINE MANSFIELD: New Dresses	43
(1911)	

Adolescence

JEAN DEVANNY: Such private things	55
from *Dawn Beloved* (1928)	
ROBIN HYDE: Little ease	59
from *The Godwits Fly* (1938)	
SYLVIA ASHTON-WARNER: On the outside looking in	67
from *I Passed This Way* (1979)	
MARY FINDLAY: Show your father you love him	74
from *Tooth and Nail* (1974)	

Sexual experience

ANONYMOUS: Delicate blossoms	85
from *Women in Wartime* (1986)	
ALISON GRAY: Leave me alone	90
from *Stepping Out* (1987)	
FIONA KIDMAN: Is this what sex is?	98
from *A Breed of Women* (1979)	
SUE McCAULEY: While it lasts	107
from *Other Halves* (1982)	
JANET FRAME: Never been kissed	113
from *The Edge of the Alphabet* (1962)	

LAURIS EDMOND: Some remote region 117
from *High Country Weather* (1984)

Close relationships

PATRICIA GRACE: He shouldn't have let me go 123
from *Mutuwhenua* (1978)

JANE MANDER: I want to see the world 128
from *The Story of a New Zealand River* (1920)

MAKERETI: Hinemoa 136
from *The Old Time Maori* (1938)

EDITH SEARLE GROSSMANN: Husband and wife 140
from *In Revolt* (1893)

GRACE MORTON (as told to Stanley Roche):
A sense of alienation 146
from *Foreigner* (1979)

MARGARET SUTHERLAND: An easy companionship 152
from *The Love Contract* (1976)

YVONNE DU FRESNE: The River 158
(1985)

Motherhood

MARY FINDLAY: Desperate remedies 165
from *Tooth and Nail* (1974)

PATRICIA GRACE: Between Earth and Sky 171
(1980)

ROBIN HYDE: I have this infant 174
from *A Home in This World* (1984)

PATTI BAKER (as told to Joss Shawyer): She hadn't died 179
from *Death by Adoption* (1979)

AMIRIA MANUTAHI STIRLING
(as told to Anne Salmond):
Hoki kino mai ra ki ahau (This is a bad home-coming) 184
from *Amiria, the Life Story of a Maori Woman* (1976)

FIONA KIDMAN: Puff Adder 192
(1986)

Work

'EMILY MORGAN' (SANDRA CONEY): I Wanted Honey 205
(1975)

MARY FINDLAY: An experienced cook-general 209
from *Tooth and Nail* (1974)

PAULINE O'REGAN: Above all, simple and joyous 218
from *A Changing Order* (1986)

COLLEEN BROWN (as told to Sandra Coney):
   A Few Problems Being the Only Girl   225
   (1980)
REBECCA JOHNSTON: Young, Female and Unemployed   229
   (1981)
MARGARET SUTHERLAND: A life's occupation   232
   from *The Fledgling* (1974)
PHYLLIS GANT: Vegetable girls   238
   from *Islands* (1973)
SYLVIA ASHTON-WARNER: The writing road   242
   from *I Passed This Way* (1979)

Old age
DARA McNAUGHT: A Gift of Life   247
   (1979)
JULIA MILLEN: Mother moves in   251
   from *Dilemma of Dementia* (1985)
MATARENA RENETI (as told to Stanley Roche):
   Of Love and Death: Matarena's Story   259
   (1980)

INTRODUCTION

The essential difference lies in the fact not that men describe battles and women the birth of children, but that each sex describes itself... And finally there arises for consideration the very difficult question of the difference between the man's and the woman's view of what constitutes the importance of any subject. From this spring not only marked differences of plot and incident, but infinite differences in selection, method and style.

— Virginia Woolf[1]

Compiling an anthology cannot be an objective or neutral process. The pattern imposed on texts has as much to do with the anthologist's experience of life and literature as it does with the texts themselves. Our pattern here is, inevitably, grounded in our past and present experience: not only as Pakeha, heterosexual, middle-class, university-educated women in post-war New Zealand, but also as workers (paid and unpaid), daughters, mothers, sisters, friends and feminists.

This anthology began, as so much feminist scholarship begins, as an act of reconstruction, discovery and rediscovery, of texts which have been submerged and forgotten, or have survived largely isolated from any meaningful context. This does not mean, however, that we set out to find 'feminist writing'. Women's writing is not of itself feminist, though some of the authors here would have applied that term to their own work. Our reading of all these texts is a feminist one, but of course every text is open to many interpretations.

New Zealand women have had little assured access to local texts in which, as Virginia Woolf writes, their own sex 'describes itself'. For all that we may have the impression of a wealth of such literature, when we look closely we find only a small number of readily available books. The priorities of those who act as keepers of the canon of New Zealand fiction have meant, for example, that John Mulgan's *Man Alone* has been in print almost continuously since it was published in 1939, and John A. Lee's *Children of the Poor* was reprinted in 1949, 1963 and 1973; but Robin Hyde's *The Godwits Fly* (1938) was not reprinted until 1973, and the rest of her fiction not until the 1980s.

Our generation was thus trained to read New Zealand literary texts which were substantially alien to women's experience. The intense contemporary interest in old and new writing by women is in large part the outcome of that narrow focus. What readers have looked for, and begun to find, is the 'different view' described by Woolf. This anthology is designed to foreground that view.

All the pieces we have chosen fall within the realistic, 'story-telling' tradition of writing that we believe dominates New Zealand literature, both fiction and non-fiction. Yet they are not presented here — nor were they in the original — as 'real' or 'true' narratives. They were not selected as the 'best' accounts of girlhood, motherhood, and so on; and they are not made out to be representative of most women's lives. As Janet Frame points out in her autobiography, 'there are no "most women" '.[2]

Instead, we have put together particular explorations and interpretations of women's experience, at different ages and in various situations. We have tried to focus on writing which deals with what are generally considered to be the 'ordinary' aspects of life for women, bringing that background forward.

We wanted stories of rural and urban, middle and working class, Maori and Pakeha women, from the nineteenth century to 1987. There are too few voices of Maori women, despite the inclusion of two pieces based on legend. Overtly lesbian voices are conspicuously lacking. Although we included interviews in narrative form, we drew only on work which had already appeared in print. That in itself begs questions about what is and is not acceptable to editors and publishers at every level as an interpretation of women's experience.

To some readers there will be obvious and perhaps irritating omissions. Two deserve explanation. From Katherine Mansfield's work, we chose an early, less familiar story of a rebellious girl. Secondly, we decided not to try to select anything from Janet Frame's magnificent autobiographical trilogy, because we felt that to do so would have done a disservice to what is the most complete account in New Zealand literature of one woman's life.

We had difficulty deciding what should go into each section; these pieces resisted being neatly categorised, reflecting the interconnected, web-like nature of women's experience. In the end the placing rested on our sense of where the main focus lies; so, for example, the extract from Jane Mander's *The Story of a New Zealand River* is about the adolescent Asia, but it is also about the important close relationship between a mother and daughter.

In some cases we had difficulty finding enough material. We had unexpected trouble, for example, with the section on childhood. Young girls feature far less frequently, even in writing by women, than would be assumed, given that New Zealand literature is supposed to be overburdened with stories of childhood. This may be a reflection of the assumption that female life becomes meaningful and interesting only once young women begin to work out what is generally seen as the most important aspect of their destiny — their relationships with men.

Similarly, writing focusing on old age (when reproduction is over,

INTRODUCTION 11

and relationships with men are assumed to fall away) was hard to find. We could have decided to drop such sections altogether; but an apparent lack of material cannot be taken to mean lack of importance or relevance. Perhaps the language is not yet readily to hand for exploring some forms of experience, or there are too few known precedents; or perhaps there will generally be few accounts of what society prefers to ignore. Accounts of adoption from the birth mother's point of view, for example, have only recently surfaced in print, although thousands of women have had that experience. Silence always has meaning, and for women in particular, what is written can only be understood in the context of what is not.

We see this book mainly as an enjoyable and useful starting place for readers who want to learn, or be reminded, how women writers have interpreted women's lives in New Zealand. As Lillian Robinson notes, 'it is essential to recognise literature that can enhance our understanding of the conditions that define women's lives . . . in order to gain insight into what women experience'.[3] We hope our anthology will be part of this continuing process of recognition, and so will help to increase and sustain the demand for women's work, old and new.

We would like to thank Elaine Linsky, Irihapeti Ramsden and Jenny Phillips for reading our draft selection and telling us what they thought of it. Geoff Walker of Penguin Books was constantly enthusiastic and encouraging about this project, and we very much appreciated that.

Anne Else and Heather Roberts

---

1. Virginia Woolf, review of R. Brimley Johnson's 'The Women Novelists'. *Women and Writing*, The Women's Press, London, 1979, p. 71.
2. Janet Frame, *The Envoy from Mirror City*, Century Hutchinson, Auckland, 1985, p. 121.
3. Lillian Robinson, *Sex, Class and Culture*, Indiana University Press, Bloomington, 1978, p. 252.

ACKNOWLEDGEMENTS

For permission to reproduce the material in this book the following acknowledgement is gratefully made.

Anonymous: extract from *Women in Wartime*, ed. Lauris Edmond and Carolyn Milward, Government Printing Office, 1986. Sylvia Ashton-Warner: extracts from *I Passed This Way*, Knopf, 1979 (republished A. H. & A. W. Reed, 1980; Reed Methuen, 1985). Patti Baker (as told to Joss Shawyer): extract from *Death by Adoption*, Cicada, 1979. Colleen Brown (as told to Sandra Coney): A Few Problems Being the Only Girl, *Broadsheet*, December 1980. Sandra Coney ('Emily Morgan'): I Wanted Honey, *Broadsheet*, June 1975. Joy Cowley: The Woman Next Door, from *Heart Attack and Other Stories*, Hodder & Stoughton, 1985. Jean Devanny: extract from *Dawn Beloved*, Duckworth, 1928. Yvonne du Fresne: Coronation Day and The River, from *The Growing of Astrid Westergaard and Other Stories*, Longman Paul, 1985. Lauris Edmond: extract from *High Country Weather*, Allen & Unwin/Port Nicholson Press, 1984. Mary Findlay: extracts from *Tooth and Nail*, A. H. & A. W. Reed, 1974. Janet Frame: The Reservoir, from *The Reservoir*, Pegasus Press, 1963 (reprinted in *You Are Now Entering the Human Heart*, Victoria University Press, 1983); extract from *The Edge of the Alphabet*, Pegasus Press, 1962. Phyllis Gant: extract from *Islands*, Hodder & Stoughton, 1973. Patricia Grace: Taranga, from *Wahine Toa: Women of Maori Myth*, Collins, 1984; extract from *Mutuwhenua*, Longman Paul, 1978 (republished Penguin Books, 1986); Between Earth and Sky, from *The Dream Sleepers*, Longman Paul, 1980 (republished Penguin Books, 1986). Alison Gray: extract from *Stepping Out*, Allen & Unwin/Port Nicholson Press, 1987. Edith Searle Grossmann: extract from *In Revolt*, Eden, Remington & Co., 1893. Robin Hyde: extracts from *The Godwits Fly*, Hurst & Blackett, 1938 (republished Auckland University Press/Oxford University Press, 1974); extract from *A Home in This World*, Longman Paul, 1984. Rebecca Johnston: Young, Female and Unemployed, *Broadsheet*, July/August 1981. Fiona Kidman: extract from *A Breed of Women*, Harper & Row, 1979 (republished Penguin Books, 1988); Puff Adder, from *New Women's Fiction*, ed. Cathie Dunsford, New Women's Press, 1986. Sue McCauley: extract from *Other Halves*, Hodder & Stoughton, 1982. Dara McNaught: A Gift of Life, *Broadsheet*, September 1979. Makereti: extract from *The Old Time Maori*, Victor Gollancz, 1938 (republished New Women's Press, 1986). Jane Mander: extract from *The Story of a New Zealand River*, John Lane, The Bodley Head, 1920 (republished Robert Hale, 1938, 1960; Whitcombe & Tombs, 1973). Katherine Mansfield: New Dresses (1911), from *Something Childish and Other Stories*, Knopf, 1924 (reprinted in *Undiscovered Country: The New Zealand Stories*, ed. Ian A. Gordon, Longman

Paul, 1974). Julia Millen: extract from *Dilemma of Dementia*, Lansdowne Press, 1985. Grace Morton (as told to Stanley Roche): extract from *Foreigner*, Oxford University Press, 1979. Pauline O'Regan: extract from *A Changing Order*, Allen & Unwin/Port Nicholson Press, 1986. Matarena Reneti (as told to Stanley Roche): Of Love and Death: Matarena's Story, from *The Summer Book*, Vol. 1, Port Nicholson Press, 1980. Amiria Manutahi Stirling (as told to Anne Salmond): extract from *Amiria, The Life Story of a Maori Woman*, A. H. & A. W. Reed, 1976. Margaret Sutherland: extract from *The Love Contract*, Heinemann, 1976; extract from *The Fledgling*, Oxford University Press, 1974.

PATRICIA GRACE

Taranga

I am Taranga. I am both of this world and not of this world, inhabiting the earthly land by night — and by day the land of the manapau trees.

Maui-potiki is my youngest child, the child of my old age. I gave birth to him on the beach, secretly. He was stillborn. Without proper ritual or ceremony, I cut off my topknot of hair, wrapped him in it and put him on the sea to be cared for by the gulls and fishes.

But I knew the power of my hair.

I returned home not fully knowing what would happen, but believing that this child could one day seek me out both in the earthly land and the land of the manapau trees.

And indeed, one day this last-born child came looking for his brothers and me. He knew our names and the circumstances of his birth, so that I recognised him and wept over him.

He was strange, and most magical, and most loving.

He was both human and godly, and one day followed me to the land of the manapau trees where I welcomed him and showed him to his father.

'This is our last-born,' I said. 'He is called Maui-tikitiki-a-Taranga.' And Makea-tutara said to Maui, 'That is a warrior's name. You will do great things for the people of earth.'

'And one day,' I said, 'you will challenge your great ancestress Hine-nui-te-Po so that people will be immortal.'

But later because of a mistake in the tohi ceremony I knew that this final deed could not be accomplished.

I felt much sorrow then. But I also felt great pride in knowing that this child was my own creation, that through my actions he had been given special powers which would be used in attaining great gifts for mankind.

Childhood

Childhood

JANET FRAME
The Reservoir

It was said to be four or five miles along the gully, past orchards and farms, paddocks filled with cattle, sheep, wheat, gorse, and the squatters of the land who were the rabbits eating like modern sculpture into the hills, though how could we know anything of modern sculpture, we knew nothing but the Warrior in the main street with his wreaths of poppies on Anzac Day, the gnomes weeping in the Gardens because the seagulls perched on their green caps and showed no respect, and how important it was for birds, animals and people, especially children, to show respect!

And that is why for so long we obeyed the command of the grownups and never walked as far as the forbidden Reservoir, but were content to return 'tired but happy' (as we wrote in our school compositions), answering the question, Where did you walk today? with a suspicion of blackmail, 'Oh, nearly, nearly to the Reservoir!'

The Reservoir was the end of the world; beyond it, you fell; beyond it were paddocks of thorns, strange cattle, strange farms, legendary people whom we would never know or recognise even if they walked among us on a Friday night downtown when we went to follow the boys and listen to the Salvation Army Band and buy a milk shake in the milk bar and then return home to find that everything was all right and safe, that our Mother had not run away and caught the night train to the North Island, that our Father had not shot himself with worrying over the bills, but had in fact been downtown himself and had bought the usual Friday night treat, a bag of liquorice allsorts and a bag of chocolate roughs, from Woolworths.

The Reservoir haunted our lives. We never knew one until we came to this town; we had used pump water. But here, in our new house, the water ran from the taps as soon as we turned them on, and if we were careless and left them on, our Father would shout, as if the affair were his personal concern, 'Do you want the Reservoir to run dry?'

That frightened us. What should we do if the Reservoir ran dry? Would we die of thirst like Burke and Wills in the desert?

'The Reservoir,' our Mother said, 'gives pure water, water safe to drink without boiling it.'

The water was in a different class, then, from the creek which flowed through the gully; yet the creek had its source in the Reservoir. Why had it not received the pampering attention of officialdom which

19

strained weed and earth, cockabullies and trout and eels, from our tap water? Surely the Reservoir was not entirely pure?

'Oh no,' they said, when we inquired. We learned that the water from the Reservoir had been 'treated'. We supposed this to mean that during the night men in light-blue uniforms with sacks over their shoulders crept beyond the circle of pine trees which enclosed the Reservoir, and emptied the contents of the sacks into the water, to dissolve dead bodies and prevent the decay of teeth.

Then, at times, there would be news in the paper, discussed by my Mother with the neighbours over the back fence. Children had been drowned in the Reservoir.

'No child,' the neighbour would say, 'ought to be allowed near the Reservoir.'

'I tell mine to keep strictly away,' my Mother would reply.

And for so long we obeyed our Mother's command, on our favourite walks along the gully simply following the untreated cast-off creek which we loved and which flowed day and night in our heads in all its detail — the wild sweet peas, boiled-lolly pink, and the mint growing along the banks; the exact spot in the water where the latest dead sheep could be found, and the stink of its bloated flesh and floating wool, an allowable earthy stink which we accepted with pleasant revulsion and which did not prompt the 'inky-pinky I smell Stinkie' rhyme which referred to offensive human beings only. We knew where the water was shallow and could be paddled in, where forts could be made from the rocks; we knew the frightening deep places where the eels lurked and the weeds were tangled in gruesome shapes; we knew the jumping places, the mossy stones with their dangers, limitations, and advantages; the sparkling places where the sun trickled beside the water, upon the stones; the bogs made by roaming cattle, trapping some of them to death; their gaunt telltale bones; the little valleys with their new growth of lush grass where the creek had 'changed its course', and no longer flowed.

'The creek has changed its course,' our Mother would say, in a tone which implied terror and a sense of strangeness, as if a tragedy had been enacted.

We knew the moods of the creek, its levels of low-flow, half-high-flow, high-flow which all seemed to relate to interference at its source — the Reservoir. If one morning the water turned the colour of clay and crowds of bubbles were passengers on every suddenly swift wave hurrying by, we would look at one another and remark with the fatality and reverence which attends a visitation or prophecy.

'The creek's going on high-flow. They must be doing something at the Reservoir.'

By afternoon the creek would be on high-flow, turbulent, muddy, unable to be jumped across or paddled in or fished in, concealing beneath a swelling fluid darkness whatever evil which 'they', the authorities, had decided to purge so swiftly and secretly from the Reservoir.

For so long, then, we obeyed our parents, and never walked as far as the Reservoir. Other things concerned us, other curiosities, fears, challenges. The school year ended. I got a prize, a large yellow book the colour of cat's mess. Inside it were editions of newspapers, *The Worms' Weekly*, supposedly written by worms, snails, spiders. For the first part of the holidays we spent the time sitting in the long grass of our front lawn nibbling the stalks of shamrock and reading insect newspapers and relating their items to the lives of those living on our front lawn down among the summer-dry roots of the couch, tinker-tailor, daisy, dandelion, shamrock, clover, and ordinary 'grass'. High summer came. The blowsy old red roses shed their petals to the regretful refrain uttered by our Mother year after year at the same time, 'I should have made potpourri, I have a wonderful recipe for potpourri in Dr Chase's Book.'

Our Mother never made the potpourri. She merely quarrelled with our Father over how to pronounce it.

The days became unbearably long and hot. Our Christmas presents were broken or too boring to care about. Celluloid dolls had loose arms and legs and rifts in their bright pink bodies; the invisible ink had poured itself out in secret messages; diaries frustrating in their smallness (two lines to a day) had been filled in for the whole of the coming year . . . Days at the beach were tedious, with no room in the bathing sheds so that we were forced to undress in the common room downstairs with its floor patched with wet and trailed with footmarks and sand and its tiny barred window (which made me believe that I was living in the French Revolution).

Rumours circled the burning world. The sea was drying up, soon you could paddle or walk to Australia. Sharks had been seen swimming inside the breakwater; one shark attacked a little boy and bit off his you-know-what.

We swam. We wore bathing togs all day. We gave up cowboys and ranches; and baseball and sledding; and 'those games' where we mimicked grownup life, loving and divorcing each other, kissing and slapping, taking secret paramours when our husband was working out of town. Everything exhausted us. Cracks appeared in the earth; the grass was bled yellow; the ground was littered with beetle shells and snail shells; flies came in from the unofficial rubbish-dump at the back of the house; the twisting flypapers hung from the ceiling; a frantic buzzing filled the room as the flypapers became crowded. Even the cat put out her tiny tongue, panting in the heat.

We realised, and were glad, that school would soon reopen. What was school like? It seemed so long ago, it seemed as if we had never been to school, surely we had forgotten everything we had learned, how frightening, thrilling and strange it would all seem! Where would we go on the first day, who would teach us, what were the names on the new books?

Who would sit beside us, who would be our best friend?

The earth crackled in early-autumn haze and still the February sun dried the world; even at night the rusty sheet of roofing-iron outside by the cellar stayed warm, but with rows of sweat-marks on it; the days were still long, with night face to face with morning and almost nothing in-between but a snatch of turning sleep with the blankets on the floor and the windows wide open to moths with their bulging lamplit eyes moving through the dark and their grandfather bodies knocking, knocking upon the walls.

Day after day the sun still waited to pounce. We were tired, our skin itched, our sunburn had peeled and peeled again, the skin on our feet was hard, there was dust in our hair, our bodies clung with the salt of sea-bathing and sweat, the towels were harsh with salt.

School soon, we said again, and were glad; for lessons gave shade to rooms and corridors; cloakrooms were cold and sunless. Then, swiftly, suddenly, disease came to the town. Infantile Paralysis. Black headlines in the paper, listing the number of cases, the number of deaths. Children everywhere, out in the country, up north, down south, two streets away.

The schools did not reopen. Our lessons came by post, in smudged print on rough white paper; they seemed makeshift and false, they inspired distrust, they could not compete with the lure of the sun still shining, swelling, the world would go up in cinders, the days were too long, there was nothing to do; the lessons were dull; in the front room with the navy-blue blind half down the window and the tiny splits of light showing through, and the lesson papers sometimes covered with unexplained blots of ink as if the machine which had printed them had broken down or rebelled, the lessons were even more dull.

Ancient Egypt and the flooding of the Nile!

The Nile, when we possessed a creek of our own with individual flooding!

'Well let's go along the gully, along by the creek,' we would say, tired with all these.

Then one day when our restlessness was at its height, when the flies buzzed like bees in the flypapers, and the warped wood of the house cracked its knuckles out of boredom, the need for something to do in the heat, we found once again the only solution to our unrest.

Someone said, 'What's the creek on?'

'Half-high flow.'

'Good.'

So we set out, in our bathing suits, and carrying switches of willow.

'Keep your sun hats on!' our mother called.
All right. We knew. Sunstroke when the sun clipped you over the back of the head, striking you flat on the ground. Sunstroke. Lightning. Even tidal waves were threatening us on this southern coast. The world was full of alarm.

'And don't go as far as the Reservoir!'

We dismissed the warning. There was enough to occupy us along the gully without our visiting the Reservoir. First, the couples. We liked to find a courting couple and follow them and when, as we knew they must do because they were tired or for other reasons, they found a place in the grass and lay down together, we liked to make jokes about them, amongst ourselves. 'Just wait for him to kiss her,' we would say. 'Watch. There. A beaut. Smack.'

Often we giggled and lingered even after the couple had observed us. We were waiting for them to do it. Every man and woman did it, we knew that for a fact. We speculated about technical details. Would he wear a frenchie? If he didn't wear a frenchie then she would start having a baby and be forced to get rid of it by drinking gin. Frenchies, by the way, were for sale in Woolworths. Some said they were fingerstalls, but we knew they were frenchies and sometimes we would go downtown and into Woolworths just to look at the frenchies for sale. We hung around the counter, sniggering. Sometimes we nearly died laughing, it was so funny.

After we tired of spying on the couples we would shout after them as we went our way.

> Pound, shillings and pence,
> a man fell over the fence,
> he fell on a lady,
> and squashed out a baby,
> pound, shillings and pence!

Sometimes a slight fear struck us — what if a man fell on us like that and squashed out a chain of babies?

Our other pastime along the gully was robbing the orchards, but this summer day the apples were small green hard and hidden by leaves. There were no couples either. We had the gully to ourselves. We followed the creek, whacking our sticks, gossiping and singing, but we stopped, immediately silent, when someone — sister or brother — said, 'Let's go to the Reservoir!'

A feeling of dread seized us. We knew, as surely as we knew our names and our address Thirty-three Stour Street Ohau Otago South Island New Zealand Southern Hemisphere The World, that we would some day visit the Reservoir, but the time seemed almost as far away as leaving school, getting a job, marrying.

And then there was the agony of deciding the right time — how did one decide these things?

'We've been told not to, you know,' one of us said timidly.

That was me. Eating bread and syrup for tea had made my hair red, my skin too, so that I blushed easily, and the grownups guessed if I told a lie.

'It's a long way,' said my little sister.

'Coward!'

But it *was* a long way, and perhaps it would take all day and night, perhaps we would have to sleep there among the pine trees with the owls hooting and the old needle-filled warrens which now reached to the centre of the earth where pools of molten lead bubbled, waiting to seize us if we tripped and then there was the crying sound made by the trees, a sound of speech at its loneliest level where the meaning is felt but never explained, and it goes on and on in a kind of despair, trying to reach a point of understanding.

We knew that pine trees spoke in this way. We were lonely listening to them because we knew we could never help them to say it, whatever they were trying to say, for if the wind who was so close to them could not help them, how could we?

Oh no, we could not spend the night at the Reservoir among the pine trees.

'Billy Whittaker and his gang have been to the Reservoir, Billy Whittaker and the Green Feather gang, one afternoon.'

'Did he say what it was like?'

'No, he never said.'

'He's been in an iron lung.'

That was true. Only a day or two ago our Mother had been reminding us in an ominous voice of the act which roused our envy just as much as our dread, 'Billy Whittaker was in an iron lung two years ago. Infantile Paralysis.'

Some people were lucky. None of us dared to hope that we would ever be surrounded by the glamour of an iron lung; we would have to be content all our lives with paltry flesh lungs.

'Well are we going to the Reservoir or not?'

That was someone trying to sound bossy like our Father, 'Well am I to have salmon sandwiches or not, am I to have lunch at all today or not?'

We struck our sticks in the air. They made a whistling sound. They were supple and young. We had tried to make musical instruments out of them, time after time we hacked at the willow and the elder to make pipes to blow our music, but no sound came but our own voices. And why did two sticks rubbed together not make fire? Why couldn't we ever *make* anything out of the bits of the world lying about us?

An airplane passed in the sky. We craned our necks to read the

writing on the underwing, for we collected airplane numbers.
The plane was gone, in a glint of sun.
'Are we?' someone said.
'If there's an eclipse you can't see at all. The birds stop singing and go to bed.'
'Well are we?'
Certainly we were. We had not quelled all our misgiving, but we set out to follow the creek to the Reservoir.
What is it? I wondered. They said it was a lake. I thought it was a bundle of darkness and great wheels which peeled and sliced you like an apple and drew you toward them with demonic force, in the same way that you were drawn beneath the wheels of a train if you stood too near the edge of the platform. That was the terrible danger when the Limited came rushing in and you had to approach to kiss arriving aunts.

We walked on and on, past wild sweet peas, clumps of cutty grass, horse mushrooms, ragwort, gorse, cabbage trees; and then, at the end of the gully, we came to strange territory, fences we did not know, with the barbed wire tearing at our skin and at our skirts put on over our bathing suits because we felt cold though the sun stayed in the sky.

We passed huge trees that lived with their heads in the sky, with their great arms and joints creaking with age and the burden of being trees, and their mazed and linked roots rubbed bare of earth, like bones with the flesh cleaned from them. There were strange gates to be opened or climbed over, new directions to be argued and plotted, notices which said TRESPASSERS WILL BE PROSECUTED BY ORDER. And there was the remote immovable sun shedding without gentleness its influence of burning upon us and upon the town, looking down from its heavens and considering our Infantile Paralysis epidemic, and the children tired of holidays and wanting to go back to school with the new stiff books with their crackling pages, the scrubbed ruler with the sun rising on one side amidst the twelfths, tenths, millimetres, the new pencils to be sharpened with the pencil shavings flying in long pickets and light-brown curls scalloped with red or blue; the brown school, the bare floors, the clump clump in the corridors on wet days!

We came to a strange paddock, a bull-paddock with its occupant planted deep in the long grass, near the gate, a jersey bull polished like a wardrobe, burnished like copper, heavy beams creaking in the wave and flow of the grass.

'Has it got a ring through its nose? Is it a real bull or a steer?'

Its nose was ringed which meant that its savagery was tamed, or so we thought; it could be tethered and led; even so, it had once been savage and it kept its pride, unlike the steers who pranced and huddled together and ran like water through the paddocks, made no impression, quarried no massive shape against the sky.

The bull stood alone.

Had not Mr Bennet been gored by a bull, his own tame bull, and been rushed to Glenham Hospital for thirty-three stitches? Remembering Mr Bennet we crept cautiously close to the paddock fence, ready to escape.

Someone said, 'Look, it's pawing the ground!'

A bull which pawed the ground was preparing for a charge. We escaped quickly through the fence. Then, plucking up courage, we skirted the bushes on the far side of the paddock, climbed through the fence, and continued our walk to the Reservoir.

We had lost the creek between deep banks. We saw it now before us, and hailed it with more relief than we felt, for in its hidden course through the bull-paddock it had undergone change, it had adopted the shape, depth, mood of foreign water, foaming in a way we did not recognise as belonging to our special creek, giving no hint of its depth. It seemed to flow close to its concealed bed, not wishing any more to communicate with us. We realised with dismay that we had suddenly lost possession of our creek. Who had taken it? Why did it not belong to us any more? We hit our sticks in the air and forgot our dismay. We grew cheerful.

Till someone said that it was getting late, and we reminded one another that during the day the sun doesn't seem to move, it just remains pinned with a drawing pin against the sky, and then, while you are not looking, it suddenly slides down quick as the chopped-off head of a golden eel, into the sea, making everything in the world go dark.

'That's only in the tropics!'

We were not in the tropics. The divisions of the world in the atlas, the different coloured cubicles of latitude and longitude fascinated us.

'The sand freezes in the desert at night. Ladies wear bits of sand . . .'

'grains . . .'

'grains or bits of sand as necklaces, and the camels . . .'

'with necks like snails . . .'

'with horns, do they have horns?'

'Minnie Stocks goes with boys . . .'

'I know who your boy is, I know who your boy is . . .'

> *Waiting by the garden gate,*
> *Waiting by the garden gate . . .*

'We'll never get to the Reservoir!'

'Whose idea was it?'

'I've strained my ankle!'

Someone began to cry. We stopped walking.

'I've strained my ankle!'

There was an argument.
'It's not strained, it's sprained.'
'strained.'
'sprained.'
'All right sprained then. I'll have to wear a bandage, I'll have to walk on crutches . . .'
'I had crutches once. Look. I've got a scar where I fell off my stilts. It's a white scar, like a centipede. It's on my shins.'
'Shins! Isn't it a funny word? Shins. Have you ever been kicked in the shins?'
'shins, funnybone . . .'
'It's humerus . . .'
'knuckles . . .'
'a sprained ankle . . .'
'a strained ankle . . .'
'a whitlow, an ingrown toenail the roots of my hair warts spinal meningitis infantile paralysis . . .'
'Infantile Paralysis, Infantile Paralysis you have to be wheeled in a chair and wear irons on your legs and your knees knock together . . .'
'Once you're in an iron lung you can't get out, they lock it, like a cage . . .'
'You go in the amberlance . . .'
'*ambulance* . . .'
'amberlance . . .'
'ambulance to the hostible . . .'
'the *hospital*, an *ambulance to the hospital* . . .'
'Infantile Paralysis . . .'
'Friar's Balsam! Friar's Balsam!'
'Baxter's Lung Preserver, Baxter's Lung Preserver!'
'Syrup of Figs, California Syrup of Figs!'
'The creek's going on high-flow!'
Yes, there were bubbles on the surface, and the water was turning muddy. Our doubts were dispelled. It was the same old creek, and there, suddenly, just ahead, was a plantation of pine trees, and already the sighing sound of it reached our ears and troubled us. We approached it, staying close to the banks of our newly claimed creek, until once again the creek deserted us, flowing its own private course where we could not follow, and we found ourselves among the pine trees, a narrow strip of them, and beyond lay a vast surface of sparkling water, dazzling our eyes, its centre chopped by tiny grey waves. Not a lake, nor a river, nor a sea.
'The Reservoir!'
The damp smell of the pine needles caught in our breath. There were no birds, only the constant sighing of the trees. We could see the water clearly now; it lay, except for the waves beyond the shore, in an

almost perfect calm which we knew to be deceptive — else why were people so afraid of the Reservoir? The fringe of young pines on the edge, like toy trees, subjected to the wind, sighed and told us their sad secrets. In the Reservoir there was an appearance of neatness which concealed a disarray too frightening to be acknowledged except, without any defence, in moments of deep sleep and dreaming. The little sparkling innocent waves shone now green, now grey, petticoats, lettuce leaves; the trees sighed, and told us to be quiet, hush-sh, as if something were sleeping and should not be disturbed — perhaps that was what the trees were always telling us, to hush-sh in case we disturbed something which must never ever be awakened?

What was it? Was it sleeping in the Reservoir? Was that why people were afraid of the Reservoir?

Well we were not afraid of it, oh no, it was only the Reservoir, it was nothing to be afraid of, it was just a flat Reservoir with a fence around it, and trees, and on the far side a little house (with wheels inside?) and nothing to be afraid of.

'The Reservoir, The Reservoir!'

A noticeboard said DANGER, RESERVOIR.

Overcome with sudden glee we climbed through the fence and swung on the lower branches of the trees, shouting at intervals, gazing possessively and delightedly at the sheet of water with its wonderful calm and menace.

'The Reservoir! The Reservoir! The Reservoir!'

We quarrelled again about how to pronounce and spell the word.

Then it seemed to be getting dark — or was it that the trees were stealing the sunlight and keeping it above their heads? One of us began to run. We all ran, suddenly, wildly, not caring about our strained or sprained ankles, through the trees out into the sun where the creek, but it was our creek no longer, waited for us. We wished it were our creek, how we wished it were our creek! We had lost all account of time. Was it nearly night? Would darkness overtake us, would we have to sleep on the banks of the creek that did not belong to us any more, among the wild sweet peas and the tussocks and the dead sheep? And would the eels come up out of the creek, as people said they did, and on their travels through the paddocks would they change into people who would threaten us and bar our way, TRESPASSERS WILL BE PROSECUTED, standing arm in arm in their black glossy coats, swaying, their mouths open, ready to swallow us? Would they ever let us go home, past the orchards, along the gully? Perhaps they would give us Infantile Paralysis, perhaps we would never be able to walk home, and no one would know where we were, to bring us an iron lung with its own special key!

We arrived home, panting and scratched. How strange! The sun was still in the same place in the sky!

The question troubled us, 'Should we tell?'
The answer was decided for us. Our Mother greeted us as we went in the door with, 'You haven't been long away, kiddies. Where have you been? I hope you didn't go anywhere near the Reservoir.'
Our Father looked up from reading his newspapers.
'Don't let me catch you going near the Reservoir!'
We said nothing. How out-of-date they were! They were actually afraid!

JOY COWLEY

The Woman Next Door

Six, perhaps seven, the child of the photograph, solid against the blur of a city, unsmiling in black and white.

She was old enough then to have learned that black and white were the non-colours, the everything and nothing that had no place in rainbows. She also knew that God was white and the Devil black, while the in-between tones, the greys of the street in the photograph, belonged to War.

And the child knew about War. It lay all the way between everything and nothing and covered the city so that no matter where one went there was no escaping it. It was a grey smoke that filled the air they had to breathe.

At school she watched the boys draw aeroplanes that resembled ducks laying eggs in flight, and she would feel the metal disc, named, numbered, on the string about her neck, and look up at the sky above the playground.

In the home the blinds were secured when sirens sounded, cups rattled on their hooks when trucks full of soldiers rolled past. Every morning the newspaper was folded over the kitchen table, plates covered with grey pictures, and above the toaster there was a voice which said, 'This is the BBC, London, calling. Here is the news.'

The child learned much by remaining silent through mealtime conversations, but she never discovered who had thrown stones through Mrs Gessner's front windows. No one seemed to know. No one seemed particularly interested. Nor could she find out where Mr Gessner had gone. Certainly he wasn't fighting with the soldiers, for one day someone, an aunt, uncle perhaps, someone had said, 'Well, what would you do if they told you to go over and shoot your relatives?' And a grey sort of silence had settled in the room.

Their neighbour had not appeared to be disturbed by the breaking of the windows. While the workmen cleared the fragments of glass and put in new panes, Mrs Gessner carried on working in her garden. The face under the straw hat was flat and expressionless. The unlaced boots never hurried. Up and down the rows, day after day, those broad freckled hands pulled weeds from the flower beds.

The child didn't speak, but she often watched. She would lie in the grass on her own side of the fence and press her face against the palings, thrilled by her own daring. Dirty Hun, they'd said at school.

Watch out or she'll get you. Spy, spy, string her up high. She would watch every movement, and when it seemed likely that the brim of the straw hat was going to tilt in her direction, she would put her head down and crawl backwards until she was behind her grandfather's bean frame, and she would stay there until the squat figure had moved away.

But nothing happened to her. Nothing. After a while the children at school lost interest in her story about the sounds of breaking glass in the middle of the night, and the mystery woman next door took on an ordinariness that defied the child's imagination. It did not seem right that a spy should put out tins of dripping for the birds or scratch down the back of her dress with a knitting needle. The child grew bolder. It was no longer satisfying to hide in the grass and stare. She came out into the open, walked along the fence, sometimes stood still and leaned on it. She met the woman's eyes, smiled when she smiled, even said hullo.

Promise not to tell a living soul, she said to anyone at school who would listen. I talked to the spy.

One day she accepted a bunch of dahlias from the garden and was thrilled to find two earwigs in the petals. She took them to school in a bottle and everyone looked. Oh yes, they were German earwigs, all right.

Then the child's father was killed. The man in the photograph on the mantelpiece was drowned at sea and everything about the child's house changed. It became quiet. People walked in it as though they no longer knew the way, and they talked in tired voices. Sometimes they would not leave the child alone. Sometimes they forgot she was there. The grey of War sat at the dinner table with them and curled up on their plates, making everything taste like the dead earth under houses.

The child took to playing in the garden next door.

Years later she would not be able to remember her first visit, but soon she was crossing the fence so regularly that Mrs Gessner cut down some of the palings to make it easier for her. And because the child was older now, and in a new class at school, she no longer felt the need to confide in other children — or relatives, for that matter.

On warm afternoons she would sit under the apple tree by a mound of green fruit, or wander along the borders popping fuchsia buds, or kneel on the path urging snails to compete on a brick raceway. Mrs Gessner used to bring out the canvas chairs, and they would sit, the two of them, drinking milk and eating biscuits with currants and lemon in them.

Then there were the days when they went into the house and the cool dark kitchen with its smells of apples and firewood and caraway seeds, and the child would climb up into the rocking chair, wriggling into a nest of cushions, while Mrs Gessner brought out the music box.

It was of dark wood, carved, with a lid which framed trees and dancing deer; and when the lid was opened it was easy to tell why the deer danced like that, for from the emptiness of the box came a song of little bells, the same tune over and over until the lid was closed and Mrs Gessner was wiping the box on her apron and smiling, ya, is beautiful? is beautiful? and the child was holding out her hands, begging for the music again.

Perhaps she talked to her family about the music box. Later, she was unable to remember that either. But it seemed that the family, slow with grief, had dragged their thinking to the gap in the wooden fence. As an uncle nailed up the boards, they took the child before her grandfather who wanted to know how long she had been going next door. How long? Weeks? Years? She didn't know. Then Grandfather talked about King and Country and the child's father. He talked to her seriously as though she were already grown up, the way he spoke to her uncles, only kinder. He had steel-rimmed glasses and grey hairs growing out of his nose. She knew that she would give her dead father a pain that was much worse than drowning, if she ever went next door again.

Some time after that, Mrs Gessner moved away from the street. The child didn't see her leave. She came home from school and was met by Grandfather, who gave her a brown paper parcel. Inside was the music box. The woman left it for the little girl, he said. She meant you, he said.

The child didn't know what to say. She felt as though she had been caught doing something wrong.

You know what your father would want you to do, Grandfather said.

Of course she knew. And as she put the music box on the fire, the aunts and uncles put their arms round her and told her she was a real little heroine, and that pleased her; but most of all she was pleased that she had made her father, who was living with the angels, very proud of his girl.

ROBIN HYDE

The glory hole

'Hullo, little girl next door. Come along over; hurry up, and I'll show you the Glory Hole.'

'What's the Glory Hole?'

'Where the fairies live. Hurry, this is just the time to catch them at afternoon tea.'

Bob's hands, firm under her armpits, swung her from the wall. They went into Mrs Malley's wash-house, Eliza holding tightly to Bob's hand. It was a very tidy wash-house, and Mrs Malley had a new rubber wringer. Augusta was always asking Providence for one, and saying it broke her back to wring the clothes out by hand. Bob pulled aside the matting on the floor, and there lay a great hole, a square filled with black velvet darkness.

'Down there is where the fairies live.'

She stared at him. Suddenly she knew that all her life she had never really believed in fairies, and always she had wanted to. Little sheeny iridescent wings, bodies like floating bluebells . . .

'Truly?'

'Want to come down and see?'

She nodded, unable to speak. 'Then come on,' said Bob; and at that very moment they heard Mrs Malley's voice outside.

'Is that you, Bob? Where are you?'

'Bother women!' muttered Bob.

Mrs Malley came into the wash-house. She was a dark woman, her navy blue print frock very clean and well-pressed over her firm bosom, and her hair drawn straitly back. She said at once, 'You're not taking Mrs Hannay's little girl down your nasty, dirty hole, Bob Malley, I'll tell you that. I'd like to know what her mother would have to say — her pinny all dust and webs when she goes home. The very idea!'

Eliza, shivering as her mother had shivered when the earthquake tipped Sandra out of her cradle, wanted to explain that she would risk all the clean pinnies in the world, all the scoldings, or even the hairbrush, for one moment to watch the fairies, one glimpse of their blue wings through the spy-hole Bob Malley had dug down under the earth. But words wouldn't come; she was tongue-tied, a silly baby in the clutches of a grown-up.

'A dear little soul,' said Mrs Malley, firm-bosomed and speckless.

Bob said, 'Never mind, Liza. I'll bring you back a present from the

33

Fairy Queen.' He swung himself over the edge of the Glory Hole. At one moment his freckly hand gripped the floor-boards, then they had vanished, and Eliza was left behind. Mrs Malley took her on her knee.

'Bob's a big rough boy,' she said, stroking Eliza's hair. 'You mustn't mind him, he doesn't mean to tease. Your mother keeps you neat as a little picture, that I'll say. My, what pretty curls. I'll bet those get combed out morning and night. I could do with a little girl of my own. Would you like to live here and be Mrs Malley's pet girl?'

Live with the Glory Hole . . . And yet Mrs Malley didn't care, she wasn't wondering where Bob was now, downstairs in the dark earth. Perhaps the big spiders had got him. Perhaps there was a stair that twisted up and up.

'I want to go down the Glory Hole.'

Mrs Malley laughed.

'You'd get cobwebs on your pinny that your mother's ironed all nice and fresh for you. You're lucky little girls to have such a good mother.'

Presently Bob's freckled hands swung into sight again, and a moment later the rest of him doubled over the edge of the Glory Hole. A strand of web lay dusty on his cheek, and he looked tired, but to Eliza his eyes seemed full of mysterious light.

'There you are, Liza.'

He put into her hands a lavender china shoe, filled with wet new violets. Their scent made a pale streak in the wash-house.

'The Fairy Queen sent you some violets in one of her shoes, and she hopes you'll come yourself next time.'

Mrs Malley's face brimmed with half-laughing, half-compassionate mischief, the face of a grown-up fixed in the attitude of being grown-up.

'There now, do look at your trousers, all dust and webs. You'll wait a long time before you get another pair, my lad, I can tell you that. How you can be bothered with your nonsense, and putting ideas into her head. Run along and brush yourself, do. Eliza, dearie, wouldn't you like a piece before you go?'

'Eliza 'ud rather have a tikky,' said Bob, and Mrs Malley's mischievous smile streaked out again. South African children say 'tikky' for threepenny-bit, and Carly, stickler for old customs, branded them as outlanders by sticking to 'tikky' even now.

Mrs Malley could smile; but one night, perhaps when the moon floated like a white terrifying balloon over the fences, Eliza was coming back to the Glory Hole; she wanted to see the Fairy Queen for herself; she wasn't afraid of dirty spiders in Fairy Land. Once, in the Magic Cave, she had been taken to a sparkly place and told, 'This is the Fairy Queen and her fairies'; but they weren't, they weren't. They were only big girls dressed up in muslin, and their faces were pink and hot, and the stars on their wands were cardboard silvered over. They smiled and looked apologetic. They didn't know. Little bodies, littler than *little*; and her voice was like a pale chime of bells.

That night, when Carly and Eliza were in bed, and Carly quite asleep, her hair spread like a branch of moonlit brown leaves over her pillow, Eliza heard Mrs Malley's tinkling laugh.

'I can't think where she's put it,' said her mother, vexedly.

'Maybe she's gone to sleep with it, the poor dear. Leave her be till morning. I wouldn't have her waked for worlds. I wouldn't have troubled you, Mrs Hannay, but it's one of a pair, though not worth sixpence, and it does come in handy for my primroses and the little things with short stems. What that boy will be up to next — tunnelling between my wash-house and my own bedroom, drat him.'

'You should put him into engineering,' said John's deep voice, sombre, and with its usual accompaniment of crackling newspaper pages. Just then it was a grievance with him that he had three daughters and no boy.

'A grave-digger would be better. At digging holes in the ground he's the beat of a rabbit, and there's a trade won't go out of fashion.' Mrs Malley's light, rainy laughter sprinkled the dark, like the scent of the dying violets in the shoe beside Eliza's pillow.

Bob tells lies, thought Eliza. That's nothing, so do I, and Carly if she's frightened. But he was pretending, like a grown-up. Littler than little . . . She saw his serious grey eyes, his freckled nose, and the sawdust slipping down to a thin, fine puddle as he flicked the saw. 'Sissy,' she said to his image, and fell asleep.

In the morning she came in from the garden, where she had broken the lavender shoe and hidden it away in the ash-can, right under the scraped cold porridge, where nobody would ever look, and told Carly she had just seen a fairy.

'You shouldn't tell stories,' said Carly. She was shelling broad beans, and to make her taller she stood on a stool, her white apron, embroidered with a red running-stitch duck, pressed against the kitchen sink. Her hands, very neat and dexterous, made the green beans jump like tiddleywinks out of their white, felt-lined houses. Sometimes she ate one raw; she thought they tasted like kidney. She couldn't bear lentils, because they looked so pulpy-yellow.

'It's not a story. I saw it on a fuchsia, so there.'

'Mummy,' called Carly, 'Eliza's telling stories again.'

Eliza burst into tears. Between her fingers, steepled across her eyes, she saw her mother come into the kitchen, flour smudged across her cheek, one auburn wisp straggling on the forehead which was marked deep between its eyebrows by two vertical lines.

'Carly, whatever is it? Eliza, don't cry like that, you're not a baby. Carly, you're the eldest.'

'She's a storyteller,' said Carly, her own soft pink mouth beginning to quiver. 'She said she saw a fairy outside on the fuchsia. You said she wasn't to tell any more stories.'

'I did see it, I did see it.' Eliza faced round, tears channelling her hot cheeks. 'Mummy, aren't there any fairies? Daddy said there were. And I did see it.'

Her mother, speaking indirectly and over her head, said, 'You should remember she's only little, Carly.'

'She's always telling stories.'

'Aren't there any fairies?' persisted Eliza. 'Aren't there, Mummy?'

'Run outside and play,' said Augusta. 'You can have a piece of bread and dripping if you like.' Eliza stopped crying, abruptly, as if she had turned off a tiny tap behind her eyes. She had never really wanted to cry, anyhow, except to find out; they fooled and fooled, and wouldn't answer when you got them in a corner. She heard her mother's voice saying, 'Carly, you'd better soak some lentils for tomorrow,' and knew how Carly would hate that. She sauntered outside. A privet border, low and scanty, cut off the oblong of grass, over which white clothes were drying, sprinkled like great snowflakes. One cypress bush was a hard, compact oval of colour, and a white butterfly made a folded triangle of its wings over the serrated leaves. The underwing had a tear in it, and the butterfly opened and shut its wings very slowly, and moved its feelers as if the effort were far too much for it. Presently it fell to the garden path, and couldn't move. She picked it up and put it back on the bush. Sun stroked its feeble body, but all the colour and passion, the ecstasy with which it had first tossed itself against the spring wind, were fled away. Eliza decided that she would make Carly pay for everyone; for Bob Malley, and Mrs Malley's laughter, and Augusta, and the tired butterfly. 'Because she told,' she thought. That night, when they were together again in the dark, she recited 'The Spanish Mother'.

> *The woman, shaking off his blood, rose raven-haired and tall,*
> *And our stern glances quailed before one sterner far than all;*
> *'Ho, slayers of the sinewless! ho, tramplers of the weak!*
> *What, shrink ye from the ghastly meats and life-bought wines*
>   *ye seek?'*

'Eliza, stop it, you're frightening me.' Carly's plaintive little voice.

> *'Poison? Is that your craven fear?' She snatched a goblet up,*
> *And raised it to her queenly head, as if to drain the cup.*

'Mother,' shrieked Carly. 'Mother, come quick. Eliza's reciting "The Spanish Mother" again. Mother, make her stop it.'

Sobs, the dark quaking hummock under the bedclothes that was Carly, a shine of light from the blue enamel light, cutting the shadows in halves. The little flame, flat as a snake's head, wasn't enough to light up the whole room. It showed only the towel-horse, with white towels over it, and Eliza's mother's hair, down and dark red over her shoulders.

'I ought to take the brush to you, young lady.'

But the voice bore no relation to the wild, somehow tameless and beautiful dark red hair, on which the lamplight crept like a rusty moth. Eliza sat up, straining her arms through the darkness.

'I love you, Mummy. I do love you, better than anything.'

'Talk's cheap. Why are you such a naughty girl?'

'I do love you, I do.'

'Oh, I suppose you do.' Eliza's mother sat on the edge of the bed and felt Eliza's hands. 'I can't think why you're so hot; you feel like a burning coal.'

Carly, lying flat and still in the other bed, felt tears round and slip down her cheeks, but she made no sound. It was just like Eliza. But she herself loved their mother best, better than anyone in the world did, much better than Eliza. Carly made even her fingers and toes still, and shut her eyes; when her mother moved away from Eliza's bed, and looking down at her, said, 'Asleep?' in a half-questioning voice, she made no answer. She couldn't bear to be listed second. Yes, she was asleep, asleep, folded away still, not asking for anything. But she made up her mind to get up early in the morning, put on her apron, and polish out the grate, and do all the forks and spoons for a surprise, and mix the porridge without any lumps, so that her father wouldn't growl. When her mother got up, everything would be done. And she would eat the lentils, great soapy yellow chunks of lentils, without a word. Carly's bed rose gently on an enormous, beautiful wave of sleep, and slid her down into a dream as she ticked off the things she would do tomorrow.

When Eliza next saw Bob Malley, she sat on the fence and swung her legs, but never said a word about the Glory Hole. Instead, she sung a derisive chant:

> Giddy, giddy gout,
> Your shirt's hanging out.

over and over. Bob's grey eyes were hurt and surprised. When she wouldn't stop singing, he turned his back and sawed away at a carefully balanced plank, making the pinkish dust fly. A curious white scent, resiny, stained the air, and the steel ribbon flashed and flashed. 'Giddy, giddy gout,' chanted Eliza, until she was tired of it. Then she clambered down and went to the front garden, where the irises pierced up in hard purple spikes, their flags furled. She felt she had paid Bob Malley out. After that, he didn't matter any more, and she could even like him.

YVONNE DU FRESNE

Coronation Day

In 1937 Cherry Taylor and I turned into Princess Elizabeth and Princess Margaret Rose. It was the Coronation that did it. And that beautiful book *Our Princesses and their Dogs* that Onkel Sven had bought me for my birthday.

Oh, the photographs in that book! They were in sepia, exactly the same colour as the mushrooms in our cow paddock. Cherry and I knew all the stories under the photographs by heart.

> 'Come along!' calls Princess Elizabeth across the south lawn at Royal Lodge. 'Time for dinner!'

And there was Princess Elizabeth, not wearing the crown or the ermine, but a simple maidenly dress, holding out a royal dog dish to an army of corgis battle-charging across a closely-mown paddock to their dinner.

'There won't be enough dinner for all those dogs,' mourned Cherry, peering at the one meagre royal dog dish. But I was concentrating on Princess Elizabeth's simple maidenly dress.

'She's wearing my dirndl,' I said, 'but with terrible great shoes.'

'*Not* terrible great shoes, Astrid,' said Cherry, in an earnest teacher's voice that set my teeth on edge. 'They have to wear strong shoes to get themselves all over the sweeping lawns.'

'I have a dirndl,' I said.

The blouse for my dirndl was a bit too bright for the simple dignity of the princesses. It had the embroideries of the wheat-ears and the cornflowers of Denmark, and blue wavy lines for the waters of the Baltic and the North Sea. We looked doubtfully at the simple blouses of the princesses. Cherry read in a reverent voice:

> Two simple little English girls at play on a summer's day. The Princesses Elizabeth and Margaret Rose show the Duke and Duchess of York how obedient their doggies are!

We gazed spellbound at the doggies, all sitting up and begging — except for one, who was slinking away into the furtive shade of a giant rhododendron. A nurse with a veil was bolting after him.

'That's Dandy,' said Cherry in an indulgent voice. 'He's a dag that one, always running away . . .'

'Are they living in a hospital?' I asked, gazing at the bolting nurse.

'That's Allah!' cried Cherry, shocked at my ignorance. 'She's their nurse.'

'Are they sick?' I insisted.

'Not a nurse. A nanny,' said Cherry deeply. Ah.

And day after day we turned into the princesses. Me in my dirndl with the vulgar embroideries, and Cherry in a dirndl made from one of my cardigans lashed together with a long brown bootlace, a very simple blouse and a skirt. We both wore our heaviest lace-up shoes with the white socks. Then we clumped up and down the south lawn of Royal Lodge, calling now and then to the corgi-horde, or waving in a ladylike way to the crowds outside the royal garden walls.

'They are locked away from the crowds,' explained Cherry, 'for they are special people.'

'Locked away?'

Cherry looked pityingly at this Danish dolt.

'Now we will take the photographs, Astrid,' she said. We peered at our favourite photograph. Underneath it the story said,

'Sit up Dandy!' says the Princess Elizabeth.

'There's good old Dandy,' we said to each other. Dandy was not only sitting up — he had lain his ears ecstatically against the Princess Elizabeth's royal chin. That dog knew where his dinner came from, I thought, but did not dare say so aloud.

'We will have to use your dog,' said Cherry firmly.

Bor the fox-terrier peered warily at us from underneath our washhouse. We hauled him out by one leg.

'Now go on,' urged Cherry, 'you are Princess Elizabeth, Astrid.' Heavens! I hung on to struggling Bor and lay my chin winningly on top of his ears. Bor gave my face his usual loving lick but, as Heir to the Throne, I did not flinch. Cherry raised her imaginary camera. She chanted slowly and reverently, '"Sit up Dandy!" says the Princess Elizabeth . . . Click.'

Then we did the next bit. We had not been able to gather much information about what the Princesses actually did, but careful research in endless newspaper photographs revealed their other occupation. They walked, outside those garden walls, from great black cars into large public buildings. Stooping modestly, they peeped at the crowds from under large felt hats, with simple buttoned coats, long socks, buttoned shoes and hands in gloves.

We gazed thoughtfully at each other and went to work on our bewildered Moders. And so we got our new winter outfits — the large felt hats, the simple coats, the long socks and the buttoned shoes.

We didn't have crowds or streets to practise with. Just the Number One Line. So we walked up and down that — practising. We peeped modestly from underneath the felts, and every now and then raised a diffident hand in a small wave. My Fader watched sardonically from the cow paddock. He imitated our small waves. A faint hoot of laughter reached us in the chill wind.

'Don't look,' hissed Cherry in my ear, 'he is vulgar.'

I looked wistfully at Fader. I would have given much to ask him to do his imitation, for Cherry, of the Duke of Gloucester travelling up the Foxton Line in his large black car on his recent triumphant tour of New Zealand. The populace had been warned to stay by their posts on the edge of the road and wave as the Duke toured slowly past. Even though the Duke had forgotten to tour slowly past, my Fader's keen eye had marked every detail — that slow wave, the Duke's well-built figure, the well-sprung car . . . Fader did the Duke of Gloucester every night after dinner.

We trailed inside to my bedroom and stood aimlessly in front of my dressing-table mirror. Cherry muttered, 'Princess Elizabeth and Princess Margaret Rose arrive at the Wembly Stadium to attend the Military Tattoo.'

We gazed fixedly at ourselves in the mirror and waved. 'Click,' said Cherry.

'You are the throne-followers?' asked an intensely interested voice. Cherry jumped, then hung her head. She found it difficult to actually look at my Bedstemoder. It was the pulled-back hair, she had kindly explained to me, the cheekbones, and the rings flashing on those long bony fingers. *Viking* rings, Cherry had breathed. Her eyes had been round and anxious. She had gathered the information from here and there, that the Vikings had actually eaten children in the olden days. I had laughed — and that, of course, had made it worse. Deep under our mushroom hats we gazed at my Bedstemoder.

'Look,' she said, having difficulty with the 'oo' sound, as usual, 'I have found this for you.'

She thrust under our noses a very black photograph album. On one page a sturdy, oil-stained young man grinned at us from his seat in a very small boat. He had his cap on back to front.

'Danish throne-follower — Frederick!' said my Bedstemoder in a ringing voice. 'He is good fellow. Always telling stories and drinking schnapps with the people. He is good boat man.'

Cherry took in the Danish Throne-Follower with one bleak peep.

'The English Royal Family don't drink schnapps, Mrs Westergaard,' said my brave, loyal Cherry. Then she went as pink as a real English rose when my Bedstemoder started on her laugh.

The next week was the Coronation. For months Miss Martin had told us about coronations. On Coronation Day, Miss Martin said, we were to come to school only for a little while. We were to have Assembly and *receive a present from the King*! Then we were to celebrate with our families, each in our simple way, explained Miss Martin, in a manner that would please the King.

On May the twelfth 1937 Cherry met me at our gate. We had on our Royal outfits. I had had a little tussle of wills with my Moder, who asked me how could we go to our picnic dressed as if to go shopping in town? 'We are to dress for the Coronation,' I told her. I could not tell her that I had turned into the Princess Elizabeth, and that, at Assembly, heavenly voices would sound from the skies and Cherry and I would walk out to greet our people, sparing a kindly thought for the multitude of loyal subjects scattered over the world in our father's Dominions.

At school, Miss Martin whiled away the time before the Coronation Assembly by giving us, once again, the story about Princess Elizabeth in our Standard One *Journal*. Cherry was called upon to read. She stood up, invisible under her hat, and read again the words we knew by heart:

> Princess Elizabeth began her birthday by going for a ride on her pony with her father, the Duke of York, and Princess Margaret Rose. Later on in the day she had a tea-party, at which she blew out the candles on her iced cake. She then cut the first slice of the cake and handed it to her father. After tea, she went, as a birthday treat, to the moving pictures.

Handed it to her father. How dignified. Went to the moving pictures! Not the flicks with all that yelling and running about of the matinée audience.

'I wonder what the little Princesses are doing — this very moment,' said Cherry, as we stood in our serried ranks on the school tennis-courts.

'All over the world,' shouted the Headmaster, warming up, 'boys — and girls — are turning their most fervent thoughts towards that great city, London, where at this very moment . . .' He paused and consulted his wrist-watch. He frowned. Then he got back into his stride — '. . . where soon our King will be enthroned.'

Enthroned. We gazed sternly at the flag hanging in the autumn sun from its noble pole. The Standard Six boy started his drum rattle; we sang, and the next moment we were shuffling out of the school gate, clutching our free Coronation pencils stamped with flags and crowns.

And there was our car — the Dodge — looking frightfully shabby, and full of our picnic lunch, and Fader and Moder and Bedstemoder and Bor the dog, looking fearfully ordinary. It was a strange day, to go bowling down the gravel road over the Plains to Foxton Beach for our Coronation Picnic, when we should be doing the Sums, the Spelling . . .

The Princesses Elizabeth and Margaret Rose, heads modestly bowed, stepped into the Royal Dodge.

'Don't trip,' shouted my Bedstemoder in a vulgar voice. Then she thought better of it. 'You have pencils there, I see,' she said.

'King George the Sixth gave us these pencils,' said Cherry repressively. She held on to hers tightly in case the Viking-Dronning would snatch it, and eat it for her dinner. We both gazed out of the windows of the Dodge, regal underneath our mushroom hats. We longed to raise one gloved hand each to acknowledge the cheers of the Coronation crowds lining the road on either side, but dared not, in case my Bedstemoder once more broke the spell.

Then we saw the rabbit. It streaked up the road before us. And Fader turned before our very eyes into a Viking.

'Charge!' he shouted. He pressed his foot on the accelerator. We reached fully thirty miles per hour. Moder laughed.

'Bor!' yelled Fader. 'Rabbit!' And Bor did his leap; his great rabbit leap. Straight through the side-curtain window he crashed, bowled over and over in the dust, and plunged like a tiger through the long grass after that rabbit. Cherry screamed, Fader braked, and we lurched to a stop.

Royal hat over one eye, Cherry said in a loud, indignant voice, '*Some*body has taken my King's pencil.'

We all tumbled out into the road. The Manawatu Plains lay all around us, bland, heavy, silent. There were no heavenly voices, no trumpet calls for the Coronation. Just that silence.

KATHERINE MANSFIELD

New Dresses

Mrs Carsfield and her mother sat at the dining-room table putting the finishing touches to some green cashmere dresses. They were to be worn by the two Misses Carsfield at church on the following day, with applegreen sashes, and straw hats with ribbon tails. Mrs Carsfield had set her heart on it, and this being a late night for Henry, who was attending a meeting of the Political League, she and the old mother had the dining-room to themselves and could make 'a peaceful litter' as she expressed it. The red cloth was taken off the table — where stood the wedding-present sewing-machine, a brown work-basket, the 'material', and some torn fashion journals. Mrs Carsfield worked the machine, slowly, for she feared the green thread would give out, and had a sort of tired hope that it might last longer if she was careful to use a little at a time; the old woman sat in a rocking-chair, her skirt turned back, and her felt-slippered feet on a hassock, tying the machine threads and stitching some narrow lace on the necks and cuffs. The gas jet flickered. Now and again the old woman glanced up at the jet and said, 'There's water in the pipe, Anne, that's what's the matter,' then was silent, to say again a moment later, 'There must be water in that pipe, Anne,' and again, with quite a burst of energy, 'Now there is — I'm *certain* of it.'

Anne frowned at the sewing-machine. 'The way mother *harps* on things — it gets frightfully on my nerves,' she thought. 'And always when there's no earthly opportunity to better a thing . . . I suppose it's old age — but most aggravating.' Aloud she said: 'Mother, I'm having a really substantial hem in this dress of Rose's — the child has got so leggy lately. And don't put any lace on Helen's cuffs; it will make a distinction, and besides she's so careless about rubbing her hands on anything grubby.'

'Oh, there's plenty,' said the old woman. 'I'll put it a little higher up.' And she wondered why Anne had such a down on Helen — Henry was just the same. They seemed to want to hurt Helen's feelings — the distinction was merely an excuse.

'Well,' said Mrs Carsfield, 'you didn't see Helen's clothes when I took them off tonight. Black from head to foot after a week. And when I compared them before her eyes with Rose's she merely shrugged, you know that habit she's got, and began stuttering. I really shall have to see Dr Malcolm about her stuttering, if only to give her a good fright.

43

I believe it's merely an affectation she's picked up at school — that she can help it.'

'Anne, you know she's always stuttered. You did just the same when you were her age, she's highly strung.' The old woman took off her spectacles, breathed on them, and rubbed them with a corner of her sewing apron.

'Well, the last thing in the world to do her any good is to let her imagine *that*,' answered Anne, shaking out one of the green frocks and pricking at the pleats with her needle. 'She is treated exactly like Rose, and the Boy hasn't a nerve. Did you see him when I put him on the rocking-horse today, for the first time? He simply gurgled with joy. He's more the image of his father every day.'

'Yes, he certainly is a thorough Carsfield,' assented the old woman, nodding her head.

'Now that's another thing about Helen,' said Anne. 'The peculiar way she treats Boy, staring at him and frightening him as she does. You remember when he was a baby how she used to take away his bottle to see what he would do? Rose is perfect with the child — but Helen . . .'

The old woman put down her work on the table. A little silence fell, and through the silence the loud ticking of the dining-room clock. She wanted to speak her mind to Anne once and for all about the way she and Henry were treating Helen, ruining the child, but the ticking noise distracted her. She could not think of the words and sat there stupidly, her brain going *tick, tick* to the dining-room clock.

'How loudly that clock ticks,' was all she said.

'Oh, there's mother — off the subject again — giving me no help or encouragement,' thought Anne. She glanced at the clock.

'Mother, if you've finished that frock, would you go into the kitchen and heat up some coffee and perhaps cut a plate of ham. Henry will be in directly. I'm practically through with this second frock by myself.' She held it up for inspection. 'Aren't they charming? They ought to last the children a good two years, and then I expect they'll do for school — lengthened, and perhaps dyed.'

'I'm glad we decided on the more expensive material,' said the old woman.

Left alone in the dining-room Anne's frown deepened and her mouth drooped — a sharp line showed from nose to chin. She breathed deeply and pushed back her hair. There seemed to be no air in the room, she felt stuffed up, and it seemed so useless to be tiring herself out with fine sewing for Helen. One never got through with children and never had any gratitude from them — except Rose — who was exceptional. Another sign of old age in mother was her absurd point of view about Helen and her 'touchiness' on the subject. There was one thing, Mrs Carsfield said to herself. She was determined to keep Helen apart from Boy. He had all his father's sensitiveness to unsympathetic influences. A blessing that the girls were at school all day!

At last the dresses were finished and folded over the back of the chair. She carried the sewing-machine over to the bookshelves, spread the tablecloth, and went over to the window. The blind was up, she could see the garden quite plainly: there must be a moon about. And then she caught sight of something shining on the garden seat. A book, yes, it must be a book, left there to get soaked through by the dew. She went out into the hall, put on her goloshes, gathered up her skirt, and ran into the garden. Yes, it was a book. She picked it up carefully. Damp already — and the cover bulging. She shrugged her shoulders in the way that her little daughter had caught from her. In the shadowy garden that smelled of grass and rose leaves Anne's heart hardened. Then the gate clicked and she saw Henry striding up the front path.

'Henry!' she called.

'Hullo,' he cried, 'what on earth are you doing down there . . . Moon-gazing, Anne?' She ran forward and kissed him.

'Oh, look at this book,' she said. 'Helen's been leaving it about again. My dear, how you smell of cigars!'

Said Henry: 'You've got to smoke a decent cigar when you're with these other chaps. Looks so bad if you don't. But come inside, Anne; you haven't got anything on. Let the book go hang! You're cold, my dear, you're shivering.' He put his arm round her shoulder. 'See the moon over there, by the chimney? Fine night. By Jove! I had the fellows roaring tonight — I made a colossal joke. One of them said: "Life is a game of cards," and I, without thinking, just straight out . . .' Henry paused by the door and held up a finger. 'I said . . . well, I've forgotten the exact words, but they shouted, my dear, simply shouted. No, I'll remember what I said in bed tonight; you know I always do.'

'I'll take this book into the kitchen to dry on the stove-rack,' said Anne, and she thought, as she banged the pages, 'Henry has been drinking beer again, that means indigestion tomorrow. No use mentioning Helen tonight.'

When Henry had finished the supper he lay back in the chair, picking his teeth, and patted his knee for Anne to come and sit there.

'Hullo,' he said, jumping her up and down, 'what's the green fandangles on the chair back? What have you and mother been up to, eh?'

Said Anne airily, casting a most careless glance at the green dresses, 'Only some frocks for the children. Remnants for Sunday.'

The old woman put the plate and cup and saucer together, then lighted a candle.

'I think I'll go to bed,' she said cheerfully.

'Oh, dear me, how unwise of mother,' thought Anne. 'She makes Henry suspect by going away like that, as she always does if there's any unpleasantness brewing.'

'No, don't go to bed yet, mother,' cried Henry jovially. 'Let's have a look at the things.' She passed him over the dresses, faintly smiling. Henry rubbed them through his fingers.

'So these are the remnants, are they, Anne? Don't feel much like the Sunday trousers my mother used to make me out of an ironing blanket. How much did you pay for this a yard, Anne?'

Anne took the dresses from him and played with a button of his waistcoat.

'Forget the exact price, darling. Mother and I rather skimped them, even though they were so cheap. What can great big men bother about clothes . . . ? Was Lumley there tonight?'

'Yes, he says their kid was a bit bandy-legged at just the same age as Boy. He told me of a new kind of chair for children that the draper had just got in — makes them sit with their legs straight. By the way, have you got this month's draper's bill?'

She had been waiting for that — had known it was coming. She slipped off his knee and yawned.

'Oh, dear me,' she said, 'I think I'll follow mother. Bed's the place for me.' She stared at Henry vacantly. 'Bill — bill did you say, dear? Oh, I'll look it out in the morning.'

'No, Anne, hold on.' Henry got up and went over to the cupboard where the bill file was kept. 'Tomorrow's no good — because it's Sunday. I want to get that account off my chest before I turn in. Sit down there — in the rocking-chair — you needn't stand!'

She dropped into the chair and began humming, all the while her thoughts coldly busy and her eyes fixed on her husband's broad back as he bent over the cupboard door. He dawdled over finding the file.

'He's keeping me in suspense on purpose,' she thought. 'We can afford it — otherwise why should I do it? I know our income and our expenditure. I'm not a fool. They're a hell upon earth every month, these bills.' And she thought of her bed upstairs, yearned for it, imagining she had never felt so tired in her life.

'Here we are!' said Henry. He slammed the file on to the table. 'Draw up your chair . . .'

'Clayton: Seven yards green cashmere at five shillings a yard — thirty-five shillings.' He read the item twice — then folded the sheet over and bent towards Anne. He was flushed and his breath smelt of beer. She knew exactly how he took things in that mood, and she raised her eyebrows and nodded.

'Do you mean to tell me,' stormed Henry, 'that lot over there cost thirty-five shillings — that stuff you've been mucking up for the children. Good God! Anybody would think you'd married a millionaire. You could buy your mother a trousseau with that money. You're making yourself a laughing-stock for the whole town. How do you think I can buy Boy a chair or anything else — if you chuck away my earnings like that? Time and again you impress upon me the impossibility of keeping Helen decent; and then you go decking her out the next moment in thirty-five shillings' worth of green cashmere . . .'

On and on stormed the voice.

'He'll have calmed down in the morning, when the beer's worked off,' thought Anne, and later, as she toiled up to bed, 'When he sees how they'll last, he'll understand . . .'

A brilliant Sunday morning. Henry and Anne, quite reconciled, sitting in the dining-room waiting for church time to the tune of Carsfield junior, who steadily thumped the shelf of his high chair with a gravy spoon given him from the breakfast table by his father.

'That beggar's got muscle,' said Henry proudly. 'I've timed him by my watch. He's kept that up for five minutes without stopping.'

'Extraordinary,' said Anne, buttoning her gloves. 'I think he's had that spoon almost long enough now, dear, don't you? I'm so afraid of him putting it into his mouth.'

'Oh, I've got an eye on him.' Henry stood over his small son. 'Go to it, old man. Tell mother boys like to kick up a row.'

Anne kept silence. At any rate, it would keep his eye off the children when they came down in those cashmeres. She was still wondering if she had drummed into their minds often enough the supreme importance of being careful and of taking them off immediately after church before dinner, and why Helen was fidgety when she was pulled about at all, when the door opened and the old woman ushered them in, complete to the straw hats with ribbon tails.

She could not help thrilling, they looked so very superior — Rose carrying her prayer-book in a white case, embroidered with a pink woollen cross. But she feigned indifference immediately and the lateness of the hour. Not a word more on the subject from Henry, even with the thirty-five shillings' worth walking hand in hand before him all the way to church. Anne decided that was really generous and noble of him. She looked up at him, walking with the shoulders thrown back. How fine he looked in that long black coat with the white silk tie just showing! And the children looked worthy of him. She squeezed his hand in church, conveying by that silent pressure 'It was for your sake I made the dresses; of course, you can't understand that, but *really*, Henry.' And she fully believed it.

On their way home the Carsfield family met Doctor Malcolm out walking with a black dog carrying his stick in its mouth. Doctor Malcolm stopped and asked after Boy so intelligently that Henry invited him to dinner.

'Come and pick a bone with us and see Boy for yourself,' he said. And Doctor Malcolm accepted. He walked beside Henry and shouted over his shoulder, 'Helen, keep an eye on *my* boy baby, will you, and see he doesn't swallow that walking-stick. Because, if he does, a tree will grow right out of his mouth or it will go to his tail and make it so stiff that a wag will knock you into kingdom come!'

'Oh, Doctor Malcolm!' laughed Helen, stooping over the dog. 'Come along, doggie, give it up, there's a good boy!'

'Helen, your dress!' warned Anne.

'Yes, indeed,' said Doctor Malcolm. 'They are looking top-notchers today — the two young ladies.'

'Well, it really *is* Rose's colour,' said Anne. 'Her complexion is so much more vivid than Helen's.'

Rose blushed. Doctor Malcolm's eyes twinkled, and he kept a tight rein on himself from saying she looked like a tomato in a lettuce salad.

'That child wants taking down a peg,' he decided. 'Give me Helen every time. She'll come to her own yet and lead them just the dance they need.'

Boy was having his midday sleep when they arrived home, and Doctor Malcolm begged that Helen might show him round the garden. Henry, repenting already of his generosity, gladly assented, and Anne went into the kitchen to interview the servant girl.

'Mumma, let me come too and taste the gravy,' begged Rose.

'Huh!' muttered Doctor Malcolm. 'Good riddance.'

He established himself on the garden bench — put up his feet and took off his hat to give the sun 'a chance of growing a second crop', he told Helen.

She asked soberly: 'Doctor Malcolm, do you really like my dress?'

'Of course I do, my lady. Don't you?'

'Oh yes, I'd like to be born and die in it. But it was such a fuss — tryings on, you know, and pullings, and "don'ts". I believe mother would kill me if it got hurt. I even knelt on my petticoat all through church because of dust on the hassock.'

'Bad as that?' asked Doctor Malcolm, rolling his eyes at Helen.

'Oh, *far* worse,' said the child, then burst into laughter and shouted 'Hellish!' dancing over the lawn.

'Take care, they'll hear you, Helen.'

'Oh, booh! It's just dirty old cashmere — serve them right. They can't see me if they're not here to see and so it doesn't matter. It's only with them I feel funny.'

'Haven't you got to remove your finery before dinner?'

'No, because you're here.'

'Oh my prophetic soul!' groaned Doctor Malcolm.

Coffee was served in the garden. The servant girl brought out some cane chairs and a rug for Boy. The children were told to go away and play.

'Leave off worrying Doctor Malcolm, Helen,' said Henry. 'You mustn't be a plague to people who are not members of your own family.' Helen pouted and dragged over to the swing for comfort. She swung high, and thought Doctor Malcolm was a most beautiful man — and wondered if his dog had finished the plate of bones in the back yard. Decided to go and see. Slower she swung, then took a flying leap; her tight skirt caught on a nail — there was a sharp, tearing sound — quickly she glanced at the others — they had not noticed — and then at the frock — at a hole big enough to stick her hand through. She felt neither frightened nor sorry. 'I'll go and change it,' she thought.

'Helen, where are you going to?' called Anne.

'Into the house for a book.'

The old woman noticed that the child held her skirt in a peculiar way. Her petticoat string must have come untied. But she made no remark. Once in the bedroom Helen unbuttoned the frock, slipped out of it, and wondered what to do next. Hide it somewhere — she glanced all round the room — there was nowhere safe from them. Except the top of the cupboard — but even standing on a chair she could not throw so high — it fell back on top of her every time — the horrid, hateful thing. Then her eyes lighted on her school satchel hanging on the end of the bedpost. Wrap it in her school pinafore — put it in the bottom of the bag with the pencil case on top. They'd never look there. She returned to the garden in the everyday dress — but forgot about the book.

'A-ah,' said Anne, smiling ironically. 'What a new leaf for Doctor Malcolm's benefit! Look, mother, Helen has changed without being told to.'

'Come here, dear, and be done up properly.' She whispered to Helen: 'Where did you leave your dress?'

'Left it on the side of the bed. *Where* I took it off,' sang Helen.

Doctor Malcolm was talking to Henry of the advantages derived from public school education for the sons of commercial men, but he had his eye on the scene and, watching Helen, he smelt a rat — smelt a Hamelin tribe of them.

Confusion and consternation reigned. One of the green cashmeres had disappeared — spirited off the face of the earth — during the time that Helen took it off and the children's tea.

'Show me the exact spot,' scolded Mrs Carsfield for the twentieth time. 'Helen, tell the truth.'

'Mumma, I *swear* I left it on the floor.'

'Well, it's no good swearing if it's not there. It can't have been stolen!'

'I did see a very funny-looking man in a white cap walking up and down the road and staring in the windows as I came up to change.'

Sharply Anne eyed her daughter.

'Now,' she said 'I *know* you are telling lies.'

She turned to the old woman, in her voice something of pride and joyous satisfaction. 'You hear, mother — this cock-and-bull story?'

When they were near the end of the bed Helen blushed and turned away from them. And now and again she wanted to shout 'I tore it, I tore it,' and she fancied she had said it and seen their faces, just as sometimes in bed she dreamed she had got up and dressed. But as the evening wore on she grew quite careless — glad only of one thing — people had to go to sleep at night. Viciously she stared at the sun shining through the window space and making a pattern of the curtain on the bare nursery floor. And then she looked at Rose, painting a text at the nursery table with a whole egg-cup full of water to herself . . .

Henry visited their bedroom the last thing. She heard him come creaking into their room and hid under the bedclothes. But Rose betrayed her.

'Helen's not asleep,' piped Rose.

Henry sat by the bedside pulling his moustache.

'If it were not Sunday, Helen, I would whip you. As it is, and I must be at the office early tomorrow, I shall give you a sound smacking after tea in the evening . . . Do you hear me?'

She grunted.

'You love your father and mother, don't you?'

No answer.

Rose gave Helen a dig with her foot.

'Well,' said Henry, sighing deeply, 'I suppose you love Jesus?'

'Rose has scratched my leg with her toe-nail,' answered Helen.

Henry strode out of the room and flung himself on to his own bed with his outdoor boots on the starched bolster, Anne noticed, but he was too overcome for her to venture a protest. The old woman was in the bedroom, too, idly combing the hairs from Anne's brush. Henry told them the story, and was gratified to observe Anne's tears.

'It *is* Rose's turn for her toe-nails after the bath next Saturday,' commented the old woman.

In the middle of the night Henry dug his elbow into Mrs Carsfield.

'I've got an idea,' he said. 'Malcolm's at the bottom of this.'

'No . . . how . . . why . . . where . . . bottom of what?'

'Those damned green dresses.'

'Wouldn't be surprised,' she managed to articulate, thinking 'imagine his rage if I woke *him* up to tell him an idiotic thing like that!'

'Is Mrs Carsfield at home?' asked Doctor Malcolm.
'No, sir, she's out visiting,' answered the servant girl.
'Is Mr Carsfield anywhere about?'
'Oh no, sir, he's never home midday.'
'Show me into the drawing-room.'

The servant girl opened the drawing-room door, cocked her eye at the doctor's bag. She wished he would leave it in the hall — even if she could only *feel* the outside without opening it . . . But the doctor kept it in his hand.

The old woman sat in the drawing-room, a roll of knitting on her lap. Her head had fallen back — her mouth was open — she was asleep and quietly snoring. She started up at the sound of the doctor's footsteps and straightened her cap.

'Oh, Doctor — you *did* take me by surprise. I was dreaming that Henry had bought Anne five little canaries. Please sit down!'

'No, thanks. I just popped in on the chance of catching you alone . . . You see this bag?'

The old woman nodded.

'Now, are you any good at opening bags?'

'Well, my husband was a great traveller and once I spent a whole night in a railway train.'

'Well, have a go at opening this one.'

The old woman knelt on the floor — her fingers trembled.

'There's nothing startling inside?' she asked.

'Well, it won't bite exactly,' said Doctor Malcolm.

The catch sprang open — the bag yawned like a toothless mouth, and she saw, folded in its depths — green cashmere — with narrow lace on the neck and sleeves.

'Fancy that!' said the old woman mildly. 'May I take it out, Doctor?' She professed neither astonishment nor pleasure — and Malcolm felt disappointed.

'Helen's dress,' he said, and bending towards her, raised his voice. 'That young spark's Sunday rig-out.'

'I'm not deaf, Doctor,' answered the old woman. 'Yes, I thought it looked like it. I told Anne only this morning it was bound to turn up somewhere.' She shook the crumpled frock and looked it over. 'Things always do if you give them time; I've noticed that so often — it's such a blessing.'

'You know Lindsay — the postman? Gastric ulcers — called there this morning . . . Saw this brought in by Lena, who'd got it from Helen on her way to school. Said the kid fished it out of her satchel rolled in a pinafore, and said her mother had told her to give it away because it did not fit her. When I saw the tear I understood yesterday's "new leaf", as Mrs Carsfield put it. Was up to the dodge in a jiffy. Got the dress — bought some stuff at Clayton's and made my sister Bertha sew it while I had dinner. I knew what would be happening this end of the line — and I knew you'd see Helen through for the sake of getting one in at Henry.'

'How thoughtful of you, Doctor!' said the old woman. 'I'll tell Anne I found it under my dolman.'

'Yes, that's your ticket,' said Doctor Malcolm.

'But, of course, Helen would have forgotten the whipping by tomorrow morning and I'd promised her a new doll . . .' The old woman spoke regretfully.

Doctor Malcolm snapped his bag together. 'It's no good talking to the old bird,' he thought, 'she doesn't take in half I say. Don't seem to have got any forrader than doing Helen out of a doll.'

Adolescence

JEAN DEVANNY

Such private things

The second happening in Dawn's childhood was minimised because Ralph, now a full-grown man, understood.

The coming of womanhood has been glorified by pen and brush. It has been depicted as an ineffable, spiritual thing creeping upon the gawkishness of free childhood, effecting by its touch a transformation into soft, trembling creatures of submission. It has been described by more common-sensible folk (chiefly menfolk who could not be expected to know anyhow) as a wonderful 'door' through which the maiden passes into the sacred precincts of life, of good and evil.

Truth is, there is nothing sacred or spiritual about it. Something beautiful there is (Into what natural process does beauty not penetrate?) but it is merely a stage in development, sometimes painful to some extent and perhaps regarded as troublesome. The beauty lies not in the thing itself but in the mental processes it engenders, in the ungaugeable potentialities of each fresh young body over which it claims dominion. The urbane and smug philistines can be assured that the actual coming of womanhood can be a very ugly thing indeed, a horrid thing, when explanations of its significance are regarded as the prerogative of the Mrs Halidays.

Dawn had left school, was as yet unwearied by the daily round of farm chores. Weekly she received a letter from Gavin Fuller and many books. And her friendship with Biddy Fane was engrossing to her. She was developing such a passion of love for the girl's beauty that even Ralph was taking second place.

Biddy loved her too.

Dawn grew more 'mannish', as Mrs Haliday called it, every day. That is, she grew closer to the free-living, natural, primitive woman type; strong in body and limb, fearless and brave. Ralph, now quite learned under Mr Glenny's and Fuller's instruction, would patiently explain to his mother how wrong she was in supposing Dawn 'mannish'.

'Can't you see, mother, that the closer a woman approaches the masculine type the closer she approaches the ideal womanhood? Women are meant to be strong and big and fine, and enduring, as real men are. How can we have a fine race if the mothers are to be puny, deformed creatures as many women are? Yes, you are deformed, mother. It is no use mincing words. Look at your drawn-in waist, your protruding stomach, your flabby breasts and drooping shoulders. Be quiet and let me finish. I know it is work and child-bearing, mother, but work and child-bearing should not do that to you, and they will not do it to Kiddo here if she keeps on with her physical exercises. It's the artificial standard of womanhood you've got, mother; you don't see Dawn right.'

But poor Mrs Haliday, thinking on the drudgery of her life, her suffering, and being unable to understand that Ralph was really pointing out the chief cause of it, would shrill out in anger against his 'fool ideas' and Ralph would be quiet for the sake of peace.

One day the young man walked into the kitchen and found a strange Dawn there. A Dawn with a white, scared face, who dodged round the table when she saw him.

'What's up?' The boy stopped and spoke quickly. But she just stood and looked at him, wide-eyed, then turned and rushed out of the back door. Ralph, following her, amazed, suddenly stopped, whistled softly and then went for his mother.

'Dawn wants you, Mother,' he said. 'Wants you quick, too.' She turned mildly and he grew impatient.

'I tell you Dawn wants you quickly, Mother. She has run away outside. Go after her quickly.'

'Why, what's the matter with her?' Mrs Haliday spoke testily.

'It seemed to me that she was frightened.' He looked suspiciously at his mother. 'Didn't you tell her?'

Mrs Haliday was outraged. She blushed vividly. How dared Ralph? How dared he know such — such private things? Tell Dawn, indeed! Bad enough that it had to happen without speaking of it before it was necessary. She shut her lips in a tight line and stalked past Ralph.

He shuffled a bit uneasily and kicked at the wall. Then he leant against the doorway and thought of Dawn's terror-stricken face.

Mrs Haliday would have found this job an embarrassing one at any time. But Ralph had outraged her, angered her and so, when she found little Dawn crouched behind the hayshed, instead of a kind silence or word or smile she was harsh and forbidding and simply said:

'Come inside, Dawn.'

She took the child's hand and led her inside without a word. Ralph saw them come in, saw the little face white and afraid and lost. A savagery boiled up within him; — but surely his mother would talk now.

In privacy Dawn looked up at her mother, so stern and really suffering that her child should have life's battle before her; she saw the woman's face work and she stammered out a choked: 'Mother!'

Embarrassed, and unable to cope with a situation so outside the scope of her experience, the woman said:

'It is all right, child. Don't worry, Dawn.'

Then, thinking such treatment sufficient for the occasion (had it not had to suffice for herself?) she hurriedly kissed the child and left her.

Ralph returned to the yard to work but found that he could not rid himself of the sight of that terrified little face. So of a sudden he flung down his spade and strode in on his mother at work in the kitchen.

'Where's Dawn?'

Mrs Haliday turned a cold eye upon him.

'You leave Dawn alone,' she snapped. 'She's resting.'

'Did you explain to her?' he asked.

'Ralph, I'm ashamed of you!' she burst out. 'How dare you talk to your mother like that? I — '

He gripped her arm and thrust his face forward in sudden rage. 'Cut that, and answer me.'

She became passionately excited and dragged her arm away.

'I explained nothing!' she cried. 'And neither will you! You dare to teach my child things she shouldn't know!'

Ralph blazed.

'Your child?' he thundered. 'Your child! Yes, that's the hell of it! That women like you should be allowed to bear little children to torture! Why — !'

But here the terrified little face rose up in his mind's eye and he became inarticulate. He lifted an arm, brawny, with the soilure of the yard still clinging to it, knotted his fist and yelled:

'Blast your toad's philosophy! From now on that child is mine! I brought her up and she's mine!'

He rushed to Dawn's bedroom and pounded on the door. He called:

'It is Ralph, Dawn! Let me in.'

A red-eyed, woeful, poor little mite opened the door. He picked her up and poured out upon her a torrent of explanation of the processes of nature.

'But why didn't she tell me, Ralph?' the child asked. 'Why didn't she?' And Ralph, sobered now and ashamed of his violence to the poor creature whose ignorance he understood well enough, answered:

'It is so big a subject and so complex that I'm not just clever enough to explain properly, Kiddo. But you must understand that Mother's ignorance is not her fault. Mother, just being a common-old-garden-variety person, has never attempted to think for herself. She is the victim of a false ethical code, a false ideal of womanhood. The world is upside-down, little Sis, and it must be the work of us young people to turn it right side up. You know, Dawn, most animals, human or otherwise, run true to type. That is, they resemble the other individuals of their race. But now and again a few minds rise above the common clay of the great majority, a few individuals spring up who do not run true to type, who refuse to draw their actions and ideas from a common mould; men and women who are bright enough to see short cuts to ultimate advancement and are brave enough to take them and blaze the trail for the slow-thinking masses to follow. They leave books, Dawn, the only real jewel-cases, and their books, sometimes by mere chance, fall into the hands of us young ones waiting and the seed is sown and grows.

'Dawn, I hate this place! These farmers and their wives and children are just clods. Talk to them of what is going on in the world outside, the world that is brought to me by Glenny's books, and they gape like their beasts; they think one mad. I want to get away to the crowded places, Dawn, to the places where men congregate and compare ideas. To where the stream of life is flowing, generating force as it goes, the force of Progress.'

Ralph, under the stress of unusual emotion, had voiced desires long brooding, and Dawn, forgetting already what had brought him to her, clung to him excitedly and interrupted:

'Oh, Ralph! Me too! You'll take me too? We'll both go away to Mr Fuller!'

Ralph laughed, his ardour cooled by her too literal acceptance of his words.

'I let myself run away, Kiddo; but you and I will go some day, though. Don't say a word, Dawn, to the Dad or the others, but, between you and me, I am going to work in the mines at Paranga when Dad is more independent of me.'

Dawn was immensely impressed and promised secrecy. They grew very confidential, talking about various things there. Ralph quite forgot his work and neither gave a thought to the poor lone woman sitting in the kitchen, her head upon her hands, the slow tears dropping one by one. Tears of parenthood! Slow drops of gall drawn forth by the alienated young.

By-and-by the two remembered their mother. Laughing, they came out to her and saw the tears. Ralph fondled her and caressed her, a thing he had never done before, and perhaps, also, for the first time a daughter's hands really touched the mother-heart.

When they left her the tears were coming quickly but Mrs Haliday was smiling softly to herself.

ROBIN HYDE

Little ease

I'm not afraid of those girls. I despise them, they are so ordinary. Then why are your eyes watering, Cry-baby-cry . . .
I didn't think it would be so big, or so lonely: so many girls in navy blue gym frocks, their thick hair plaited, bobbed or tied behind with plain black ribbon. Mother won't let me cut mine; it won't plait, and it's so curly that, when it is tied, it stands out in a red bush. School regulation costume: navy serge gym costume, with plain white blouse, black girdle, black woollen stockings, black heel-less sandshoes. Chisholm House tie; black band with college colours about your hat, which is in winter a straw cady, making a thick red furrow on your forehead; in summer — much better — a panama.

Some of the IIIA girls are very tall and sophisticated. They have been a year in the form already. Common sense tells that they are the slow ones, the left-overs, but it's hard not to be impressed by them. They know their way about, Christine calls to Fifi, 'Here, I've kept our desk,' and gives a scathing glance at any little cuckoo who flutters near.

If you have the slightest symptoms of a figure above your waist, the gym frock makes you look like a navy-blue barrel.

'Can't you climb up the ropes hand over hand? Can't you do somersaults from the horizontal bar? At our school, we always had gym. Watch Simone Purcell, she's *good.*'

'That's not bad, Eliza. Oh, did you hurt yourself? Didn't she come down hard on her head?'

'Girls, atten-*shun.*'

'That's old Griffin. You don't have to take much notice of her. Betty Peters is her favourite. I'd rather die than be a favourite, wouldn't you? Miss Griffin's got a young man. He can't be very particular, she must be old as the hills. She's always thinking of him, you watch the way she sits with her mouth pursed up. She writes letters to him behind her exercise book, when she's supposed to be correcting our work. One day Fifi Longford picked up a sheet of letter she had written, and it began "Sam, darling." Sam, darling! Fifi handed it back before all the girls. She was nearly bursting. I'll bet Miss Griffin must be forty. I'd rather die, wouldn't you?'

Dismembered pieces of buttercup: light, cold voice. Girls, this is the calyx . . . this is the corona . . . here are the stamens . . . If you hold a buttercup under your chin and it makes a shine like painted metal, you steal butter; but they don't say that. All the King's horses and all the King's men will never put dismembered buttercup together again. Two rolls of pink crinkly paper have vanished from the classroom. Miss Adderley wanted them to make paper roses for the school bazaar. When she can't find them anywhere, she stalks out, two bright spots of displeasure on her cheekbones, to report the loss to Miss Verriam, the head mistress. The girls chatter volubly. Of course, old Mrs Macarthy, the caretaker's wife, must have moved them by accident.

A voice, flickering cold as a sword, whips out of its scabbard.

'Why don't you ask Eliza Hannay where they are? She's sitting right next to the windowledge where Miss Adderley left them.'

Of all the aviary voices, not one is chattering. Why don't you ask Eliza Hannay? There is a spot of ink right in front of her blouse, and her hair sticks out behind. The bush smells purple and golden-brown. They have put high wire-netting over these classroom windows, so that you can't look out. I was dux of my school, but the girls from Oddipore are all scattered, like the frail little pink and indigo blobs of jelly washed up at Island Bay after a big storm. What on earth would I do with two rolls of pink crinkly paper? At St Monica's church socials they always had it, festooned in streamers across the roof, pink lattice work and dusty roses over the walls. Two iced buns and a glass of weak pink lemonade. Carly went as Cinderella, in a pink sateen frock and a white apron; her little Cinderella slipper was tied to her waistband, and her long hair touched her waist. Sandra was a forget-me-not . . . Mother nearly worked her eyes out scalloping the blue satin petals, and I was Union Jack, though I didn't much want to be. I recited, and that girl with the red hair danced. She looked like wavering smoke. Anyhow, Calver Street was next door to a slum. I hate this clean place, the too many voices, too many bodies: too large. But I'm not going to cry.

'You needn't have made Eliza cry, Simone Purcell. You might just as easily have taken the crinkly paper yourself.'

'She's a baby. Fancy snivelling over a joke.'

'Well, you've no right to say she's a thief. If that's your idea of a joke, you might as well keep quiet.'

'Let her alone. Simone's only showing off.'

A queer face, Simone's. The forehead is bumpy, like a young boy's, and beneath very black brows stare out pale-green eyes, leopard eyes. They have a slightly vacant, wandering look, and are not quite straight. She has just missed a squint. Her hair is fine, perfectly straight, neither gold nor Saxon tow-colour, but fine gilt. Her lower lip thrusts out, sullen, and her hands are ugly, the blunt, ineffectual hands of somebody who should have been an artist, and can't. Always those blunt fingers are scribbling things on paper, nymphs almost lovely, but preposterously lean and long, profiles of hideous Austrian-looking wenches, all nether lip and top eyelash. And they aren't any good. The neat little unimaginative drawings of Fifi Longford come off, Simone's don't. Her body, in its shabby clothes, is lithe and slender.

Simone Purcell, I am going to make you sit up and take notice. Simone, why did you say I took the pink crinkly paper, when you knew I didn't, and you could just as easily have picked on anyone else? Because you knew I'd cry? But I'm not soft all the way through . . . Or because the others hadn't interested you?

I can hit back. I can say clever things quickly, without stopping to think. At the end of a month, the girls laugh, and say, 'Eliza Hannay is rotten at games, but she *is* witty.' 'Look at the doorstep sandwiches her mother cuts her for lunch,' pipes little brown Alice Fagan. And when I am beaten, in a class debate, Fifi Longford, one of the big, handsome left-overs served up cold from last year's IIIA, says under her breath, 'Serve you right, Miss Eliza Hannay.' They're hostile, but they had three pretty good speakers against me, and mine were duds . . . poor little Kattie Bryce will giggle. Simone and I together could wipe the floor with them.

I hate Simone Purcell; and I can make her look round whenever I like. You don't say in your head, 'Simone, look at me — Simone, look at me'; that's a dud way. You just look at the back of her head, and make all the thoughts go bobbing out of your mind, like corks on a slack tide. The most absurd words and ideas go bobbing past. Then she looks. . . . When Miss Adderley or Miss Codrington says something funny without meaning to, she looks of her own accord, and poor old Coddie throats, 'Girls, I will *not* have undercurrents of understanding in my classes.' Simone's laughter comes up in little bubbles behind the pale-green iris. We know we'll never forget the phrase, 'undercurrents of understanding'.

But we are enemies. Our looks cross like daggers. I am only waiting my chance. Only her eyes are like grass with the sun on it . . .

From the big hall where prayers are said every morning, and lessons read out of the Old Testament, rusty as if with dried blood, a wooden staircase mounts up beneath a wall hung with deep-coloured prints. Every stair is slightly crooked and hollowed, where the feet of girls and girls and girls, some of them wearing the great mushroom hats and muslin blouses of the 'nineties, ran up and down. They used to play croquet and archery, and this school was then an establishment for young ladies, with no scholarship or Government subsidy brats. Somehow I love those wooden hollows, inside me; but I will not tell. There is a dusty museum upstairs, and the long, stained rooms are labelled 'Chemical Laboratory', 'Botany', 'Home Science'. But we never do anything by wholes, it is all dismembered, like the buttercup, and nobody has the energy to stick it together again. It comes as a little clean thrill, a shock of surprise, when your mind makes even the most trifling discovery for itself, puts two silly little bits of picture-puzzle together. I was thrilled when I discovered that matter has the property of contraction and expansion — and yet, look how easy. We were young and keen when we came here, we had passed our examinations well. Now they get out their textbooks, and slap bits and pieces into us. Things equal to the same thing are equal to one another. Common are to either sex, artifex and opifex. Nobody ever says, 'You are learning this *because*,' and gives a reason. It's all cold, like jellied sauce set around a dismal pudding. Only sometimes things explain themselves — poetry, English, French. And then they dare, they dare, to laugh at William Morris, and Miss Hebron simpers too.

Not worth learning. I translated for myself —

> Les sanglots longs
> Des violons
> De l'automne —
>
> Autumn's violins
> In lengthened sobbing,
> Wound my heart with restless
> Dullness of their throbbing,

but nothing in English could be as lovely as the sound of 'les sanglots longs'.

At the bottom of the garden are two great oak trees, their leaves a green murmuring summer. You can eat your lunch alone or in groups, though if you sit alone you look left out. The girls get up lazily and play croquet, or bump the seesaw against the ground, but the real sports play basketball and cricket. Once Cassie James sliced a cricket ball right over the high tin wall and into the street. She is ugly, stupid, and so round-shouldered that she is almost hunchbacked, but the college is proud of her, as of some terrible hunting trophy, a pair of elk's horns brought home from the mountains.

Eliza on the basketball court faces the enemy. Run — dodge — splodge. 'Pass, can't you, pass.' As the hard leather smacks her palms, a sudden acute pain runs up the little finger Sandra once broke. When the whistle blows, her finger is beautifully swollen, and the ache red-hot.

'Back to your places, girls. Pass, there, pass.'

At half-time Eliza goes up to the nut-cheeked young sports mistress, whose bosom and sturdy haunches look absurd in just the same navy-blue gym frock as that worn by the girls.

'Please, Miss Jamieson, I'm afraid I've broken my finger.'

Miss Jamieson starts to say, 'Nonsense.' Then she changes her tune.

'Cold water, bandages and a sling. Run inside, and Miss Hebron will fix it up for you. You've sprained it, anyhow.'

The finger is not broken, but dislocated; and, blessed sequel, it pops out again at the first impact of the leather. 'You'll be no good for basketball,' says Miss Jamieson, sourly. 'How are you going to fill in your spare time?'

'I'm on the Library Committee, Miss Jamieson' — but at sight of the young mistress's face, Eliza hastily added, 'and I'll learn to swim, and walk a lot, and play croquet, and perhaps next term my finger will be all right.'

And I love climbing the hills, especially when they're grey, and the two old oaks down at the bottom of the garden, and writing poetry, and the hollows in the stairs, and the colours in the Wars of the Roses prints — you know, the ones in the outside hall. And I like English sometimes, and French, but I've read to the end of the book while they're still on Chapter Two, and it's so dull sitting about. And I *hate* mathematics — to listen gives me a sick feeling in my spine, like cramp; and I read Tacitus from a crib, one of my father's books, because it's so interesting, and better to get the whole sense than blundering on from phrase to phrase, like caterpillars in a nightmare. And Miss Farquhar was not right in her translation about getting vermin and diseases from swine. But I love 'And the pearls there are darker than the pearls of other seas,' that's Tacitus, and 'Nox atra, qui abstulit colorem res,' that's in Virgil. Can't you see it? 'Black night, that steals away the hues of earth.' And you've got a skeleton monkey upstairs in the little museum. I like that too, I don't know why, except that skeletons look so clean and wise. I love Rostand's *Chanticleer* in the library, and so does Simone Purcell, the girl with the green eyes, whom I hate. You think she's a good sport because sometimes she can throw a goal at basketball, but you wait, Miss Jamieson — she's as bad as me, if not worse. And, Miss Jamieson, I hate the wire-netting over the windows, and the way the girls laugh about poetry, and the size of them massed together, because the navy-blue costume makes us look as if we were all bits of the same substance, overflowed into different vats. And I hate Miss Verriam, because she's a snob. But she's like my Aunt Bernardine. It's not our fault she had to take State School girls instead of remaining an academy for mushroom hats with respectable pinheads under them. Oh, and I do conversational French because Madame Renault is like a damson — there's a little dark bloom on her skin, and her lips are velvety. And I don't carry Miss Cairn's books to be a favourite, but because I am rather sorry for her. She means well and looks silly, doesn't she?

'Try bandaging with iodine,' advised Miss Jamieson. She was rather a nice girl, but too hearty, and her eyes popped.

A little while after, Eliza had her chance with her darling enemy, Simone. Simone slipped and fell on the basketball court, tearing one knee right out of her stocking. Her cheeks turned wild rose, her green eyes looked bewildered, then filled. Eliza suspected that the Purcells, like the Hannays, hadn't much money. Simone's clothes were almost worse than hers. Afterwards in the classroom, Miss Hebron asked Simone a question which anyone could have answered. She stood up; the leopard eyes looked about her in a hunted way, then she stammered, burst into tears.

'Sit down, Simone. Don't be such a child.'

'Coals of fire,' thought Eliza. She stood up.

'Please, Miss Hebron, Simone isn't a child.'

'Eliza Hannay, sit down at once.'

'Please, she isn't. Simone fell and hurt herself. She hit her head on the asphalt, I saw her. She has the most terrible headache, and she didn't want to tell anyone.'

'Oh.' A long pause. 'Well, in that case you'd better take Simone's terrible headache home, Eliza, since you're so concerned.' Miss Hebron was being sarcastic, but it didn't matter.

'Thank you, Miss Hebron.'

Outside, Simone, still crying, said, 'Liar. Dirty little liar.'

'If you howl any more, people in the street will think you've just come back from a funeral, or been expelled,' Eliza advised dispassionately. The hills were quite near, delicate hard grey. At one place a quarry made a high scar, hacked out of the grass. Eliza thought, 'Wherever she goes, I'm going too.' Water splashed down the misty threads. Simone climbed and climbed, as if she could never get tired. There was a glint of berry-red in the grass, and Eliza picked up a necklace of red beads strung on tarnished silver. She felt disappointed that somebody else had been there before, but the beads were pretty. The rocks were now like living things, animals with flat, out-thrust faces. They rattled and slithered underfoot, and suddenly Eliza's stomach felt sick. She heard her voice, too high, saying what her mind ordered it not to say.

'I can't climb up there. I'm not going any farther.'

Simone climbed on. Eliza scrambled ineffectually at a rock-face, got on a ledge six feet up, looked, and was not quite sure if she could get up or down.

'That's right, cry. You hate me, don't you?'

'I don't hate you, I despise you.' But to despise anyone, clinging straddled against a rock-face like a baboon, only a ridiculous little drop of six feet below, was just talk. And beyond that, she didn't hate Simone any longer, didn't despise her. The shadows of clouds moved mighty over the rocks and grass, and they weren't tainted by Simone's presence there. Trees had been planted farther along, little pines thrusting their nuggety brown-flowered heads into the arc of the air. They lay beneath them and laughed, sliding the pine-needles between their fingers. Eliza gave Simone the red beads on the tarnished necklace.

Next day in class Simone told it all, imitating Eliza on the rock-face. 'I d-don't h-hate you, I d-despise you.' One of the big girls said crushingly, 'Don't tell tales out of school.' Eliza didn't greatly care: Simone was hers. In a strange way, it was pleasant to look up in dream, look up the ridiculous inaccesible rock-face and see her friend's face above.

'Mother, I'm in IVA this year.'

'Of course you are.'

Eliza's name wasn't in the senior scholarship list, but there was an Elsie Hannay. 'It's a misprint. Of course you won your scholarship,' said Augusta firmly, and the gods obeyed her. Of course it was Eliza . . .

'Mother, I'm in VA this year.'

'Of course you are.'

Carly, who was a year ahead in time, was among the B girls. But she didn't mind. She said, 'I know I'm not clever,' and didn't want to be. Carly hadn't to sit for matriculation, which would have frightened her out of her life. The ugly red mark scored by the school hat across her forehead made her look like a worried marmoset. She was dying to throw it away, to put on soft, floppy hats and dresses right down to the ground, dresses of flowered voile and organdie. While you were in school uniform you must never be seen talking to a boy, not even your own brother, but Trevor Sinjohn still took Carly walking over the hills every week-end, and she went up to the Sinjohn's house on Sundays to help with the cooking. Mrs Sinjohn, a tiny woman with swollen varicose veins, said Carly was a dear, good girl, a true daughter.

When Eliza was nearly fifteen, she thought she was in love with Trevor Sinjohn too, and wrote verses about him:

I bring thee passion-flowers of my dreams —

Trevor never knew. The grey hills, the oldness and dirtiness of the cemetery, leaned through the windows of her little room, leaned on her heavily. There was a clay road slanting up between far rows of pines, and the dying sun dwelt on it. She thought if she could one day walk up it alone she would be happy. At other times she cried: 'I'll run away. I'll run away and live in the bush.'

Augusta provoked her, and Eliza told her, 'I do love Trevor Sinjohn, so there.' 'You must be mad. You ought to be ashamed of yourself,' retorted Augusta. She was growing heavily middle-aged, her face in the light of the little green room was hard and uncompromising. She distrusted Eliza, and for a moment thought, 'Better she had never been born.' To take Carly's boy away, even to look sideways at him, would have been the unforgivable sin. But she need not have worried.

After Eliza had thought of Trevor's cat eyes for a month, and written him several ardent poems, she forgot him.

It was Simone who understood, in her off-hand way — sometimes striking out, sometimes as good a friend as the black pine-tops. Augusta called Simone 'that little harlot', because she put on lipstick; and because Augusta had intercepted a letter in which Simone said that they would have lovers when they were grown up, but not too many babies.

'Girls, atten-shun. Right wheel. Forward march. Touch your toes. Swing the trunk from the hips. Keep your abdomens in and your chests out. Stand at ease. Atten-shun.'

SYLVIA ASHTON-WARNER
On the outside looking in

In summer we four did a great deal of swimming at the town baths and often the other three played tennis at school, Penelope with the boys. You'd be amazed at how well Cupid plays tennis. In winter, coached by Miss Cumberland, we played tough basketball which made me later home still. Penelope made the A team but I could only make the B, dammit, no matter how arduously I practised. I wasn't quick enough and nothing could make me that. My canvas basketball shoes fell off the carrier of my bike one day and I didn't see them again. A terrible row blew up at home and Muriel emptied her purse to buy me some more which at once fell off the carrier again, brand-new, same day, so that she put an advertisement in the paper: 'Lost: one pair of white canvas shoes. Return to Sylvia Lost-Warner.' A story still endures from those times that when Sylvie brought home the mail from the corner they used to send one of the younger children to walk behind her to pick up the letters as she dropped them, so that they'd get their full quota.

By great good fortune our form teacher was Miss Cumberland who loved concerts and music and drama. On account of my freak memory I was useful at the piano and successful with drawings in the class magazine, not sketches and cartoons as Miss Cumberland called them. She and the others loved me drawing them and I took fine care not to ridicule them, and finer care still not to offend Dr Roydon though I must say he was a cartoonist's dream come true; maybe I did. I remember a drawing I made of him from the back view, swaying along the corridor with a strap swinging in one hand. He may not have liked that. And a poem or two but the boys could beat me there and the girls wrote the articles. But in this area at least my wares marketed and it's a good thing I had *something* to offer.

We were extended to the limit and very happy. There was no doubt in the minds of the four of us that we were excessively excellent, that the new school had been built specifically for us and that if there were anything we didn't know it was obviously not worth knowing. You should have seen us outside our classroom door at morning interval in the crowded corridor talking at top pitch with all stops out and the loud pedal on.

I was not unaware of other people in high school but they had to be stars or I didn't see them; people of charm, breeding and brains. I remember Portia in a form ahead telling me even as far back as that, 'I'm going to be an author,' to which I replied, 'I'm going to be an artist.' Not that we friended up, she was already indivisibly united with her Latin suffix Gwen, but we've kept an eye out for each other since. Also included in those out-loud sessions in the corridor were the Mannering girls, a form behind me, Ursula and Madge, whose people had produced a Minister of the Crown, and the new master's sensational step-daughter Jancy, the most beautiful girl in town. I could draw Jancy now with my eyes tight shut.

The nearest I got to actually loving anybody was Ursula Mannering; you often get a pleasant face equalling a pleasant nature, but the real thing, whether love or hate, the inspiration, came from a girl I rarely encountered, again from the third form, Veronica Dundonald; a rather solitary girl, a soprano, who sent word would I play her accompaniment. In the privacy of the schoolroom at home at the weekend I painted, practised and wrote for her my ultimate best. She was rich, cultivated and authentically exclusive but I avoided her in the crowded corridors, too shy of the reality to stand it. Exposure to the source of one's inspiration is a shattering business. Automatically she took her place in the succession of my ideal girls.

What taxed me was the way people paired off. Once you had chosen your mate like Jessica-and-Lila, Portia-and-Gwen, the twosome was unassailable. No third could push in. At best you could be a plus, not a part. You picked each other at the start and that was it. I'd never picked a mate at the start of any of my fourteen schools but it concerned me now that people had paired at the district high school before I'd ever got there, which had something to do with the continuity in a school like that where a newcomer remained a plus, excepting Penelope, who also had not paired, yet was never on her own, having a wonderful gift of integrating with a group. Circumstance alone had put us together although I liked her very much . . . popular, pretty, brainy and sporty, though I was not at ease with her. For her part, she'd visibly weighed the pros and cons in 4A, saw no alternative and opted to make the best of it. For these first two terms in 4A I was not alone and I too was popular in a hit-and-miss way. I had no enemies that I was aware of. I was not a marked man.

Indeed a glamour lit up my living. I had been accustomed to this in the world of fantasy but now it spilled over into reality like lights flashing from one mirror to another. A sense of miracle was my companion assuring me I could do anything I set myself to so that, astride two worlds, one foot in fantasy and the other in reality, I behaved a bit larger than life. Dazzled and less than responsible. Yet the context suited one like me and it was my happiest time in any school.

Out of school was another thing. I could not join in their social life not being in the position to exchange hospitality and I didn't have a white dress and racquet and all that. However my vanishing after school without trace was not something they accepted as they couldn't take readings of my background; in place of a visible respectable home in an identifiable street was a vacuum of impenetrable mystery, which I suppose I romanticised and, if I didn't, I should have: you can't waste good stuff like that.

They tackled this theorem in their own way by organising picnics halfway home beneath Wardells Bridge where we swam and ran and climbed the willows and talked about teachers and boys. But all it engendered was an unrest in me. Wardells Bridge was too close to home and their company too close to the bone.

Then they tried inviting me to their homes for weekends but instead of enjoying the elegance and affluence, a language my blood nevertheless understood, these visits were unsettling. The domestic proximity was not for me, besides, since I could not ask them back to my place, I felt I was walking on quicksand and I sensed a trembling at base.

This may well have been the time when the walls of personality began eroding, not only from the traffic between reality and dream but from the wear and tear of feeling. Joy can corrode as much as sorrow; from either you get the battering within as well as the battering without so that the walls which enclose you become thinner as you live along, whereas you need strong walls round your personality to prevent the intrusion of the personalities of others. Feeling is so contagious it can penetrate anything. What was once your own distinct personality becomes a fermenting hotch-potch of everyone else's and you find yourself thinking from so many facets that you don't know what you think yourself.

In my journey through life so far this time spent in 4A with the first and the best was like the highest point on the road where stood an inn with lighted windows. Inside it was crowded where people drank hot fresh tea. To a wayfarer like me the portal was open and I was welcome by right, if not for what I looked like then for the wares I had. In this crisp air I was holding my own within the company, on the inside looking out. The world had stopped taking it out of me and was giving with both hands.

So far none knew of my Te Whiti background of smouldering explosive secrets but there was always the chance they would. At thirteen in that society I believed the dimensions of a person were defined by place and circumstance. I was decades off realising that accident of dwelling place does not necessarily mean parochialism of the soul.

In tracing the course of my schooling in Masterton I am somewhat circumscribed because it took place less in the classrooms than on the roads getting there and back. My real schoolrooms were the countryscapes, my desk the saddle of a bike or a horse and my teachers the wilful weathers. It astounds me how little I remember of what went on in the actual classrooms; I could contain in a few chapters what I learnt in all those schools, whereas about what happened outside of them I could go on ad infinitum without repeating myself.

I had an idea I was missing out. I wanted to do my work. I liked schoolwork but you couldn't hold a book on a bike. Maybe I could on a horse. The high school did have a horse-paddock handy so, as Ashton had once said he'd see to my education if I stayed in Masterton, I asked him for a horse. He and Mumma did succeed in buying me something on four legs but it was hardly an Arab steed. To be fair it had traces of pedigree, cream in colour with white mane and tail and slender flowing bones except that you could see each one. Her head was not such a bad piece of drawing but her 'dark and fiery eye' had been quenched somewhat and she 'snuffed not the breezy wind'. True, her nostrils must have quivered one time but her lower lip by now drooped like a little basket you could carry your homework in, or your lunch.

In the poem you'd get lines like, 'Thy proudly arched and glossy neck,' but although Creamy's neck was long and shapely it did not arch like poetry. Her head hung down in a disillusioned way till her pendulant lower lip all but scooped up dust. You got the feeling that her dreams had not come true, or as though they had, which is worse. As though some thumping stallion had indeed ravaged the best of her but had got off scot free.

Her movement could have been worse when she moved at all but she seemed so short of energy that you'd think she had a temperature or something and although they bought me a saddle it was only one of those pads with a girth-strap used on fat ponies which did little to nullify her backbone. I could write a strong feature for the editorial page of a newspaper on Backbones I Have Known.

'Fret not to roam the desert now with all thy wingéd speed . . .' Creamy had no speed, much less wingéd. All told, no sheik would have thrown down his gold for this steed.

However, I was not ashamed to be seen on her especially in the spring when the greener grass made her a little frisky when she'd lift her head at least to the level of her shoulders and she was better than the bike. What two wheels could pick their way down a bouldered track under Wardells Bridge to graze among the buttercups? No bike had the amble of a lazy horse like the rhythm of stirring the porridge. Headwinds meant nothing. I could learn my French declensions on Creamy and even tried writing out geometry theorems until the day when Mr Bee held up this mangy bit of paper to the class like an

Exhibit A and said in his lofty upper-class English voice, 'Solvia Oshton-Wonner. Do I take this to be your hommwok?' After which I put the time into excuses instead, which called for no writing on horseback, so that when one of the boys had missed his homework too Mr Bee suggested he ask Solvia to supply his excuse.

The girls liked Creamy though. They saw her to be romance itself and fell over each other to catch her after school to ride her as far as the gate; an unforeseen fringe benefit. Also, ambling on the grass at the side of the road continued to be a good time to learn aloud French and Latin grammar and English figures of speech, to memorise passages of Shakespeare set by Miss Cumberland, as well as passages not set by Miss Cumberland, the pages she skipped in class about Othello throwing his leg over Iago's thigh in bed when dreaming of Desdemona. Had Creamy not known the way home herself we could have ended up anywhere; none of which befell the others when walking on peopled pavements.

One day I met a man on a horse and we got talking he and I. His horse was enviably fat and frisky while mine was shamelessly thin. Why, he said, didn't I leave her home to graze for a few months and ride some of the condition off his fat thing. He said I should start next Thursday and come to school on the service car and meet him after school at the post office at four o'clock. I would ride his horse home and he'd return on the service car.

On Thursday I cut basketball and ran off and on all the way down Renall Street and was at the post office at four. The town clock said so. All I could see in mind was this shiny fat horse to ride to school for months but he wasn't there so I waited. At five I was still waiting on the kerb gazing down the road that came from Te Whiti and feeling a little hungry. It would make a better story to say it was also sleeting and cold but in fact it was a lovely pre-spring afternoon as soft as a note of music.

At six I was waiting. I had no money for food of course and would not have left my vigil if I had. What I remember most about that afternoon is how lovely it was as an afternoon in its own right. Even though it was the main street with traffic and people it was movingly tender, momentous and still as though holding its breath, a feeling unrelated to any fat horse. The cars had a dreamy gliding, the people walked by with less haste it seemed and no one I knew passed by.

The hours turned over into evening, it was seven by the clock and the street lights were on, glamorously unreal to a country girl. The service car had departed long ago and no man brought me a horse. By now a night chill was fingering through my winter uniform though not a breath of air lifted my hair. On the kerb I waited watching. I did not allow it to occur to me that the man may not come. Some dreams are too strong to reject.

'Sylvia,' astonished, 'what on earth are you doing here at this time of night?' Miss Cumberland with a coat on and carrying a parcel.

A sudden blurt of tears. She stands over me on the kerb. Several good moments of the evening are wasted before I can say a thing. At last I manage to tell my tale upon which she takes me home to her place, the Holy of Holies. This was worse than the boarding house night and what would Daphne say.

The streets give way to a winding lane, unpaved and grassy at the side, named Hope Street. A small cottage shows up, two-storeyed, old-fashioned and narrow, a picket fence set close to the road and the whole painted white. Her mother is inside who sits and smiles with serene compassionate eyes while Miss Cumberland lays a blinding white cloth and gives me a meal which I try not to choke on, then a virgin white bedroom which I try not to die in. Her personality is too close, her composure lethal and my soul exposed to withering point. 'Shy' is not the word. Not one single white minute do I sleep all night and by morning I'm ill, unspecifically . . . Dr Roydon takes me home from school with two of the girls. . .

I never saw the man on the horse again.

About this time Mumma began to show characteristic signs of restlessness, lifting her nose to the breeze scenting fields afar, and Puppa too for all I know. It was not inspector trouble this time and not chairman trouble either. Mr Trate remained nobly patient though we 'little ones' must have tried him to the limit. We deserved to fear him but we didn't.

She must have done quite well at her teaching in Te Whiti because she applied in the open market for and was appointed to another sole charge school with a far better house and glebe, Rangitumau. The district was still within reach of Masterton. It had to be on account of my high school. For her it was a relatively short move as she favoured changing provinces. All we left in Te Whiti were our names carved on desks, banks and cliffs.

It was spring. We'd not seen Mumma so happy about a residence before. For a start it *was* a house, as distinct from a whare, cottage or dungeon; it was modern, equipped with facilities and for the first time we had a bathroom. It was fairly new, freshly painted, near the road with a lawn in front and a stone's throw from the school. No I'd not seen her so uplifted and inspired over her home before. After making the tea for her and Puppa she laid her plans. She bought a few dozen Lawsoniana trees and planted them herself round the fence for a hedge as nice people did and put in a vegetable garden at the side, the whole response unheard of. True, the new chairman and school committee failed to bring us a load of wood, help with our meat or lend us a cow but the service car went right past our place, stopped at the gate with the mail and bread and delivered the big ones when they came. Luxury indeed.

We found ourselves in a house we were not ashamed to say we lived in. When Daphne came home for the holidays she took one dive into that front garden, making paths, planting flowers and ferns and clipping the lawn till it looked, as Ashton said, 'like a bloomin' park'. Gracie was so relieved that she studied the idea of getting engaged since she could bring a young man home here, I forget which. If for no other reason than to pacify Mumma who would flatly say, 'Why don't you get ma-a-rried.' And Puppa too who hinted, 'I'm lonely for my grandchildren.' It was something the big ones had no answer to, other than do something about it. From her own salary Gracie bought cane mats for the living room floor and two brand-new cane chairs; you wouldn't believe it, we were like other people at last, that elusive desired state. As things were now I could have asked the girls at school to Rangitumau had it not been already a flick of fate too late. Since they'd uncovered my background at Te Whiti when Dr Roydon drove me home ill I'd been de-registered, de-frocked and dropped. Not that I would have asked them inside to meet everybody since there'd be no telling what different ones would be doing, or what they'd say in such crisis, but they could have seen it from the top of the road in the distance and said, 'So *that's* where she lives. Passable.'

Too late. Too bad. Schools as such were overrated as places of important learning. Give me a tree-fern any day to one of your Latin prefixes. In the meantime Rangitumau was a glorious classroom, one of Nature's own; tucked in the foothills of the ranges within sight of the forest fires at night and within smell of the smoke it was a painting of a place like Te Pohue and Umataroa; hills of bush, risky ravines and mysterious lanes all over again leading through the valleys to nowhere and many a fine bank to carve drawings on and sign your name to them. Me and Norma and Marmie and 'Vadne, and in that order, off we'd go into the morning to claim Rangitumau and sign the whole place. Bread we'd carry in a paper bag and we'd drink from a tingling stream. On the lowland was a wistful river with willows gazing at themselves in the water where we'd swim and play an hour away in blank forgetfulness. Talk, sing, laugh and dream like heaven had fallen down.

Singing one evening up some soft glade to an innumerable audience of trees it did not get through to me that this kind of celebration would not qualify a girl for exams or for confrontation with life. By whatever measure ye measured, Rangitumau was a glorious place except for one flaw: my seven miles to school were now eleven.

MARY FINDLAY

Show your father you love him

'Could you please tell me why I wasn't selected for the team?'
'Certainly, Mary, if you're sure you want to know.'
'Of course I want to know.'
'Well frankly, you're too dirty. Your blouses are scruffy, your hair needs washing and your fingernails — ugh!'

I had asked for an explanation and I got it. How was she to know the hot-water tank at home had rusted away? What use to tell her of flat irons which, when heated over a fuel stove, made black marks on blouses?

'Soap and water cost very little,' she commented.
'What do you know about it?' I shouted and fled precipitately.

I expected to be punished for this outburst but Miss Grove took no action. A few days later, while performing on the wooden horse in the gymnasium, I fell and dislocated my shoulder. Miss Grove took me to the doctor who cut off the sleeves of my blouse and snipped my singlet at the shoulder. My pitiable underwear was thus exposed. I felt more embarrassment than pain. The doctor manipulated the joint and put my arm in a sling, and the teacher drove me home. As we reached the gateway, the big ugly man whom my father had called the bailiff was waiting.

'Mrs Wilkinson?' he said to the teacher.
'No, but this is Mary Wilkinson,' she replied.
'Thank you,' he said and walked away.

She helped me to undress and get into bed. As she left, she said, 'I'm very sorry about the basketball, Mary. If I'd realised how difficult things were for you I would never have spoken to you the way I did.'

The apology scarcely registered. I was worrying about the bailiff. She had told him my name. What would my father say? I decided to keep quiet about it. I had worries enough. The doctor had ruined my second blouse, so now I was reduced to one. It was the middle of winter with many wet days. How on earth was I going to manage to wash and dry the remaining one?

The school dance was coming up. It was known as a 'hen hop', that is, an all-female occasion, girls dancing with girls. Attendance was compulsory for fifth and sixth forms. Floor-length evening frocks were worn but the Head had announced in Assembly that this year, in view of the times, gymfrocks or summer dresses would be acceptable. I took no part in the enthusiastic discussions preliminary to this great event. In the classroom, paper patterns and scraps of material were handed around. Most of the girls' frocks were being made by their mothers, but some few were going to dressmakers. At home I tried on each of my three dresses. All had the same fault, they wouldn't go over my shoulders. Disastrously, I had grown! I turned them inside out but found there was no seam allowance, as Belle had let them out to the limit. I would have to wear the gymfrock and I knew for certain that I would be the only sixth-former to do so.

Resentment turned to anger and anger to deceit. I wouldn't go! Why should I be subjected to more humiliation if I could avoid it? Two days before and one day after the dance I stayed away from school. I knew without asking that my father would not write the required note explaining my absence, so I successfully forged his handwriting and gave a bad cold as my excuse. I got away with it.

I had bought the gloves and evaded the school dance. There remained the question of the blouse. If I were to continue at school I must have a second blouse. I asked my father for the money and he refused it. I counted my cash, yes, I had enough to buy a blouse but would have nothing left if I did so. God, I was sick of it all. Sick of pennypinching, sick of schoolgirls, sick of Dirty Dicks, sick of petty problems. School had lost its appeal; being in the sixth form was hollow without prefect status, and being without suitable clothes and pocketmoney excluded me from many activities. To hell with them! I'd keep my few bob for the emergencies which were bound to arise and I'd manage with one blouse — and if it was dirty that would be just too bad.

My father was drinking again. I avoided him as much as possible. The midnight shift was the problem. On the four o'clock he was gone by the time I got home and I simply locked my door and sneaked out in the morning before he woke. But when he had his day off and when he was on the midnight he would come home after the pubs closed at six o'clock and expect me to attend to his wants. I would always hear him coming. He would yell from down the street, 'Mary, Mary, where's my girl?' As he drew nearer, it would be 'Mary! Where's the bloody girl?' Then he would burst into song: 'Ta ra ra boom de ay' and become more cheerful. 'Mary! Where are you, daughter?'

I used to stay indoors for this stage, otherwise I became a public spectacle. By the time he reached the door he was full of maudlin sentimentality. He wanted to kiss me. I loathed the smell of alcohol and his drunken embraces revolted me. 'You're getting a fine big woman, like your mother. Kiss your father, my girl, he's your best friend. Oh if only your mother was here to see you, my poor dear darling girl, she's gone — gone.' Then he would weep and demand more kisses. He would slump in a chair and talk about my mother.

If I were lucky I could humour him at this stage and he would go to sleep but often he turned nasty. 'Get my dinner, you big ugly lump and shake yourself. I keep you, don't I? You're nothing but a useless bitch. Time you went to work, I don't see why I should have to keep you.' If I said nothing, he would say, 'Bloody sulking, are you? Don't you treat me like that! Smile, damn you, or I'll belt you.' If I made any reply whatsoever, it was, 'Don't you answer me back. I'll thrash you within an inch of your life.'

These were not idle threats. He used either his belt or his fists. Sometimes both.

I grew cunning. About the time he was due home I would lock my door. He would bash and bang away, but he never broke the door in as he threatened to. Occasionally he did his drinking at home and then it was more tricky. I would creep down to the house and try to find out whether he was there or not. If he was asleep I would sneak into my room and lock the door, but if he was awake I had to hide in the bushes.

Those nights were interminable yet pride held me back from telling anyone. It was winter, dark soon after five, cold, and sometimes wet, waiting outside till 11.15 p.m. when he left for work and it was safe for me to go inside. After a while I improved my technique. If I found him at home I went back to town and sat in the lounge of a department store till 5.30 p.m. when they closed. From there I went to the public library which closed at 9 p.m. A half-hour's walk home took me to 9.30, which meant I had less than two hours to wait till his alarms went off.

All this was not helping me with my homework and I was in constant trouble at school as a result. I was afraid I would run out of money as I was buying my lunch (a pie) and evening meal (fish and chips). There was hardly any food in the house even when I did come home. All that was provided for me was bread and golden syrup which I supplemented with quantities of sugar. I ate it by the basinful. That winter I had seventeen boils on my back and shoulders.

One afternoon I was unlucky. I had just arrived home and, after making sure that my father was out, I stretched out on my bed. Hearing a noise outside, I remembered I hadn't locked the front door. 'It might be the bailiff' flashed though my mind. I tiptoed to my window and as I did so my father said, 'Now we'll see who's boss around here.'

I swung around in horror. He was in my room. His eyes were bulbous and bloodshot. He was rotten drunk. He swayed in the doorway, blocking my path, but even in drunkenness he was nimble on his feet. I had no hope of escape. He dragged a chair to him and sat down. 'Come here, my dear and kiss your father.' There was neither kindness nor sentimentality in his voice. 'Do as you are told,' he roared.

He undid his belt. 'Do you want me to come and get you?' Terrified, I moved towards him.

'Shake it up! Show your father you love him.'

As I advanced he stood up and wrenched my hair, bringing me to my knees. Through the pain I was conscious of the vile smell of excrement.

'You can kiss my boots, you bloody bitch. I'll teach you to avoid me!'

One hand held my hair, the other held his belt. He lifted his arm and brought the belt down over my head. 'Go on, kiss the shit. That's what you are, just shit.'

Another blow and another. He pushed my head down till my face was wet with the contents of his bowels.

He wasn't finished yet.

'Now my fine educated lady. Nobody sent me to college. Take my boots off and scrub them clean.'

This time he used the buckle end of his belt. The blow struck my breast and the pain was searing. Slowly and painfully I undid the laces. At last I finished. Quickly he grabbed my arm and twisted it behind my back.

'Now pick them up and clean them.'

Holding my arm, he pushed me to the sink and turned the tap on. As I lifted the boots, he let go of my arm and twisted my head under the running water. The tap caught my eye and I screamed. He let go my head and as I fell to the floor I caught sight of another man in the doorway.

'You're a bloody bully, aren't you? Call yourself a man? Why don't you tackle something your own size?'

'Who the bloody hell are you? And mind your own business, I'll do what I like with my own child.'

'You are James Lewis Wilkinson and you are hereby summoned to attend the magistrate's court on August the 5th at 9 a.m.'

My father stood quite still as he was handed a blue paper entitled 'Judgment Summons'. Then, turning to me, the bailiff said, 'Young lady, I'm taking you to a doctor.'

I gave the address. Dr Alan Hamilton, Seatoun.

I was growing up. I faced the doctor dry-eyed.

'Why Mary,' he exclaimed. 'What on earth — '

'My father did it.'

He patched me up. Cuts and bruises and a black eye where the tap had caught me. Calling his wife, he said, 'Mary will stay with us

tonight, Grace. After she's had a bath I'll give her a sedative. Will you see to her?'
   I accepted his ruling and allowed myself the luxury of bath, bed and a pretty nightgown. I swallowed the sedative and slept.
   It was raining when Mrs Hamilton brought in my breakfast.
   'Wake up, Mary.'
   'What time is it?'
   'Nine o'clock. Get up as soon as you've had your breakfast. The doctor is taking you to the Child Welfare Department and the appointment is for ten-thirty.'
   Mrs Hamilton had washed and pressed my clothes, and when we arrived my father was already there. I was surprised to see Aunt Elsie as well. We were all shown into an inner office. I kept beside the doctor. I was both hopeful and afraid.
   The Child Welfare Officer was a mannish-looking middle-aged woman. She had straight iron-grey hair and a homely face. She wore a suit with a shirt-blouse and tie. She addressed the doctor.
   'Dr Hamilton, as you have brought this matter to the notice of the department, will you outline the case?'
   'As you wish, Miss Duggan. I've known Mary Wilkinson for some months. She is an intelligent, able girl. She has been striving against considerable odds to educate herself. Last night she was brought to my surgery suffering from cuts and bruises inflicted by her father.'
   'It's a lie,' shouted my father, 'I never touched her!'
   'Mr Wilkinson, please don't interrupt. You will have your say later. Doctor, can you prove these injuries sustained by Mary Wilkinson were in fact caused by her father?'
   'I can bring a witness to prove it.'
   'Thank you, Doctor. Mr Wilkinson, what do you have to say?'
   'It's a lie. The girl is a liar. She came home in a mess. She had been fighting somewhere. She's uncontrollable, out all night. Put her away!'
   'Thank you, Mr Wilkinson.' She turned to Aunt Elsie. 'Mrs Cooper, you are Mr Wilkinson's sister?'
   'Yes.'
   'Has your brother, to your knowledge, ever ill-treated his daughter?'
   Aunt Elsie looked uncomfortable. 'He is my brother . . .' she faltered.
   'Mrs Cooper, I know that. Answer the question please.'
   'I don't wish to speak against my own family.'
   'I have no legal power to make you, but if this case comes to Court you will be obliged to answer. Already you have implied that you have some knowledge which stands against Mr Wilkinson. What you tell us will not go beyond this room and it may help towards a solution to this problem. Well, Mrs Cooper?'

Aunt Elsie went red and gulped. She turned to my father. 'I don't like saying it, Jimmy.'

My father was on his feet. 'Miss Duggan, my sister is unreliable. She's had nervous trouble. She's a sentimental fool and easily deceived.'

He was unfortunately right about this, but Aunt Elsie surprised me. 'Miss Duggan,' she said. 'My brother has an uncontrollable temper. He tortured me when I was a child and has struck me since I've been grown-up. He drinks heavily, I'm afraid.'

'Have you seen him strike his daughter?'

'I am sorry to say, yes. On many occasions.'

The Welfare Officer stood up. 'I wish to speak to Mary by herself and I must ask you all to wait in the outer office for a short time.'

When were were alone, she looked at me thoughtfully. 'Mary, I want you to listen very carefully and then think hard. You must understand, firstly, that you are past the school-leaving age of fourteen and over the age of consent, which is sixteen. You may leave school and leave home if you wish. Neither your father nor anyone else can stop you, provided you support yourself and keep out of trouble.'

'I didn't know that. I thought I had to be twenty-one.'

'Do you wish to leave home?'

'Oh yes!'

'Do you wish to leave school?'

'Sometimes.'

'Why?'

'I'm not very happy there.'

'Why, Mary?'

'It's mainly clothes. I've only one blouse and my underclothes are awful.'

'Have you asked your father to buy you clothes?'

'Yes, but he won't.'

'Do you like your aunt?'

'Yes.'

'If some arrangement could be made, would you be happy to stay with her?'

'I would, but my Cousin Claire wouldn't. She doesn't like me and I don't like her.'

The Welfare Officer rose and opened the door. Mrs Cooper, would you come in here for a minute, please?'

Aunt Elsie looked shaken but she smiled at me and patted my hand.

'Mrs Cooper, could you take Mary into your home till the end of the year?'

'I don't know, Miss Duggan. I'd like to but to tell you the truth, I can't afford to.'

'Your brother would pay board for Mary.'

'I'm sure he wouldn't. Unless you can make him? Nobody can get money out of Jimmy, even his own mother couldn't when she was destitute.'

'Thank you, Mrs Cooper. That will be all. Would you wait in the outer office and ask Mr Wilkinson to come in?'

My father seemed subdued.

'Mr Wilkinson. I suggest that you board your daughter with your sister till the end of the year.'

'She can go there if she likes.'

'You are prepared to support her?'

'Yes, I'll support her all right, but not at my sister's. She can stay in her own home where she belongs or she can pay her own way wherever she likes.'

'Thank you, Mr Wilkinson. That is all just now. Would you kindly wait outside?' He glared at me as he went out.

'Now Mary, I must tell you this. The department has no power to force your father to support you, other than in his own home. Your aunt is well intentioned towards you, but she can't be expected to keep you. In any case, she says she can't afford to.'

'I don't think it would work anyhow, staying with Aunt Elsie. Claire and I fight and Aunt Elsie always takes her side naturally.'

'Would you like to leave school and get a job?'

'I guess I'll have to, after this.'

'It would be better for you to continue your education. The employment situation is bad at the moment.'

'I know.'

Miss Duggan played with her pen, considering the position. I wondered why I had been brought here; we were only going over old ground. So far nothing concrete had come out of the interview. I was feeling uncomfortable and very conscious of my father sitting outside. As if reading my thoughts, the Welfare Officer addressed me.

'What is it, Mary? Have you any ideas yourself?'

'No, I thought you might be able to put me in a hostel or something.'

'If you had been under fourteen we would have done that, and when you turned fourteen you would have been placed in domestic service and remained under our supervision until you were twenty-one.'

'I'm glad I'm sixteen then.'

'Ask Dr Hamilton to step in, he may have some suggestions. And Mary, while we are talking you will please wait in here.'

She opened a connecting door to a small office behind her desk.

I waited for what seemed a very long time. I could distinguish the voice of the doctor, the Welfare Officer and later my father, but I couldn't hear Aunt Elsie. Nor could I hear what any of them were saying. Finally, I was called in. My father and the doctor were in the room, but not Aunt Elsie. They were all looking very serious.

Miss Duggan spoke. 'Sit down Mary. The doctor and I have explored all avenues of employment. There are simply no jobs for girls, other than domestic service. On the other hand your father has given his solemn word that if you return home and continue your schooling, he will never again lay his hand on you.'

She turned to my father. 'Mr Wilkinson, if you assault your daughter again, she is to report to this office immediately. We will then take police action against you and place her under the protection of the department. Do I make myself quite clear?'

'I won't touch her. I'll do my best for her.' His voice was choked and he didn't look at any of us. I wondered what had happened to Aunt Elsie.

Miss Duggan's voice interrupted my thoughts. 'You have heard what your father has said. It is now up to you to make a decision. You are free to leave school and find whatever employment and accommodation you wish, or you can go home and continue your schooling. I am not prepared to advise you, only to protect you. The choice is yours.'

I looked from one to the other. They all looked grim. I wished Aunt Elsie were in the room. I spoke my thoughts.

'Where is my aunt?'

'She's gone home. The doctor and I felt she was not in a position to help you.'

That was about it. 'Not in a position to help.' Suddenly I was angry. They were all the same, the doctor included. Advice, they all had plenty of that. But give me board and bed, no! 'They were not in a position.' I was on my own.

Anger brought clarity to my mind. I regarded the doctor, kindly disposed towards me, doing his professional duty. I viewed the Welfare Officer, impersonally sitting in judgment, and lastly I looked at the crushed figure of my father. A fraction of my mind registered the word 'protection', the sole outcome and justification for this harrowing experience.

Miss Duggan spoke gently. 'We're waiting, Mary.'

Desperately I tried to organise my thoughts. 'You mean, it's either home or being a servant?'

'I wouldn't put it quite like that, Mary. You are above average intelligence and, given further education, you are capable of better things than domestic work.'

The same old stuff. They just didn't care. They wanted to get rid of me. They would go back to their comfortable homes and forget me. Only my father was really involved with me, and what a father!

The doctor cleared his throat. 'I don't want to hurry you, Mary, but I'll be late for my surgery.'

'I'm sorry, Doctor.'

My father stood up. 'I've given my promise, Mary. I can't do more. I'm more sorry for last night than I can say. I was drunk and I didn't know what I was doing. You'll be all right from now on. We'll look after each other. What do you say, my girl?'

I had no real choice. It was Dad or more Dirty Dicks.

'All right, Dad. I'll come home.'

Sexual experience

ANONYMOUS

Delicate blossoms

I entered Wellington East Girls' College in 1939. When war was declared in September, I was thirteen, and from then until 1942 when I left, the war was filtered through the influences of the school — the essays set for homework, the topics we debated, and the talks we heard at morning assembly. Wellington East Girls' College interpreted the war for its pupils, informing us what we should think about it (right was on our side), how we should feel about it (indignant but proud), and what we should do about it (make the kinds of things that were useful in World War I).

I can remember a call from the Red Cross for girls who wished to help our soldiers. At that age, I was programmed to respond to all and any calls for help and soon found myself making a hussif. My friends and I were not entirely sure what we were making. We rather hoped that the loops of tape that we sewed, by hand, onto a strip of khaki drill, would ultimately hold bullets. It was disappointing, therefore, to discover that they were intended for sewing implements such as scissors. We attached spare buttons to the hussif and stitched on little flannel patches for pins and needles. The school pinking shears, generally kept under lock and key, were released for this important task, so that girls could prevent the flannel from fraying. My imagination was not equal to visualising how soldiers would use these examples of our industry. I could not recall anything written on the topic of hussifs by G. A. Henty or in any of the World War I stories in the *Boys' Own Annual*. I needed convincing that men would use their spare time sewing buttons on their underwear and mending holes in their socks.

The school did a lot for 'our boys' in the Navy. The Senior Service appeared to depend upon voluntary labour for its scarves, mittens, and — 'for more capable knitters' — seaboot stockings made from greasy home-spun wool. I made a pair of navy blue mittens too tight and tiny to fit on my own hand. Women representing the Navy League and wearing what appeared to be admiral's uniforms came to the school and ceremonially received our products. I felt bad about my mittens and only hoped that there was some brave sailor with very tiny hands. Some of the girls wrote little notes which they tucked into their completed knitting. I cannot remember anyone ever reporting that a grateful sailor had replied.

We also ran sweet stalls until sugar was rationed early in 1942, made copper trails of pennies, and earnestly sought new ways of making sacrifices. Looking back I consider that eating burnt toffee and dry coconut ice was one of our sacrifices.

Although, like everyone else, we spoke of 'our boys', the war did not at first touch many of us personally. We heard of local boys volunteering and applying for various branches of the armed services. The Fleet Air Arm was popular. However, the boys I knew were still at school, and the limit of their military involvement was blowing a trumpet in the school cadets. The early war was very much a British war, a BBC war; David Niven and a nightingale singing in Berkeley Square.

Wellington East Girls' College is perched on the side of Mt Victoria, directly above a tunnel bearing traffic to Hataitai. Below the school, on the flat, and set in spacious grounds is Wellington College, which was then, as it is now, full of boys. Wellington East and Wellington College shared a boundary fence, but while this fence was readily accessible to the girls, the boys would have had to climb a steep slope in full view of any teacher on duty to come anywhere near it. Nevertheless, the thought that some of the boys might make the ascent was ever present in the minds of the Wellington East staff, and a rule was promulgated that no girl was to be closer than six feet to the fence in order to prevent any conversations with stray mountaineers and to reduce the risk of girls deliberately enticing boys up the hill.

But wartime brought about some concessions regarding permissible relationships between the two schools. In my 6th Form year there was exciting news. In response to the prospect of a Japanese invasion Wellington College was to be taken over by the Army. The classes were to be distributed around local schools and halls, and five were to be relocated at Wellington East Girls' College. Our 6th Form was to inhabit one end of the Assembly Hall and one of the classes of boys the other. We were to be separated by screens. At least one girl invested in a 'curly cut', confidently expecting that we would get some boys to match ourselves. On the day that the boys were to come, girls gathered discreetly in the playground or observed from second storey windows. At last the boys arrived. The teacher of the class with whom we were to share the hall was not a man but a young woman (a concession to wartime conditions), and behind her came a straggly line of the smallest boys we had ever seen. They must have been chosen on the basis of size. They squeaked desks, banged books, cuffed each other, got into scuffles, threw paper darts, and kept up a general din at their end of the hall. We could hardly hear our own teachers speak, and were heartily glad to see the last of them when they finally left at the end of the term.

Supervised contact with the boys from Wellington College had always been allowed. Some of the boys, for example, were students in the ballroom dancing classes held in the Wellington East Assembly Hall. These occasions were not conducive to flirtation, the boys generally sweating profusely, and the girls trying to avoid sticky palms and contact at chest level. The school dance was a different matter. The senior boarders from Wellington College's Firth House were all invited and arrived looking very neat and tidy. However, the dance occurred at night-time, and the boarders were, therefore, viewed as a potential threat to the girls. At the completion of the dance, the headmistress, a gentle, sincere, other-worldly woman, who might have lived a more satisfying life in the Middle Ages, always asked the girls to remain seated in the hall. The boys were then sent back to Firth House. After ten minutes or so the headmistress telephoned the headmaster. 'Is that you Mr Armour, are all your boys back?' Assured that all the boarders were safely back, the girls were then permitted to go.

Caring for the girls of the eastern suburbs of Wellington was hard enough in peacetime for someone who viewed Wellington College boarders as a threat. The arrival of American troops in Wellington in June 1942 seemed to bring about a state of severe anxiety. Our headmistress delivered allegorical messages at morning assembly, read obscure passages from the Old Testament, and constantly alluded to protection of purity, self respect, and womanhood. It was over the heads of the junior girls. The seniors understood but took little notice. In 1942 at Wellington East Girls' College the menace of war was the threat presented by our American allies rather than that presented by the Japanese.

The control of the girls had always centred on seeing that they covered most of their bodies when out in public. The gym tunic with its box pleats was designed to produce a slab-sided, androgynous effect. Girls were also required to wear long-sleeved blouses, ties, gloves, hats firmly placed on the head, and long black stockings. Special attention was paid to covering heads and hands. It took very little time for it to be demonstrated that the United States Marines who roamed the streets of Wellington did not recognise the Wellington East uniform as a protection of feminine purity. Moreover, some girls from Wellington East began to bring a change of clothing to school and shed the hated gym tunic before going 'shopping' in town on Friday nights. The rumour was that these girls were all from the commercial course and not from the Latin course. If true, this probably meant that the commercial girls displayed more daring — certainly the Latin course girls were no less anxious to meet Americans.

There was an atmosphere of suppressed excitement throughout the school at the thought of the possibilities offered by the American troops; money, romance, a passport to the United States. Some girls reported meeting Americans in the street and going to the pictures with them. A Greek girl whose family owned a milkbar was helping to serve the customers when an American began to talk to her. To their mutual delight they discovered that they were both Greek. The father of another girl saw a young soldier wandering in the street and asked him home for a meal. How wonderful to have such a helpful father! One day a senior girl came to school wearing a diamond ring. She was engaged to a Marine. We imagined that her future life would be bound up in some way with Hollywood. As time went by we became more sophisticated, and assumed that the girls who left school before the end of year were going to have American babies.

At the end-of-year prizegiving the headmistress decided that firm measures were needed. In the presence of parents, staff, and distinguished guests, and after her report on the state of the school, the examination passes, the scholarships won, the school's success on the field of sport, the number of pupils, and the staff arrivals and resignations, the headmistress, dressed in her customary white blouse and grey serge suit, her grey hair drawn back into a bun, launched into an impassioned speech even more indirect and metaphorical than usual. It centred on the theme of delicate blossoms and how easy it is for these to be crushed, bruised, and damaged. The purity of a flower growing in a garden was contrasted with flowers cut, cast down on the pavement, and trampled underfoot.

For once her message was understood even by the juniors. The blossoms were her girls, and more and more of these blooms were to be found in the city streets, where they were in grave danger of being flattened by United States boots. To illustrate her meaning the headmistress firmly grasped her presentation bouquet with her left hand, and with her right, tore off the flower heads and threw them onto the stairs leading to the stage. 'There!' she said. 'As each girl comes up for her prize she will trample a blossom underfoot. Let this remind us of the fate of so many of our girls today.' As the names were called, each girl walked up the flower-strewn steps, delicately avoiding the roses, carnations, and larkspur, picking her way through the flower heads or gently moving them to one side with her toe. At the end of the ceremony not one blossom had been crushed by a black brogue. The headmistress still clutched a bundle of leaves and stalks.

The presence of the American Forces made the war personal and real for us in a way that the black and white films of the day, and the patriotic messages, had not. There were standard phrases that came to be used. We learned that the Americans were not all 'after one thing', that many of the men were very young and 'just out of high school', and that they were often 'lonely and homesick'. We learned some of their names: German, Polish, and Russian names, unfamiliar to New Zealand ears. Later, many of these names appeared in copperplate writing in the long lists on the noticeboard outside the office of the

Evening Post which announced the casualties of the battles of the Pacific.

Wartime created conditions in which new ways became permissible. It redefined the lives of men and women. Even to schoolgirls it revealed new possibilities and ways of behaving. Indeed, the crisis situation created by our entry into world conflict allowed a number of changes that might otherwise not have occurred so soon. Under the pressure of war, shortages of various kinds, both real and imagined, and the patriotic duty to save, many of the earlier dress rules were relaxed and gradually arms, legs, and hands were exposed on Austin Street. We girls continued the time-honoured practice of disguising the holes in our stockings by using our fountain pens to colour the flesh underneath them with blue-black ink . . .

ALISON GRAY

Leave me alone

Barbara stirred and woke. Beside her, David lay curled in sleep, his back brushing her breasts, his hip against her thigh. She turned carefully onto her back so as not to disturb him and put her hands behind her head. Through the crack under the door she could see yellow light gleaming from the hall. Melanie was not home. With her left hand Barbara groped on the bedside table for her watch, feeling gingerly among the tissues and books, the ashtray and the radio cord. One forty-five a.m. Sunday morning already. Last night it was twelve thirty. Two nights of worry in a row. No wonder she was always a wreck. She put down the watch and lay back. There was no comfort in the ceiling. Not even a fly moved to keep her company. The clothes on each side of the bed had no thought for Melanie. Nor did her scarves hanging motionless from the edge of the mirror. When she and David made love she liked the way the walls wrapped round them like a tramping hut in a storm. But when the loving was over and she surfaced to look around, she became aware of the world outside her room. And its terrors.

Cautiously, she put one leg then the other over the edge of the bed and slid out from under the covers. David stirred but slept on. The cool air ran its hands over her skin and she lifted the dark hair from her neck to let it through. Quietly she pulled back a corner of the curtain, opened the window and leaned outside. It was black and still. The last plane had left three hours ago. There were no boys on the playing fields of St Pat's; no soccer players on the green; no yachts in the bay. All the dogs were quiet and the seagulls slept. She could see the orange lights curving round Cobham Drive to the airport and a scattering of streetlamps below the house. They lit the tops of the trees in the gully and made tiny pools of green and gold in the dark. None of the neighbouring houses showed a light. The stars were out of reach and the moon was high and white.

She felt small, alone and irresponsible. Somewhere out there was her daughter. Sixteen. In a car. With a boy. Drunk, maybe. Raped. Dead. Bleeding in an accident. Wiped out on drugs. Ripped off her face. Slapped in a cell. The night made no response to her pain although she did hear a car whine irritably somewhere in the distance. It was as though the city had turned its back and shrugged, finding her anguish of no interest.

With her body shrunk round a knot in her stomach she turned away and let the curtain fall. In the bed that smelt of sex and cigarettes, David slept on, sprawled over onto her side. She hesitated briefly, took down her dressing-gown and went into the hall.

The light stung her eyes and made her head ache. It was like an interrogation and she screwed up her face against it. Leave me alone, she wanted to say. I know she's not home. I don't know where she is or how to get hold of her. I don't know Craig's phone number or the registration number of his car. Maybe she's with Caroline. That'd be all right. No, Caroline will be in bed and her father would die if I ring at this time of night. Oops, that's a Freudian slip. It's her mother who'll be awake.

She walked down the hall to the kitchen, talking to herself to shut out her fear. First I'll have a cup of tea and then I'll ring someone. But who? I'd have to tell them the whole story. Say I don't know where she is or who with. Describe her clothes and her hairstyle. It's me they'd come for then. It's me they'd lock up.

She filled the kettle slowly at the sink, watching the laburnum moving in the wind like the Welfare tapping at the glass. She remembered Melanie telling her about Timothy Barnes, outraged. His father was on his own and found it hard to manage a fifteen-year-old son who dyed his hair pink and wore four-inch dangly earrings. Every time they had an argument he threw him out, literally, and locked the door behind him. Yet it was Timothy who got put in a Home, said Melanie, breathless with indignation. Timothy, who wouldn't hurt a fly. Not his father who didn't know how to look after him. Barbara had clucked sympathetically at the time, secretly smug — about time some of these men got a taste of what it was like. She'd had to manage for years without help. Yet now, at two in the morning, in the blank tidiness of her night kitchen, she understood his hopelessness.

She sipped her tea, staring with unseeing eyes into the yellow brightness of the hall. Both hands were wrapped round the mug, the only comfort she had.

Five more minutes and the mug was cold. Ten minutes and her feet were chilled to the ankles. Okay, this is it. I'll have to get help. She stood up, and the noise of her chair on the lino cracked through the house. Phone book. Right. Police? No, not them. The hospital? Not the hospital, please, not that. McDonald's Restaurant, perhaps? They went there a lot. You nitwit, she thought, McDonald's wouldn't be open at two in the morning. Even Ronald McDonald has to sleep sometimes. Well, where? Jesters Nightspot? The piecart? The lookout on Mount Victoria? Where did they go? What did they do at this time of night? Drink? Smoke dope? Make love? God knows. She slammed a blind down on her thoughts and gave in to tears. It was hopeless. You could dial to your heart's content and never make a connection.

There were five hundred pages of numbers she could ring and every one could be wrong. She pushed the phone book back in its slot and fished in her pocket for a handkerchief. She was so absorbed in blowing her nose she didn't hear the bedroom door open. David stood in the doorway naked, his arms crossed over his chest to keep out the cold.

'What on earth are you doing out there, Barb? It's two in the morning.'

'Melanie's not home and I don't know where she is.'

'Don't be such an old fusspot. You over-protective mothers, you're a real pain. Come back to bed and get warm. It's cold without you next to me.'

'She might be hurt or in an accident or something. It's so late.'

He lifted her to her feet and hugged her, his body still warm against her blue satiny robe. 'You'd have heard by now if there was something wrong. She'll be all right. She's probably boozed or stoned or blissfully happy cavorting with Craig in the back seat of Bridget. Time flies when you're having fun, you know. She's probably forgotten where she lives.' He slipped his hand over her breasts and across the curve of her belly. 'Come on with me, and leave her be. It's freezing out here.'

She clutched the front of her dressing-gown over her breasts and let him lead her down the hall like a child. Andrew stirred as they went past the boys' room and she felt a rush of warmth for her two small sons. They were safe and predictable. She loved them, they needed her. She was their mother, they were her children. It was all perfectly straightforward.

Back in bed David wrapped her in his arms. 'Hey, you're so tense, hon. Come on, let go and give me a cuddle.' He kissed her gently along the line of her shoulder, enjoying the softness of the hollow in her neck. When he pressed her close, Barbara could feel the hardness of his hips and the soft bulge of his cock.

'Do you think Craig and Melanie really do it?' she whispered.

'Of course they do.' He pulled back, surprised. 'What makes you think they wouldn't?'

'She's only sixteen.'

'So?'

'What if she gets pregnant?'

'Surely you've talked to her about that. Come on, you're not that slow.'

'Yes I have, sort of, generally.' She spoke in bursts, defensively. 'But it's not easy to say to your daughter, "Excuse me, but are you having sex with someone?" If she's not she might think she should be and if she is she's more likely to tell me to get lost than say "Yes, mother dear" — especially if she's Melanie. Sex is very private stuff. You don't want your mother nosing round in it.'

'Nosing round is not in our repertoire, my dear,' he said.

'Get away.' She kicked him gently and thought again about Melanie. The way Dave talked she felt even more irresponsible, as though she'd refused to acknowledge what was happening right under her eyes. 'She knows about contraceptives because she's heard me talk about them. And she knows you can get condoms at the chemist. Some of the kids in her class go to Family Planning and I said she could do that. In a way I don't want to talk to her about it because I can't bear the thought of her doing it, so I don't know what she's done or where she's at. I don't even know where she is — or who she is, for that matter. I'm out of touch.'

She sat up on one elbow and looked at him, bewildered. 'More and more I feel like there's no connection or feeling between us. It's like she's a stranger in the house and we've always been so close.' She began to cry and brushed the tears away angrily. 'On nights like this I think of the headlines and the scandal — Sixteen-year-old in drunken orgy. Mother in bed with boyfriend — but it's not quite as simple as that. I don't know what's happened or how it got to be this way but it's not what I want. No way.'

'But surely you were the same. Can't you remember? Didn't you fight with your parents and stay out till late and drink?'

'Not at sixteen, I didn't. She's only a child.' The wail of Barbara's anguish stopped short as the front door opened.

'There she is,' said David triumphantly. 'I knew she'd be all right. Now you can stop worrying and concentrate on other things — seeing we're awake and all that.' He slid his hand down over her soft triangle of dark hair and in between her legs. 'Just to keep our hand in, you know.'

'More than a hand, I suspect,' said Barbara and rolled towards him, feeling her body yield to the pleasures of relief while her mind hung back, unsatisfied.

It was eleven o'clock before Melanie appeared, dressed in a man's shirt five sizes too big for her and a tight turquoise skirt that stopped three inches above her knee. There were dark rings around her eyes and her hair stuck up in random but half-hearted spikes. She slouched into the kitchen ignoring Barbara who was warming her stomach against the stove while the coffee perked. Barbara watched her daughter's bent head as Melanie drank glass after glass of cold water.

'You were late last night, dear.'

'Mmm.'

She saw the ghost of herself filling the kettle in the middle of the night. 'Did you have a good time?' Melanie nodded briefly into her glass without turning her head. 'Where exactly were you? I was worried sick about you and I didn't have a clue where you'd gone.'

'I was at Simon's. I told you that's where I was going but you were so busy with Andrew you didn't listen.'

Just at that moment Andrew and Jamie burst into the kitchen sporting cowboy hats and guns.

'Scones ready, Mum?'

'Two more minutes. Here, have a biscuit while you wait.'

'Christ, you kids are noisy. Can't you go and hoon about somewhere else?'

'What's wrong with you, then? Got a hangover or something?'

'Oh piss off, you little jerk.'

'Melanie.' Barbara remonstrated without conviction.

'Well, he's a pain in the arse. Can't you tell them to go outside?'

'That might be a good idea, my smalls. I'll call you when the scones are ready.' Barbara winked at them and reached into the cupboard for mugs. 'Do you want coffee, Mel?'

'Oh yeah, I suppose so. David still here?'

'Mm. He's in the living-room.' Melanie pulled a face. 'But he's going to squash this afternoon.'

Placate, placate, knead and smooth, juggle and twist. She busied herself with plates while Melanie made herself a sandwich and wandered into the living-room. David looked up from the *Sunday Times*.

'Hallo, Mel. Have a good night?'

'Yeah, it was all right.'

'Any bottle fights?'

'Oh, get off, David.'

'Well, it has been known to happen.' He grinned and went back to the sports page.

'Yeah, sure, once two months ago when I wasn't even there and only heard about it three days later. Anyway, it was Andrew and Damien who started it and everybody knows they should never be allowed in the same room.' She picked a banana from the fruitbowl and began to peel it. 'One day you'll get sick of that story and think of something new to hassle me about.'

'I'm only teasing.'

'Yeah, but you never know when to stop.'

'Did you say you were in a bottle fight?' Barbara came in with the tray and put it down on the kauri table. The light glowed through the glass coffee mugs and bounced off a vase of spring flowers behind them. It made a bright contrast to her white face and frightened eyes.

'Fuck, Mum, you're bloody paranoid. Of course I wasn't. It's just David's idea of a joke.' She picked up her coffee.

'Well you worry me, you know. I never know where you are or what you're doing. And you don't bring your friends home any more.'

'Are you surprised, with those two larrikins around? Who'd want to come? Anyway, I'm sick of this house. I hate this room since you painted it and my bedroom's too small.'

Barbara looked round, surprised. The room was a soft rose pink, trimmed with mulberry, with a low ceiling and long narrow windows looking out over Evans Bay. The polished wood floor was covered in the centre with an oriental rug. Round its edge were two dark red sofas, an old easy chair and the rectangular table where Melanie sat, drumming her fingers while she stuffed scones into her mouth. Barbara stretched her legs into a patch of sunlight on the floor. She couldn't imagine how anyone could dislike this room. It was her favourite space in the whole house and Melanie had nagged till it was done. She'd suggested they had shelves and David had made them. She'd helped choose the curtains and the lampshades and had the final say on the rug. What more did she want? Barbara felt herself turn like a caged bear poked once too often.

'I'm surprised to hear you say that after all the work you put in. It seems you'd hate it whatever colour we painted it.'

There was a silence in which Melanie backed off and concentrated on the scones. She couldn't afford a confrontation at this stage. Not with Labour Weekend coming up. She tilted her chair onto its back legs and looked her mother up and down.

She wasn't a bad old stick really in a middle-class sort of way — fairly tall, about five feet five, dark hair neatly cut, good figure considering how many children she had, and a face you looked at twice. Mostly because of the eyes. They were dark brown and liquid and sparkled like a deep pool when she laughed. Her nose was a bit long and her teeth weren't quite straight, but she wasn't too bad. Her clothes were boring, though — typical Lambton Quay, trendy but timid. Neat checked shirt tucked into a wide leather belt. Well-cut trousers, bright blue, but careful, always careful. The way she acted didn't do her any good either. She poked at things as though they'd bite her, and said 'No' unless she was forced to say 'Yes' and even then she was nervous.

Melanie took another bite out of her scone. If Barbara wanted to live like that she could, but doing it to her children was a different matter. What on earth did she imagine they did when they were out? Have wild orgies and group sex? Lie round smashed off their faces, pock-marked with needle holes? Perhaps she imagined evenings of violent crime where they beat up old ladies and ran off with their handbags to get dollars for drugs. Melanie sniffed impatiently. She felt like the lion in the Newtown Zoo. It was boring at home, boring, boring, boring. Anyone could see that. There was nothing to do but watch telly and eat. She'd done that night after night for sixteen years. She'd looked out the same windows and seen the same boats and the same planes. She knew every plant in the garden and every mossy step to the clothes line. She needed a change and a chance to express herself. She wanted to find her own way in the world in her own style.

Barbara finished her coffee and put down her mug. Carefully. She went across to the sofa and sat close against David so she could read the paper over his shoulder. Without looking up, he slipped his arm over her back and brought his hand round to fondle her breasts. Melanie saw her mother's face soften as she kissed his ear and the soft hollow of his cheek. He had her hooked, the jerk. Melanie felt excluded and angry. It was bad enough having to negotiate her life with Barbara. When David began horning in on the act, it added a whole new dimension.

She took her cup to the kitchen and rinsed it thoughtfully under the tap. Somehow she had to get him on her side. He'd be better as an ally than an adversary. It probably wouldn't be too difficult. He wasn't as anxious as Barbara, and he wanted her to like him. That had to be worth a fair bit.

She came back into the living-room and looked at them curled together on the sofa, heads bent over the sports page. She put her hands behind her head and fired her first shot.

'Are we going anywhere Labour Weekend, Mum?'

Barbara looked up in surprise. 'I don't know. I hadn't thought about it. Why?'

'I just wondered. Some of us thought we might go away somewhere.'

'What do you mean, go away? Who are you talking about?'

'The usual crowd. Craig and me for a start, and Simon. Caroline if she can come, or Jacquie. We're not sure yet.'

'Where would you go?'

'Don't know. Up to Dad's maybe. Or to a place called Manutuke, near Gisborne. That's where Simon's people come from. And there's probably going to be a rock festival at Brownwoods so that's another possibility. Depends how we feel at the time.'

Barbara sat up slowly. Her body felt as if it had been taken over by her heart which pounded blood at a frantic rate down to her fingers and toes and up into her throat. She leaned against the arm of the sofa and regarded her daughter with something approaching fear.

'I couldn't say just yet, Melanie. I'd have to know more about it. Where you were going and how. Where you'd sleep, how you'd eat. Who was driving if you're in Bridget. It's not the same as a Sunday outing, you know. There's a whole big, dangerous world out there.'

'That's exactly what we want to try out. We're old enough to leave school and get married — well, legally — so surely we're old enough to have a little adventure. We don't want to have to have rules and check-in times and name tags and stuff. It would ruin the whole point of it. We want to explore and see what's there before we decide what to do. I can cook, so can Craig and Simon's got a tent. We'll be all right.'

'But you can't just take off from Wellington and not know where you're going. What if it rains? What if there's no camp-sites or you run out of money or have an accident or something? You're only children.'

'You always say that and we're not. I look after the kids. Remember? I pay adult fares on the bus and I have a credit card. Even Huckleberry Finn was only thirteen when he went down the Mississippi and he didn't have any parents. We're only going for three days, for Christ's sake. It's not a lifetime voyage.'

Her mother looked bewildered. 'I don't know, Melanie, I just don't know.' Don't ask me this, don't make me decide.

Barbara saw her family like a spider's web, carefully spun and easily broken. She'd patched it when Colin left, stitched and glued and fought to keep it in one piece. Now it was stretched again, beyond her strength. She looked down at David, studiously reading the paper, then across to Melanie, head back, jaw out, sticking to her guns. It's not fair, she thought, parenthood is not fair.

'Let's talk about it later,' she said. 'There's plenty of time.'

FIONA KIDMAN
Is this what sex is?

Elvis started to sing 'Love Me Tender'.

Now all of her melted, the voice dissolved round her like marshmallow held in her mouth and sliding down her throat. She throbbed, she was spellbound, the voice was molten gold. She noticed that her free hand was wet, and saw it was with her own tears. This was a dream world and she was part of it. She had been admitted, songs were being played for her, she had friends, and, it seemed, she was in love.

When the song was over, it was time for her to go again. 'Next Thursday?' whispered Sydney against her ear.

She nodded, as if hypnotised. Her world was loving her and she loved it back. 'I'd run you home, but I've got another job to go on to,' Sydney said. 'I'll be better organised next week.'

Outside in the crisp dark, more than the cold hit Harriet. Certain inescapable facts had to be faced.

For a start, there was no way she was going to typing the following week, which meant that she would have missed three nights out of four. She could only type things about sitting on tits, and Cousin Alice seemed to think that she was almost ready to go on to higher things.

There was no way that she would be able to learn to do better than that by the time the job became vacant, and what she would do was a question with such frightening ramifications that she quailed. Even if she were to give up Sydney after the following week (and she had already come to think of him as somebody valuable) she still wouldn't be able to type in time to take the job. The May holidays were almost there, with only one more typing lesson left before the end of term, and on that night she was committed to Sydney. It was disturbing, and yet somehow comforting, because it was abundantly clear that her misdemeanours would catch up with her whether she went to that last typing lesson or not; it would not be a miraculous cure-all for her past failures, so meeting Sydney wouldn't make all that much difference.

But that brought up a new and even more devastating problem. If the May holidays were only one typing session away, she would have no excuse to go out on Thursday nights for two whole weeks. The situation was oppressive. There was no other single solitary excuse for staying out late in Weyville.

'I'm thinking too far ahead,' she told herself sternly. 'I must concentrate on next Thursday night. One thing at a time.' And, suddenly

buoyant, she went in to face Cousin Alice.
Her relative looked at her approvingly. 'I'm glad to see you looking so happy, my dear. I can see you're ready for that job. I must have a talk to your typing teacher about your speed before the end of term.'
Harriet reached over and kissed Cousin Alice swiftly on the cheek, something she had never done before. 'Don't do that. I want it to be a surprise for you,' she said, and Cousin Alice's face shone with pleasurable anticipation.
The following Thursday dragged endlessly. She couldn't find zips that were the right colour for people, she gave wrong change, and when Mr Stubbs heard a customer complaining, he sharply rebuked her. His words brought home to her the desirability of change, and reminded her that a change might be more disastrous than the way things were. It was a nagging discomfort. Something she would face tomorrow. Though that wasn't far away.
At last it was time to go. It was almost dark as she walked down the street to the milk bar. A quiet wind was stealing through Weyville, scattering lolly papers in the air. A newspaper wrapped itself around a lamp post, and as she rounded the last corner before the milk bar, it caught her, sending chill little shudders through her like a premonition of something she was about to lose forever. She put her head down and hurried on.
Outside the milk bar, an electrician's van was parked, and sitting at the wheel was Sydney. As she approached, he leaned over and opened the door. 'Hullo, there,' he said softly. 'Ready?'
'Aren't we going inside?' she asked, with a stab of panic.
'They told me you didn't have much time on Thursday nights. They gave us blessings and said they wouldn't keep you all to themselves when we haven't got much time together.'
Harriet got in uncertainly, not sure whether to shut the door or not. Sydney leaned across her and pulled it shut, his arm leaning heavily against her breast as he did so.
'Where are we going?' she asked, fearfully, now that this adventure had begun.
'To my place,' he said cheerfully, as he started the van.
'You have a place of your own?'
'Not my own. My parents' place. I live with my parents.'
'Oh.' A great flood of relief passed over Harriet. She was going to meet Sydney's parents. It occurred to her that she didn't know his surname.
'Merrott,' he told her. Sydney Merrott — it seemed a safe reliable name, even one that you could live with. Mrs Sydney Merrott. Taking her home to meet his parents. Already. And he had a steady job. Handsome in a sort of way, too. Not that she'd want to get married straight away of course. All sorts of things would have to be planned,

and they'd need to know each other a bit better.

At least she wouldn't have to worry so much about a better job; she could just stick this one out. Being Mrs Sydney Merrott and an electrician's wife would take up so much of her time that she wouldn't need to get involved in anything else much.

Now she found it easy to talk. As they drove through the empty streets of Weyville, she told him about the bad day she'd had, and how she wasn't too keen on selling haberdashery. She supposed his mother must come into the shop, and he said he supposed she must, and Harriet said wouldn't it be funny if they'd already met, and Sydney said, yes, wouldn't it be funny and did his curious little act of ducking his bottom teeth over his top ones as he looked at her out of the corner of his eye. That didn't seem to matter very much because she felt so beautiful and happy. Already she was planning how she would tell Cousin Alice about Sydney, because if he was taking her round to his parents' place so early in the piece, she would certainly have to invite him to Cousin Alice's. Maybe that was quite a good thing because sooner or later she would have to take him to Ohaka, and he might never have met people like her parents before; not that she was ashamed of them, but Cousin Alice was Weyville. He would understand that she came from a mixed background and might even find it quite quaint and see his new wife as somebody rather exotic.

They pulled into the driveway of a wooden bungalow. It was difficult to see in the dark, but by the lights of the van Harriet discerned that Sydney might be quite impressed by Cousin Alice's house. There seemed to be nothing wrong with the Merrotts' house, but Cousin Alice's looked better established. This house had the slightly raw look of a place that had been built recently, but it seemed prosperous enough. Maybe the Merrotts hadn't been rich for very long.

One outside light was on. Harriet thought this curious, and supposed that the family must all be on the other side of the house. On the whole, though, the place had a strangely bleak and uninhabited air.

She became conscious that Sydney was nervous. Perhaps after all she didn't come up to standard. She watched him take the key out of his pocket in an idly detached way, and the truth hit her. Silently he let her in, and turned on a light, shutting the door behind them.

'Your parents aren't here, are they?' she said, matter-of-factly.

'No.'

'Why did you tell me you were taking me to meet them?' she asked.

'Hey, wait a minute,' said Sydney. 'I never told you that.'

'You said you were taking me to your parents' place.'

'That's right. I didn't say they were here.'

The simple truth of this statement was irrefutable. 'When will they be home?' she asked.

'In two weeks.'

'You mean they're away for two weeks?'

'That's what I said. Bit of luck, isn't it?'

'Can I sit down?' she said, at last.

'We'd better get on with it if you're short on time,' said Sydney, and now there was no doubt that he was nervous.

So this is what it comes down to, thought Harriet, as she followed him silently to his bedroom. I am now about to be introduced to the great mysteries of life. After wondering all this time, she hadn't even had time to anticipate the event — or even to decide whether she particularly wanted to find out what 'it' was right now.

Sydney's room was very neat. Twin beds were made up just in Cousin Alice's style with bright bedspreads and matching curtains. There was very little to indicate Sydney's interests in life except for a guitar standing in one corner.

'Do you play that?' asked Harriet, running her finger across the strings and making them twang.

Sydney shrugged. 'Used to. Nearest my mother ever got me to learning music.' He pulled off his shirt.

'How old are you?' she asked.

He looked faintly exasperated. 'You ask a lot of questions, don't you?'

'I just wondered,' said Harriet.

'Twenty-three. Are you going to take your things off?' He seemed much more in command of the situation now that he was shedding his clothes. He abandoned his socks quite briskly.

Reduced to his underpants, he observed her standing motionless. 'You're a cool one, aren't you? Look, do you want me to do it for you, and all that stuff?'

She thought of Jim and standing naked before him. It seemed to have happened a hundred years ago. She remembered his gentle finger stroking her where the hair had started to grow; now it was a wild bush.

She wondered if Sydney would be as gentle. Something told her that he might not be, for he was beginning to looked decidedly impatient.

'It's all right,' she said. 'I can do it myself.' Quickly she took off her clothes, until she was down to her brassière and panties. Sydney still had his underpants on. 'Shall I go first?' she inquired, noting that his bump was most pronounced. She sat down on the bed and watched him, pleasantly fascinated that she was about to see what the thing actually looked like uncovered.

'God, you're cool,' said Sydney again, with some agitation. He pulled his underpants down, and Harriet gave a startled cry. The revelation of this very large piece of apparatus pointing at her like a witch doctor's bone was quite terrifying.

'Ah, you want it, eh,' said Sydney, pleased. 'Come on, get them off.' Obediently she took off the rest of her clothes. What did she do now?

Muttering a series of ahs and ohs, which she took as an indication that he was pleased, Sydney sprang on her and threw her backwards onto the bed. Remembering her previous effort with Jim, she settled herself back while he rolled onto her.

As it was quite obvious that he expected her to know what to do next, she felt somewhat embarrassed at the prospect of asking him. She really had no idea what was expected.

'Come on, get 'em up,' said Sydney. He was crouching intently between her legs. Harriet put her arms around his neck, as she couldn't think what else to put up.

'You do want to do this, don't you?' said Sydney.

'Oh yes,' she said fervently.

'You don't seem all that keen. You going to make me work for it? Here, let's see if we can work you over a bit.' He fastened his mouth on hers, grinding away with determined licking and snorting. His skin felt very sweaty against the palms of her hands.

Suddenly he grabbed her under the knees and pulled them up into the air. This seemed an extraordinary posture to Harriet, who began to laugh.

Sydney froze. 'What's so bloody funny?' he snapped.

'Nothing. I'm sorry. I was just . . . thinking.'

'Just thinking, were you? Don't you like me?'

'Oh yes, I do,' Harriet assured him.

'You looked me over enough — didn't you fancy what you saw? Never had a girl look at me like that. It's bad manners to look at a bloke the way you looked at me.'

'Oh, damn,' he suddenly groaned. He levered himself up on his hands and knees, and they both inspected the splendid penis he had been sporting a few moments earlier. It hung limp and shrivelled, like a fleshy little carrot that had been kept too long. Harriet wanted to laugh again, but she had the nasty feeling that Sydney might hit her.

'Will it come back?' she asked, now genuinely interested.

'You could help,' said Sydney.

'Could I?'

He shook his head in wonder. 'Christ, you're not frigid, are you?'

'It's not very warm in here,' Harriet admitted.

'I don't know whether you're putting me on, or what. I've never met one like you before.'

Harriet toyed with the idea of confessing all, but before she could say anything, he got to his feet and said huffily, 'I'll do it myself.'

'Will you? What will you do?'

'Are you going to watch?'

'Shouldn't I?'

'You've got no feelings at all have you,' he said. 'I'm going to the bathroom to do it.'

At the door, he turned and said, 'Don't try any funny tricks, will you. I'm not going this far without getting it up. No going off on me, just because my hard's gone. It'll come back, you know.'

'Of course not,' said Harriet. She was beginning to feel quite sorry for him. It seemed that even if she didn't know what to do, he wasn't much better off than she was. Curiosity was getting the better of her, and the wish that he had correctly guessed to dress and get out as quickly as possible was fading. She pulled an eiderdown from the end of the bed and lay there in a small cocoon. Nestling against its feathery warmth, she felt almost luxurious. Taking her clothes off had always been a pleasure, disastrous as the consequences could apparently be.

Soon Sydney returned, holding his penis carefully in one hand. It seemed respectably large again, though somewhat softer than the first time it had come in contact with her legs.

He climbed under the eiderdown, and pressed himself over her again. He continued to hold his penis and said softly under his breath, 'Grow, grow.' Interested in this process, Harriet put her hand on it. Immediately it sprang to life.

'Aah,' sighed Sydney. 'I knew you were all right. Let's get it up before we have any more problems, eh?'

Following the previous course of action Harriet raised her knees as far as they would go. This seemed to please Sydney considerably, for his penis started probing her with great enthusiasm.

'Christ, you're tight,' he said with perspiring admiration.

Then the pain started. She had never been hurt there before, and now he seemed to be raining blows into her. Her body started to shake in anguish.

'I — can't get — into you,' Sydney panted. 'Ah, there we go. We're away,' and her body seemed to disintegrate in a great spasm of pain, so searing, so terrifying that she screamed aloud, again and again.

'Wowee, I knew you were great, whoo, you like it, don't you?' Sydney shouted. 'Yah, that's right, writhe, I love it, God that's beautiful, keep it up baby, that's great stuff.'

Is this what it's always like? moaned Harriet to herself. Does this pain happen every time? Is this what sex is? Why does he keep moving in and out like that? I thought he just put it inside me. Perhaps he's doing something else to me — *am* I having sex? When's he going to stop?

Finally Sydney did stop, after a lunge that seemed to go right up to her breastbone. He lay on top of her, panting and exhausted.

'Worth it, eh?' he said when he had recovered a little. Harriet whimpered in reply. He pulled himself out of her, and for an instant her body exploded with quite a different sensation. She supposed it must be the relief of being unpinned from the bed, but years later she recalled that feeling, and thought with a kind of wonder that that miraculous little orgasm had saved her from instant retreat to a nunnery. Certainly she regarded Sydney with a tender and more forgiving glance that she would have thought possible moments before.

As they disentangled themselves, Sydney looked down at the bed. It was covered with blood.

'Kerist,' he yelled. 'Why in the hell didn't you tell me you had your period?'

'I didn't know I had it,' Harriet said, as startled as he.

He looked at it furiously, then disappeared, coming back in a moment with a damp towel. He started dabbing at the blood on the bed, but the stain seemed to spread more widely.

Harriet had started putting on her clothes. 'I'm sorry,' she said.

'So you bloody well ought to be. Haven't you been watching your dates? You must have know it was due.'

'They don't always come right on the day. If you know so much, you ought to know that,' Harriet pointed out acidly.

He pulled on his clothes, and stood staring morosely at the bed. 'Oh, for goodness sake,' said Harriet, beginning to feel cross with him. 'If you wash it, it'll be dry long before your parents come back.'

'Yeah, I know,' said Sydney. 'But I'm picking up my girlfriend when she finishes work tomorrow night. I won't have it fixed by then.'

'Girlfriend?'

'Fiancée.'

'You're engaged to her?'

'Yep. Getting married at the end of the year. I've got a section, nearly saved up for the deposit on the house. We're going to have ranch sliders and things like that so it'll cost a bit. Still, I reckon I can get it together by the end of the year. Not bad, eh?'

'No. Not bad,' said Harriet numbly.

'Still, it's not going to help her seeing that, is it?'

'Take it to the dry cleaners in the morning and tell them it's a rush job,' said Harriet.

'I can't,' wailed Sydney. 'She works in the dry cleaners.'

'Oh, that's really too bad, then. For goodness sake! Change the covers over on the beds and put the eiderdown over the spare one.'

'Hey, that's good. That's a swell idea. Thanks, Harriet.'

'Glad to help. D'you mind if I go home now?'

'No, sure I don't.' His spirits had recovered quite remarkably, and her crime seemed forgiven.

As they drove past the milk bar, Harriet felt the cold despair of loneliness descend again. They'd known, they must have known, that Sydney was engaged to be married. They'd set her up with him. There was no way back to the milk bar. She had been betrayed.

'Please don't stop outside my gate,' said Harriet, as they approached Cousin Alice's house. Sydney parked the van a couple of doors up the street.

'Next Thursday?' he asked.

'Night school's finished for the term. I can't get out. Unless of course you'd like to call on Cousin Alice and ask her if I can go out with you!'

'Oh, come on now! Jeez, I can see why the kids call you Twanky Doll. You're putting on the dog a bit, aren't you?'

'I think I'd better be going in,' said Harriet.

'Well, look, Harriet, you know I can't do that. What would your — what would Mrs Harrison think of me, with a fiancée and all that?'

'Quite,' she said coldly.

'So if you knew I couldn't, what did you want to say a thing like that for?'

'I really had better go in.'

'Hey.' He suddenly caught her arm fiercely. 'You won't tell them about you know what?'

'What?'

'You know.'

'I don't.'

'Oh, Ker-ist! Me not being able to get a hardie, you know. I mean, I did in the end, didn't I?'

'I won't tell,' Harriet promised wearily. 'Now, please . . . I'm late.'

Another thought struck Sydney. 'That blood. You weren't a virgin, were you?'

Harriet hung her head. 'Oh, Ker-ist,' he said. 'You shouldn't have let me do that to you.'

'I thought men were supposed to know all those things.'

'Yeah, well, I never . . . you know, with one before. I just didn't think. You know, you stuck round with those kids.'

The last part was an accusation. She said nothing.

'I didn't hurt you or anything, did I?'

The pain was solid, from sore heart to aching genitals. Harriet climbed out of the van without another word. If there was any point in what had happened, she couldn't see it.

As she walked up to Cousin Alice's front gate, Sydney cruised beside the footpath, the door of the van swinging open. He was calling out, anxious little noises asking for reassurance. She turned into the driveway and didn't look back.

In the night she wondered again if that was what 'it' was really all about. She wondered if she had really, at long last, done 'it', and if so whether she might ever expect more from 'it' than she had had tonight. For a moment she recalled the strange pleasure right at the end of the act, but the memory was swallowed up in a great black hole of grief and loss.

SUE McCAULEY

While it lasts

Friday night. A car slowed down on the street; all evening, cars had been passing and slowing, but this one had no muffler. Liz went on reading but the words were just words on their own and would not link into sentences. The car stopped. Definitely it had stopped. There were shouts and a slamming of doors, then the car drove off again. She began again at the beginning of the sentence; the street was full of houses expecting visitors.

The door was locked and he hammered on it with unnecessary force. Liz got out of bed and went to open it, remembering how much he could irritate her.

'You was in bed?' He smelt of beer.

'It's quite late.'

She went back to the bedroom, he followed her and stood leaning against the wall.

'You glad I'm back?'

'Well, I'm glad you're still alive anyway.'

'You was worried?'

'I suppose the car was stolen?'

'It was and it wasn't. Fat Boy paid the deposit. Only under another name.'

'What did you do down there?'

'Nothing much. Just mucked about. They wouldn't let us in at the prison.'

'But you had a good time?'

'Not really,' he said. 'I's homesick.'

She was going to laugh, but she saw he meant it. 'Well, you're home now,' she said.

He looked past her at the window with its curtains drawn and she knew in a curdling instant what he was about to say.

'You remember the other night, what you said . . . Did you mean it?'

'I was drunk.' Her cowardliness shamed her. 'Yes, I meant it.'

He was crouching beside the bed holding her hand. The whole of her was a hand being held. His face was hidden against the bedspread; when he raised it his eyes seemed huge. Blue eyes, she thought, were intrusive, they invaded you. Brown eyes looked inward; they went deep, you could float in them. Possibly drown.

107

At eleven Liz had been religious. She had planned to be a missionary in some dark tropical land tending the sparrow-legged bulbous-bellied children who had eyes like Tug's eyes. She longed for selfless dedication and righteous anger. She wrote to Trevor Huddleston, care of his publishers, but he was no doubt too busy to reply.

Her mother sang in the Anglican church choir on Sundays, but Liz was privately scornful of her mother's style of religion — social introductions, descant harmony and a Sunday spiritual inoculation. The daughter waited to be overcome by some dark, tumultuous force; she longed for surrender and dedication and intensity. The feeling was strong in her that she had been Chosen, yet she hesitated, wanting confirmation; a sign; however small. She created opportunities for this to happen beyond the bounds of coincidence, but when no bushes burned, no telegraph poles split in two and the messages of the clouds remained obscure she finally lost interest.

She committed herself then to Ralph and his various successors — stray cats and broken birds. A few died but most of them recovered. The birds flew away or stayed around the home as semi-pets; the cats she took eventually to the SPCA where they were probably destroyed. Liz was aware of this likelihood but remained committed to tending her ailing strays.

After a time her spiritual aspirations began to seem nothing more than a childish phase. Watching her battered birds flap off awkwardly into the suburban skies she would tell herself that if there was some infinite truth this was it and it was beyond question or comprehension — just *there* like the hillside, like the sea.

And sometimes when she was alone, out riding Delilah, entranced by the shape of her horse's ears and the fall of her mane, she would get a sensation of pure happiness. Although the feeling itself was beyond description it was accompanied by a vague sensation of thirst. For herself she defined it as rapture. She had no doubt it had something to do with that infinite truth.

And now, absurdly, with Tug's hands and mouth moving over her body she thought of religion. She remembered the sharpness of her longing for intensity and surrender and she recognised that incomparably exquisite thirst. *Of course*, she thought. *Of course*.

He was shameless. He presented his body as a chef might present his finest cuisine, confident that every morsel — every hair, every pucker and crevice — was delicious and desirable. And gradually, as he explored her own body without permission or hesitation she felt three decades of caution and apprehension crumble and fall away. For the first time in her life she felt unreservedly — well, *almost* unreservedly — lovable.

They lay tight in each other's arms.

'What are you thinking?' She whispered, feeling that dull thirstiness all through her.

'I's thinking what a lot of time we wasted.'

'That was your fault; you turned me down.'

'I's scared. I mean you're sort of . . .'

'Like your mother?'

'Not now you're not.'

She laughed. 'So what happens now?'

'We start again.'

'I meant . . . I won't regret it,' she told him. 'Whatever happens I could never regret it.'

She woke at eight, exultant. She felt as she had felt after the birth of her children — permanently, cataclysmically altered. She had looked at the clock before she fell asleep and it said half-past five. Tug had fallen asleep about an hour before her, his arms still tight around her. When she slid a hand down over his buttocks he had thrust against her even in his sleep. Now, remembering that, she grinned to herself wanting him to wake so she could tell him.

He was buried beneath the bedclothes. She pulled them down carefully, wanting to look at his face. Unveiling it like a national treasure. His eyes flickered then opened wide and he grabbed at the bedclothes and pulled them back over his head.

'Tug?'

'I thought it was a dream,' muffled through the blankets.

'It wasn't, and you can't stay under there forever.'

He lowered the blankets slowly, fearfully, to make her laugh.

'What happens now?' he asked when they reached his chin.

'I guess we make the most of it while it lasts.'

'How long d'y' reckon we'll last?'

She thought about it. In her experience euphoria had never been more than momentary. 'Two weeks?' she ventured in wild optimism.

'I'd say nearer two months.'

She shook her head.

'Two months,' he repeated. 'D'you wanna bet? Two dollars, ay?'

'I don't want to bet.'

'Come on,' he urged, grinning already at his own joke. 'Make it a bit interesting.'

She cuffed at his head but he ducked. His face grew solemn. 'You wanna know something?'

'What?' Anxiety welled.

'It wasn't me who had the weedy feet. It was Bones.'

'You realise,' she said, searching for blackheads in the border forests of his hair, 'that we both happen to be at the peak of our sexuality.'

'How d'you know?'

'It's a known fact. Research has shown that men are at their horniest around sixteen and women when they're in their thirties.'

'So it'll wear off they reckon? What'll we do then?'

'I'll go back to knitting,' she said, 'and you'll just have to find another hobby.'

'Never. I like this one too much.'

'There's other things,' she said a little wistfully, trying to remember them. Insatiability had a lot going for it in terms of immediate reward, but she suspected it was an affliction and not the natural order of things. She could not decide whether she was supremely fortunate or helplessly depraved, but she acknowledged her addiction.

Nevertheless, apart from one lapse where she pleaded sickness, she dragged herself out of their voluptuous bed in the mornings and caught the bus to town. She buttered bread, cleared tables, poured coffee, smiled at strangers, chatted to Irwin and counted change into palms. And all the while her mind wriggled ecstatically over memories of the night past and anticipations of the night to come. Customers who had once been only smiles, frowns and small talk became bodies proclaiming their personal preferences and possibilities and Liz, checking her reflection in the washroom mirror was surprised, each time, to find that her compulsion was not etched there like graffiti.

Her fancies were most reckless in the mornings. By afternoon she would have tempered them, and sometimes by the time she wearily climbed off her homeward bus they would have diminished to minor and regrettable aberrations.

But in the living room or in the bedroom Tug would be waiting naked and erect ('What if it wasn't me but the meter reader?') or limp and languorously submissive. Once he was dressed in her long white nightgown and wearing her make-up. And though on close inspection the cosmetics lacked a certain expertise of application the general effect was quite lovely. It occurred to Liz, a bit resentfully, that even in younger days she had never looked as feminine and devourable.

Liz introduced games of another kind. They weren't as much fun but they were the kind she knew best and her playing of them was compulsive.

'Why me?' she would say. 'I mean, do you think of me as old? Doesn't it bother you?'

And Tug, ignoring the unwritten rules of play, would be flippant. 'Nah, doesn't bother me. I like a few wrinkles. I'm kinky.'

So, after a few attempts, she played it alone, except that he kept interrupting with interjections.

'It's like brown velvet,' she said. 'I'd wondered about that. Whether dark-skinned men were dark everywhere.'
'Did you think . . . ?'
'I had no way of knowing. I thought maybe all men were that motley purple. I find dark skin so much more attractive. They say a lot of white women do. Like in America there's this mystique about sexy black men which attracts the white women. Maybe it's something like that with me and you.'
'Well aren't I sexy?'
'Of course.'
'Then what are you talking about?'
'Just that it's the wrong reason for wanting someone.'
'But I like Pakeha women.'
'Ah, but why?'
'I jus' do.'
'There must be a reason. I mean it could be revenge; a way of getting back at Pakehas for things they've done to Maoris.'
'Who told you that shit?'
'It happens.'
'How d'y'know?'
'I just know. I suppose I've read it.'
'Oh.' Eyes popping in phoney awe. 'Then of course it must be right.' Silently laughing at her.
'You're hopeless,' she sulked. 'I can't even have a proper conversation with you.' (Was *that* it — his lack of learning? Allure of the primitive; the Lady Chatterley syndrome?)
'You know,' she said one evening, digging into the stew he had cooked for them, heady with herbs. (Did she have a subconscious need to dominate — an unnatural desire to relegate her partner to the submissive wifely role?)
'You know,' she said, 'in some cultures young men are encouraged to get their early experiences of sex with older women.'
'So?'
'Just thought you'd be interested.'
'Well you'da been a waste of time. I had to teach you everything you know.'
'Not quite everything.'
'Near enough.'
She wondered; if they were sinning and, if she as the instigator and the adult was the guilty party, would her comparative inexperience be a point for or against absolution?
For guilt was always there lining the gingerbread of her passion. As his mother, she thought with doleful sentimentality, her love for him could have been pure and unconditional. (It being so much easier to

love a child that is not rightfully yours — such love being free of the demands, self-accusations, duties and complex divisions of loyalty associated with true motherhood.) As his lover she was gross and tormented. She watched him for signs of emotional devastation due to their altered relationship, but on the whole he seemed happier.

Sometimes, glancing apprehensively into the future, she envisaged a time when they would revert to a platonic maternal/filial relationship. She would cast herself, convincingly, in the role of the dependable anchor in the drifting tidal confusion that seemed to have constituted Tug's past life and might be expected to constitute his future life. She would be his occasional refuge from an otherwise rootless and stormy life; he would be her vicarious excitement, her passing breeze of chaos and insecurity.

Beyond that she invented a tranquil day in the future when Tug, into his mid-twenties, would appear on her doorstep. (And she, having not heard from him for nearly two years, sometimes saying to her husband — that kindly, solid, good-provider whose features remained indistinct — 'I hope Tug's looking after himself. I do worry about him.') Then there Tug would be at the door with a pretty young woman beside him and an infant — a boy — in his arms (wide-mouthed, black haired, the image of Tug). And Tug would say, 'Liz, you've got a grandson,' and he would introduce Liz to his wife, proud of them both. And Tug and Liz would exchange glances; a bond of understanding, of shared memories and affection, of a rare and fragile secret shared.

She described to Tug this happy vision. He thought about it for a while.

'You wouldn't be jealous of her?'

'No. As long as you were happy I'd be delighted for you.' She believed herself. It was such a satisfactory happy ending.

JANET FRAME

Never been kissed

Yes, Zoe was getting better. But talk of truth was the first sign that *It* was going to happen.

She could wash herself now, and sometimes sit in a chair in the ward or on the crew deck. The passage of time was no longer strewn with buttercupped menus and lit with distorted omelettes hanging like electric bulbs to be switched on and off with each rising and falling of the *Matua*. Yet it was taking so long to be rid of the sickness, and her body was buried by huge stones that had to be shifted inch by inch every time she moved; and for so many days her body had lain flat and folded, printed with trademarks for soup and cream and chicken, like an empty paper-bag carrying its own advertisement.

She wished the film would end, the screams and the noise on deck, so that only a swish of quietness and shaded peace lapped the room, only a small quaker-cap of light hung from the ceiling. She wished the steward would bring the Horlicks, and the Sister come with the pills; then sleep, and the waves telling all, in sighs and sea-shells.

Then *It* happened. It was so strange. Someone darted swiftly into the ward — a member of the crew, dark, unshaven, wearing a striped jersey. A pirate perhaps. He crept towards Zoe. He did not say Hello or Good Evening. With the languor of seasickness, buried under the stones, Zoe lay silently staring. A waiter off duty? One of the men from the kitchen? A stranger come to say goodnight?

Then he stooped suddenly over the bed and kissed Zoe on the lips. She was so astonished that she did not withdraw her mouth, made no protest, and his lips rested upon hers for many seconds when he stood up quickly, looked guiltily about him, and crept from the room.

Now you who were kissed for the first time early in your life before the hair at your temples was beginning to turn grey, before your neck became corrugated sacking and your oval knees like two old tennis-rackets with sagging strings, why, in your earliest life when you were blushed like cherry-blossom and facing each day the glossy side of the light — you may remember the pleasure of saying to yourself, *My First Kiss*, and the need to describe it, to confide in best friends, even in objects like walls and furniture. But if your first kiss happens when, like Zoe, you have lived for over thirty years — shall I be honest and say you are nearly forty? — then the best move is silence, no matter how much you long to tell, otherwise people know it never happened to you before; and they wonder, or pity; and children cry after you because children trail kites of seeing that follow the wind and supervise the complete vision spread out in the sky — Old Froze-nose never been kissed! Old Froze-nose never been kissed!

After it happened Zoe had kept her eyes closed. It was important to think, to realise the meaning of the incident, to separate it from the motion of the ship and the gleaming fittings of the ward and the sound of the waves cornered gripping scooped building liquid shells which dissolved, fell apart, or were broken to pieces on faraway shores and became dust in sightless eyes, and sand, warm sand over the eggs placed there in faith, the reptile eggs hatched to new, ancient life.

Tell whom?

My first kiss. A swift dirty deed. Comfort. Self-pity. Horror.

And a host of lonely thoughts broke into Zoe's mind, sweeping away the customary furniture, the knick-knacks, the cosy draperies of usual language that for so long had spread their flatulent warmth; like the worn verses in autograph and birthday books —

> *Whatever is, is right.*
> *Whatever you are be that,*
> *Whatever you are be true,*
> *Straightforwardly act, be honest in fact*
> *Be nobody else but you.*

And

> *Never be sharp, never be flat, always be natural.*

A member of the crew kissed me, Zoe said to herself. A first kiss from no one to no one, like those cables which swing between mountain peaks and carry nothing.

And then she laughed aloud to think that she had never known, that she had always believed that people were separate with boundaries and fences and scrolled iron gates, Private Road, Trespassers Will Be Prosecuted; that people lived and died in shapes and identities with labels easily recognisable, with names which they clutched, like empty suitcases, on their journey to nowhere.

— Well it is a mistake, Zoe said smiling. — I am interested now in traffic lanes, in byways, highways, in the terrible hoover at the top of the stairs, and the way my identity has been sucked in with the others so that in the dust and suffocation of the bag which contains us all I cannot tell my own particles, I am merely wound now with the others in an accumulation of dust — scraps of hair and bone welded in tiny golf-balls of identity to be cracked open, unwound, melting in the fierce heat of being.

Something's burning.

A dirty member of the crew kissed me. Who was he?

You see, one is not satisfied with wraiths and breezes, with visiting Gods.

Was he myself, my parents, my dream-husband, lover? Zoe wondered. Now I shall never rest until I know. My life has been sucked at last into the whirlpool, made shapeless as water, and here I am trying to carve it as if it were stone; and how beautiful is water which never shows the marks of age and decay!

A dirty member of the crew kissed me and like a creature in a fable, stole my identity, left me naked, in rags; I must make something, quickly, recapture a shape, pin, hook, net the milling ocean — but oh my God!

Zoe touched her lips with her tongue, feeling a soreness there, remembering the splash of notices inside the doors of public lavatories in the city. Veneral Disease is Dangerous. Treatment is Free and Secret. Do not delay. Supposing . . . was it not a sign when the lips were sore . . . one never knew with people on board ship . . . sailing here and there to all countries . . . the crew mixing with all types of men and women . . .

It might be different, Zoe thought, if the man were English . . . brought up, say, in Liverpool or somewhere local but . . . one never knew with people from abroad . . . ships take anyone these days. Yet . . . I used to think this way . . . I used to be suspicious of foreigners.

Oh my God, hell is local.

Again she touched her lips, aware of the soreness. What would happen if in the few years left to her she had children? They would be born blind, with a yellow crust over their eyes. When she grew older she herself would perhaps become paralysed, lose her power of speech; her face would be twisted to a permanent grimace, she would have to stay in bed in a tall narrow bed in a back room overlooking someone else's allotment, with the district nurse visiting on Tuesdays to rub her back and feed her with barley soup . . .

But the children. They mattered most of all. They would be born blind.

Zoe's heart was treadling against her ribs, faster and faster. Again she felt the sore spot on her lips. Gradually, however, her fear diminished, soothed away by the rise and fall of the ship and her need to concentrate on its motion, to assure it in some way that she could not yet explain that she could not help rebelling against it, that the only means of surrender would be death; and death does not transform people into sailors, though it frees them and allows them eternal restlessness, independent of sunlight, wedged among pearls and a dim, flowering ballet of trees.

Calmly now Zoe considered the fact that she had been kissed for the first time in her life by a stranger. Yet who can deny that kisses between those who love are also kisses between strangers? A kiss that was neither a beginning nor an ending, it was isolated from the pattern of Zoe's spinsterish life with its secret desires and dreams and dreads; it was, in a way, a mythological act, as when the gods in the shape of birds or animals or human beings descend from the sky to touch the human maid. It was an act beyond reason. No doubt the sailor had his reasons. No doubt he was startled to find that his prospective evening's pleasure was an exhausted timid woman with greying hair, and cheeks flecked with vein-spots as if tiny arrows had found their mark; and eyes coerced by inward pressure to commit (and instantly regret) fantasies of arson upon areas of human property.

To Zoe the kiss was like a divining-rod which twists suddenly and trembles in a desert where no one believed in the existence of water — or of wine.

A dirty member of the crew had walked into the room and kissed her . . . at a quarter to eight in the evening, fifteen minutes before the steward was expected to bring her Horlicks and the Sister her pills.

And now it was eight o'clock.

The steward appeared with the Horlicks upon a tray. He put the glass on Zoe's locker.

— Thank you.

I have a secret, she thought. What will it lead to? I am changed. Tomorrow I will ask to get up and eat my lunch in the chair. I must make an effort. Seasickness, they say, is only suggestion. My path is certain now. I even think differently. I am changed, like those people who after the visits of the gods begin to sprout wings (or horns) or give birth to monsters.

I wonder who kissed me? What is he doing now? If I ever have children they will be born blind and deformed. Soon it will be too late. I will lie in my labelled box, divided and arranged in overlapping portions like wrinkled dried fruit . . . Will I have children some day, or will they always be mere dreams dispensed by absent-minded Gods?

LAURIS EDMOND
Some remote region

The embattled territory that awaited them on the other side of the frontier they would now never cross they scarcely mentioned. I, having almost finished making my act of total recall — so confusing, hazardous and painful — I am glad of it. Glad that in the end they weren't influenced by images of (for instance) Eileen Murdoch relishing their wickedness on her party line, or in Mr Dumfries' shop . . . the fascinated outrage of Mrs Reid, the shocked excitement of all conversations in every house in Arawa for months to come . . .

It wasn't even, as perhaps it should have been, the weight of domestic responsibility that dragged them back at the last minute from that alluring horizon. However, Terry's measles and Hilary's skin grafts must not be underestimated as agents of family cohesion (just because Louise and Nigel themselves did so underestimate them, not quite recognising, I think, the forces that drew them apart).

There is one event yet to recover from the obscuring deposits of the years, and I am glad of that too, although I do not propose to let anyone else in to the quite small, now far distant room where those two slept that night, finding there a delight and anguish which it seemed they had to realise before they could bring themselves to let it go. It may be that I am suddenly secretive about this final and perhaps most important recollection of Nigel and Louise (think how often the possibility had risen, shone, faded) because it is the last I shall ever have. The last, that is to say, of my composition of him — the beautiful, contradictory, desolate puzzle that is all that remains of him in my memory and my imagination.

But I can say that they went together into some remote region which most of us enter rarely, if at all, even when making love and knowing it is love. Or believing it is. Now I am on the brink of the most elusive definition in the entire language; but since Louise at that time had got no further, I think I must leave that too. It's enough to say that 'love' as glimpsed, fought for (and against), finally realised, between Nigel and Louise was love in one of its better definitions. One of its best, in fact.

That's why they could go together in those few hours, on a starless summer night, to a place to which no one can give a name, because if any of us are allowed to enter it we can do so only by losing ourselves entirely and re-discovering the names of things when we come back to the world of places and people, time, information and rational awareness.

So, they found themselves eventually in a room with an indistinct lattice-work pattern on the wallpaper and the long dark shape of a curtain. Behind it a window which would have shown them, had they looked, the outline, still white from the winter snow falls, of three or four of the nineteen peaks of the mountain that stood always over Arawa and the griefs and confusions of its people.

Nigel left before morning and Louise lay awake, trying to draw into herself, inside one skin at one moment, the shocks and reverberations that it would take years wholly to absorb. Her grief was not simply a matter of loss, but a sorrowing for the perhaps greater desolation of having made her choice. It was all you could have, she saw, half a life. There would never be more than that.

Always before there had been alternatives. The most she had had to decide was what order they came in. She could agree to go and live in a little country town, and the more congenial life of the city would wait for her. She could fall in love, yet want no one to suffer for it, take something from one person, one life, something from another. Nothing was final.

But in the end, it was. She saw her life as a pattern of easy, shallow impulses. Tom was different, he had made his choice, and part of him was diminished by it. Well, she would be diminished too. Already she could see herself as less charming, less open, less idealistic. All these aspects of herself she had taken such pleasure in — they would go. There would be something gained, perhaps? Some new maturity . . . it didn't feel like it. The only certain thing was that she had chosen because she could do nothing else. It was almost not a choice, but a compulsion.

She thought of the last moments of Terry's birth, that surging propulsion in which her body was nothing but the instrument of the force of birth itself. She had known an absolute powerlessness, felt herself as merely a place in which this immense cataclysm occurred. Again and again the tumultuous thrust of the birth had racked her body; it was not the tiny creature who was to be Terry — that too was helpless, merely an instrument. It was life itself seizing them both, with the blind insistence that a child was to be born, another repository of the irresistible energy of existence.

She lay there in the dark watching the first faint greyness of the dawn touch the long window. What had Terry's birth to do with all this? There is relief, fulfilment, delight, after the birth of a baby. *I feel only that I am terribly impaired. But the inevitability — that's the same.* That night in the hospital events had taken her over. And it was the same now. All the events of the year, the pleasure of recognising in Nigel her own self, her most natural, most absolute self; the discoveries of the tangle of other lives, here where they were all inextricably tangled. All the misery of Tom's instant, easy, oblivious commitment to his work here . . . that was the beginning.

She had said, in the first confusing weeks in Arawa, that you had to be for Tom or against him, there was nothing in between. She understood now, at last and painfully, that you had to be for or against *something*, something greater than yourself. Perhaps it didn't much matter what it was. She'd learnt that from a thousand small experiences — everything that had happened since the day she and Tom had first stood at the gate of their house and looked up at the beech tree with the mountain glistening behind it. Rupert — brilliant, elf-like, tragic Rupert, dangling on a string that would one day drop him for ever. Toddy embarking on his delayed growing up with about as much idea of where he was going as if he'd taken a leaky boat and lost both oars. Wilfrid, fighting his losing battle against all that threatened his doomed kingdom. Even Muriel with her triviality mixed up with a mindless endurance, a plain common sense; her unexpected ruthlessness, the secret weapon. It was all of them. And Tom. Dedicated, incomplete, noble old Tom.

She got no further. In the early morning dimness there appeared a strange figure: Terry with a man's sports coat dangling round his knees and hanging over his hands; his small face pale, his eyes enormous.

— Mum! he whispered. I came home because we took Tess with us and she's had her kittens. In the tent. And Robbie's mother won't open her door. We've got to find a box.

— All right, said Louise. Let's look.

Close relationships

PATRICIA GRACE

He shouldn't have let me go

It was nothing to say goodbye for twelve days. I kissed each one quickly, scarcely, and got into the bus. Hardly waved. Flint-eyed Nanny with her old white face, quick eyes. Enfolded in a great coat that had fitted her once or that she had once fitted into. Shrivelled ears keeping warm under the scarf knotted against a serrated wind. One old hand in a pocket keeping warm, the other held up to wave, frail as paper, a bit of crinkled litter blowing. My father was beside her with an arm to steady her and his hat pulled down. Under it his green eyes protruded like two Granny Smiths. He looked worried now, was wondering if he should have let me go, jingling keys in his pocket.

My mother and auntie, arms hooked together, glowed like twin coins. Proud, they smiled and waved, wanting to cry. And Toki turned up at the last minute. Just out of bed; singlet and jeans; jandals. Making faces and waving. Leaping at the cold snapping and stropping of the wind.

It was easy to wave one hand as the door flushed shut and the big wheels pulled us away. Sneaking to the lights and stopping, with the engine thudding softly, away again past the library with its doors still shut on the rows of silent books. And Neilson's. In an hour I would have been sitting at my typewriter watching the pages fill and would have set out the cups and made tea at exactly 10.30. A smell of old varnish and ink, and Mr Neilson's tobacco, Annette's roll-on underarm, and my own. Good to go sidling past.

Good sitting in the bus with the others all dressed the same, new tabs sewn neatly on the pockets of new blazers, and money in the pockets. Speeding up now, bowling along like a rolled ball.

At lunch-time we stepped down into nettled cold, rushing into the café over footpaths black and pocked with rain. It was easy not to think of them then, all of us together huddled in the steaming shop, and soup going down hot, puffing out hot breath. Hot breath dispersing, rising to the steam-stained fly-pitted ceiling or running in patterns down the cracking walls and bending glass.

Then finding the lavatories. Peeing together in rows, boxed. Washing, paper towels overflowing the bins in sodden heaps and our wiped hands fuzzed with paper as if they were suddenly crumbling.

And into the bus again, thankfully. Fitting easily back into the places we had left. It was easy to be warm and comfortable, launching out on to the blacked road, with the windscreen wiper making a fan-shaped hole in the rain.

Near the end of our journey the motorway was a trick wheel turning in two directions at once. Winding out cars, trucks, vans, bikes, buses. Ours was one. Crossing, changing, speeding up, slowing, so that there was no time to think of anything else. It was easy to watch and to feel the excitement, the great wheel looping down the long curve and out between the sharpening hills. And then!

Coming suddenly to an expanse of sky tiered above an expanse of rocking sea. And the hills all round, reaching up out of that sea and touching, only just, that speckled moving sky.

Buildings. Boxes, windowed. Of every size, reaching or crouching between and among the hills, still and watching. Waiting and listening as though they'd been caught that way in a game of statues. There was nothing else to remember as a few lights began ferreting the dimming afternoon.

It was not the end of the journey, however, only the beginning. Before boarding the ferry we sat down to a *good meal*. Mrs Rowley saw to it. 'You must have a *good meal* . . . You can't travel on an *empty stomach* . . . *Eat up*.' She didn't like picky eaters and in that way she was like my father. No matter what else you had on your mind, no matter how worried you had suddenly become — not knowing how to order, wondering which knife and fork — you still had to *eat*. Get something *good* into you. Wanting to do everything right.

At home they would have been starting their meal too, the two of them, and Toki probably, Nanny Ripeka perhaps, helping themselves out of the big dishes on the table. Tonight they'd be having boiled mutton and cabbage, and there'd be a dish of fish-heads boiled white. The whole place would stink to high heaven. Well. Rough sort of kai that anyway. Much better to be sitting at a little round table for four, eating, what was it? Beef curry, rice, and vegetables. Picking. Not wanting to finish first or last. Watching, and wondering if your manners were all right. Hoping the napkin you had spread on your knees wouldn't suddenly slide to the floor.

He would lift a plate-sized fish-head on to his dish and put salt on it. Then he'd begin expertly, pressing the flesh away from the flat bones with fingers and a fork. Lifting each piece carefully so that it wouldn't break, to put it between his teeth, steaming. He would let it cool for a moment, then into his mouth, his expression saying that this was the moment he'd been waiting for all day. One side of his mouth would have small bones shooting out of it, and they would somehow land in a tidy row round the edge of his plate. Each large bone he would take and suck; each loud suck would cause his already popping eyes to pop even more. And the climax would come when he was eating the eye. A mighty suck with a great noise to it, and the eye with all its soft flesh and juices would land on his tongue, busting on the roof of his mouth and flowing down his throat. Except for the little ball that would shoot forward and pop out. Nothing would be left when he'd finished except a tidy row of cleaned bones and two little white marbles from the eyes.

'I hope I don't spew it,' one of them said. It was an awful word to utter in such a place. 'Later. When we sail.'

'It's better than dry retching,' another one said. 'You've got to have something to bring up. Just in case.'

Hadn't even said goodbye — well, hardly. And I was last after all, trying to hurry, rice toppling and gravy dripping down my fork.

Then walking up the gangway, gripping my bag as though it was the only thing left that I knew about. Not believing the size of the ferry or the cold of the wind cutting through or the violent stench of the sea. Most of the others had had someone on the wharf to see them off, someone pushing little parcels into their hands, saying Good, Good on you, and Good luck, and Goodbye. When are you coming back over. Over? We were going Over. I wondered why my father had let me come. He was at home eating the head of a fish and I wanted *them* there waving and huddling in the cold, looking up at me as I leant on the rail.

I saw someone then, and it was my mother surely. But no. Pulling a little boy by the hand. I couldn't . . . Looking up and frowning into the dull light. Not my mother but her sister, my Auntie Rangi, seeing me and waving. With her grandson Richie that I'd never seen before. My mother had rung and told her . . . She had a parcel in her hand but she was too late to give it to me.

Quite suddenly there was a wide band of sea between me on the ship and Auntie Rangi and Richie on the wharf. The tear that dropped would make no difference to the strip of water. I hoped no one had noticed.

I kept on waving towards the wharf in case Auntie and Richie had gone along to the end with the rest of the crowd, but the end of the wharf was dark and far away. I couldn't see.

Then I wondered what was in the parcel that Auntie Rangi had brought with her. Probably some of her home-made bread. She had held it up and her mouth had moved, telling me but I couldn't hear. The others had home-made biscuits in their parcels or fruit. Oranges, apples, and reeking bananas. Chocolates, a thermos of soup. Bread might have seemed — different. Perhaps it was better after all that Auntie had been too late to give me the parcel. And I wondered how different I was, wondered if I really had packed enough underwear and pyjamas, wondered if my things were the same, or different.

'Come on you're in here with us.' They were being good to me, but

I couldn't help thinking my pyjamas might be funny, wondering why my father had let me come.

For a while we lay on our bunks looking at some magazines Georgina had brought with her. I stared at the pages, watching the print blur, but staring, not wanting to look out of the porthole and be reminded where I was.

Later we changed for bed, and I noticed that my pyjamas were no different after all and felt relieved. Having a bunk with your own locker and bed-light, your own air-vent and hand-towel was all right. Good. And having the same pyjamas.

But only till the light was out: it all disappeared in the dark. In the dark there was my father with green apple eyes, jingling keys in his pocket, and my mother and auntie laughing and waving, waving and crying. Toki arriving from somewhere. From where? Slapping his skin, hopping about and waving. Nanny with her knotted scarf, her knot of a hand. Auntie Rangi and her parcel, mouthing words ripped away by the wind and lost in the shambles of sea and waterside sound. Suddenly I wanted some of Auntie's bread. I wanted some of her bread very badly. Putting my head down under the stiff sheets, hoping no one would know.

We were Over. Legs trembling. Eyes and head sore.

Seasick by the looks . . . Make sure . . . Home with your billets . . . Have a *good* breakfast . . . Make sure. Home?

The billets in a huddle on the station platform remembered to smile. They smiled grey-faced into a grey morning, holding slips of paper with our names on them and sounding the names over to make them real. A tall woman with a military chest looked at the list and brayed out names, voice matching chest. My name was among them and I walked towards a young man and a young woman as we showed each other our teeth. Just call us May and Greg, they said. My mother would have liked them.

I thought it would be all right then, motoring through the city in May and Greg's VW, in the early traffic, with a flat sky lighting and the city beginning to yawn and stretch.

I could almost eat the *good breakfast* that May had cooked for me. Their house wasn't much different from ours. I was thinking of my mother; she would have liked to know that May's and Greg's house wasn't very different from our own. I decided I'd write a letter after breakfast telling my mother and father what a good time I was having.

I wrote to them every day, telling them about the games we'd played, describing Greg's and May's house and garden, telling them all the new things. About riding to a high place and looking down over the tessellated patterns of the city, and about the willowed river with its droving ducks and its quick trout swimming. The thin awning of

smog that on a still day laid itself between you and the arena of sky.
  Not mentioning how I dreaded each mealtime, choking down unwanted food, and how I pedalled to the courts each morning on May's bike exhausted from not sleeping. Wondering if he was sorry he'd let me come. Wondering if twelve days could be forever.

But it wasn't forever. On the night we went back to the ferry I put myself to bed and waited to be home, knowing I never would be. Knowing they would all have died or gone away by now. Twelve, eleven days. Knowing there was no Over any more. Only a Here, lurching and staggering above the shudder and drum. Only the vomity stink in undulating darkness.
  'I was talking to Mum and Dad,' Auntie Rangi said. 'This morning on the phone. They're all right. You're not. Not all right — are you, my love? You been away too long. But never mind, not long now, no crying.
  Then waiting out the bus journey in pretended or occasionally actual sleep. And getting down from the bus at last. At last. Going towards them slowly, not running. Watching my mother's eyes fill, listening to the jingle of keys.

JANE MANDER

I want to see the world

Asia was eighteen.

For months the inevitable fact that she would be eighteen had dominated her thoughts, and her mother, watching her, sensed with her uncanny aptitude for presentiment that something was in the air. What that something was she feared so much that she refused to think about it.

Now Asia's birthday was two weeks behind her, and Alice had seen for days that the dread something was fast approaching. As she paced the beach below the cliffs one evening, with the river running silently beside her under the cool spring stars, she knew she was only indulging in her old habit of putting off the evil hour. As she walked, she hated the thought that old habits could still dominate her. She hated her own exhaustless capacity for suffering. She hated her terrible dependence on the people she loved. She hated her inability to be just where she suffered.

At last, shivering, but not with cold, she set her face homewards. Ahead of her, across the river, she saw the moving lantern of the mill watchman going his rounds, and the red lamps on the ends of the wharves, and the headlights of a big Australian barque that lay moored to one of them.

Tom Roland's dream was coming true. He had built his mill and enlarged it, and was considering enlarging it again. Almost as fast as the logs could be run down from the bush they were sawn and loaded into the timber vessels that now came from all parts of the world in a continuous procession up the river.

By day the whole bay vibrated with the whistle and screech of the circular saws, the tear of the breakdowns, the rasp of the drags, the rattling of chains on the skids, the hum of the belting, the scream and clank of the donkey engines as they loaded flitches into the voracious holds of the ships, and, as a running accompaniment to all these, the triumphant roar of the great engines that drove every wheel and chain and belt.

The shutting off of all this fuss and buzz now intensified the silence of the nights. Even Alice was conscious as she walked home of the absence of the throb of the engines, of the vacant stillness of the hushed machinery. The intermittent sounds of the night were dwarfed by the memory of the day's loud speech. She heard, as it were, from a long way off, snatches of song from the barque, and the sounds of an accordion played somewhere at the head of the bay.

She turned wearily round the cliffs, and proceeded to climb steps now cut in the clay up the bank to a path above which joined at the boss's front gate with the old path leading directly down to the store. She paused several times, trying to fortify herself with the freshness of the night. Once she lingered, listening to the cry of the new baby, the second, at Bob Hargraves' house, a chain or two on the other side of the store path. As she stood, sweet scents floated down to her from the shrubs and flowers that now hid the foundations of her home.

Roland's picnicking days were over, and with the prospect of prosperity he had been willing to make of his house something more of a setting for his increasing success. The year before he had practically rebuilt the whole structure. A narrow central hall now ran from the front door to a large lean-to containing a porch, a scullery and a bathroom with a fitted tin tub, the latter creating a precedent for the entire northern end of the Auckland province. The distinction it gave his house in the eyes of passing travellers was a source of great satisfaction to the boss. Two bedrooms had also been inserted into the middle of the cottage, just behind the enlarged front rooms.

Alice would have appreciated the changes much more if she had been consulted, or any notice taken of her wishes. But the only people whose advice Roland had deigned to consider were Mrs Brayton, Bruce, and Asia. It was Asia who had had most to do with the scheme of interior decoration. Each stage in the furnishing of the rooms represented a stage in her artistic development, and each stage was the result of a visit to the Hardings, now removed to Auckland, and of explorations into the latest fads from America, which country largely influenced the evolution of household art in New Zealand.

As Roland was not as susceptible to the progressive nature of art, or as inclined to take it seriously as Asia was, he could be persuaded each time to impose only a little of the new upon the old, with the result that the patterns of the wallpapers and the linoleum did not always agree, nor did the furniture balance properly in the room space, nor did the colours always harmonise. But Asia had high hopes of some day seeing it as a perfect whole.

At first Alice had been enthusiastic about the changes, but later she resented them. She could not see why it should be good to have a flowered wallpaper admired at one time, only to have it scorned and discarded for a tinted one three years later. If it was beautiful once why was it not beautiful for ever? Mrs Brayton's wonderful rooms had not been changed since the day they had first seen them. But in spite of her, and it was this that hurt, the evolution of art in the house on the cliffs had proceeded.

From the beginning she had been so thankful herself for every hard-won addition to mere comfort and convenience that the claims of art seemed ridiculous. For a person who had a passion for one great art she was singularly indifferent to others. Also, it seemed hard to her that Asia should be given money to make a show, when she had had to fight for every inch of comfort she had ever gained.

It was not that she was jealous of Asia; it was rather that Asia's success at managing people, and particularly Roland, brought home to her her own continued failure in this direction. It was true that she now got on much better with her husband. With success he was less irritable, and in ways he had become more considerate, particularly, she had noticed, during the last year. But she knew that her victories had been mostly Asia's victories. One instance came again to her memory, as she stopped for the last time before entering, outside the fence, at the corner by the cliffs.

It had been their first fight to get help in the house, help that was badly needed, as Alice grew less able to do her share. Asia was fourteen when she first began to question whether washing Roland's heavy flannels was part of the fixed duty of woman. Alice, though physically and temperamentally unfit for housework, had never protested against anything, realising that it was all in her marriage contract, and she told Asia it was no use to resent it. But Asia was a young rebel, fast developing a fierce hostility to anything that savoured of a law or an order, and she finally drove her mother into asking Roland for the extra money to pay for help.

'Good heavens! What are the girls doing?' he had demanded. 'If they want luxuries of that kind where will it end?'

And Alice had succumbed immediately, and had wept about it in secret.

Asia stood it for a few weeks longer, and then, one morning, when the flannels were heavier and dirtier than usual, she had burst in a white heat upon Tom Roland, who happened to be lying late in bed, and had told him that his flannels and his boots would stay dirty in future unless he got someone in to clean them.

He had stared back in amazement at her raging face, and then a flicker of amusement crossed his eyes.

'Holy Moses,' he snorted, 'if it's as bad as all that, get two washerwomen.'

'You don't know how to manage him, mother,' said Asia wisely, later in the day.

That stung Alice to make a stand that night when her husband tried to get even with her. He had said only a few words when she turned on him.

'You stop annoying me about nothing,' she commanded, and turning half dressed, she walked out of the room and left him alone for the night, to digest his astonishment as best he could.

No one was more surprised than she was at the happy results of this incident. Asia calmly requisitioned one of the men's wives for all the washing and heavy cleaning, sending for her sometimes two days a week, and never again was a word said.

There was one thing for which Alice was supremely grateful to her husband. Never had he given a sign to show that he misunderstood her friendship with David Bruce. Though she knew they gave him no real cause for jealousy, she was none the less surprised at this apparent indifference to the amount of time they saw each other. She rightly took this to be a tribute more to Bruce than to herself, and it was one thing that was independent of Asia's influence.

For three years now Alice had felt something growing between herself and the child she idolised. It had begun with Asia's first visit to the Hardings in Auckland, and it had been increased by later visits, and especially by the theatre going that had risen up like a bogy to affright Alice. In vain Bruce told her that every girl got stage mad and got over it. In vain Asia told her mother that she was not going to the dogs because she loved plays. The unforgettable fact was that Asia continued to go to plays even though she knew it hurt her mother. Alice knew she had slipped into some other world of thought, and was shaping herself by a philosophy that she herself feared. And it was the end of all this that she feared. And somehow, in her mind, the beginning of the end had become associated with Asia's eighteenth birthday.

It was because she had felt it coming nearer that she had gone out this spring night to try to bring herself to face it.

After closing the front door behind her Alice stood in the hall listening. The stillness of the house seemed ominous. She moved to the sitting-room door, and when she saw Asia sitting alone by the fire she had the feeling of a creature trapped by something that has lain in wait for it.

Hearing her there, Asia raised a pale and uneasy face towards her.

'Mother, I want to talk to you.' She tried to make her voice casual, but it sounded strained.

Throwing off her cape, Alice walked slowly to her chair on the other side of the hearth, her face growing whiter.

'Where are the girls?' she asked weakly, feeling that she wanted no interruptions.

Betty and Mabel, who were now thirteen and eleven, were no longer referred to as the 'children'.

'They've gone to bed.' Asia leaned down to put more wood on the fire.

'Is Tom home?'

'No. He won't be back tonight. He has sent word.'

Alice sat down, seeing Asia through a mist. The worst thing of all about this to her was the sense of her own utter helplessness to prevent, or postpone, or alter by one fraction the purpose of the clear, fearless, arrogantly youthful eyes that looked up at her with a tragic pity.

Asia was beautiful with a radiant vitality that stung everyone to life when she entered a room. Her features were not classic like her mother's, nor faultlessly regular like the ideal of the adolescent, for they were too strong. But she had a fine white skin, delicately tinted, eyes with the subtle draw of deep pools, and masses of soft gold hair that waved with a dozen tints as she moved. She was eager and hungry for life and beauty, voracious for adventure, tremendously sure of herself and her right to live as she pleased. She had no conception of the chasm that separated her at eighteen from her mother, either at the same age or now. But she knew only too well the likely effect of what she now had to say.

The attempts she had made to show her mother whither she was tending only convinced her it was best to wear a mask, and when the inevitable break came to make it as short as she could. For years she had lived more closely to Mrs Brayton and to Bruce than she had lived to her mother. She realised the tragedy of it. She knew what she had meant in her home. She knew what a blank she would leave behind.

As she looked at her mother's head bowed to the fire, she saw afresh what the years had done to that drooping figure and that pale, proud face, mellowed and more gracious certainly, and in ways more beautiful than ever. She wondered if she would ever solve the everlasting enigma of strength and weakness behind those suffering eyes. She set her teeth on the thought that she was now going to add to the grey hairs, the lines and the droop.

As she braced herself to speak, her mother raised her face, with a manner suggestive of noble resignation.

'Well?' she said patiently.

'Oh, mother,' began Asia miserably, 'I know I'm going to hurt you dreadfully, but, oh, please, do try to understand.'

Alice resented the implication that she might not understand all the more because she knew it was deserved.

'What is it?' she asked coldly, inviting the worst.

'I want to go away. I want to earn my own living. I want to see the world.'

'Yes?'

They were both looking into the fire. Those three sentences were what Alice had feared to hear, and she felt her heart set in her chest like a ball of plaster.

Asia had known beforehand that she would get no help, but she had determined to say everything there was to be said as shortly as possible. She clenched her hands on her knees, for she knew the look

in her mother's eyes was just as bad as she had expected it would be.
'It isn't a new thing, mother. I've wanted it for years, but I made up my mind I would wait till I was eighteen. I've thought about it till I've been sick — I know what it will mean to you — but I cannot help it. I must go, I can't be a parasite — I just can't.'

A flood of shame swept over Alice's face, and blinding tears rushed to her eyes, but Asia did not look at her as she forced herself on jerkily.

'And I want to see the world. It's all so wonderful to me, and I'm not afraid, and I know I can get on. You needn't worry about me, and, of course, I will come home to see you; but I can't stay here any longer. I have used this place up — I've breathed every breath there is to be got out of it. I would have gone two years ago but for you. I have thought of you. I've tried to tell you, but you wouldn't listen, and so I went on keeping it to myself till I couldn't any longer. I had to tell others — Uncle David and Mrs Brayton.'

Alice sat up stiffly.

'You've told them first!'

'I had to tell somebody, mother.'

The pain of this hardened Alice.

'And what do you think you can do?' she asked with a shade of scorn.

Asia winced, but kept anger out of her eyes and voice.

'I have music.'

'Yes, so had I.'

'Well, mother, I've got to try, even if I fail, and I won't fail.'

'Oh, you foolish child, what do you know of the world?'

If there ever was a question better designed to make youth hate age and fight it, it is not on record.

Asia bit back the words that leapt to her lips. If she had not been so conscious of her mother's misery she would have said things that neither of them would have forgotten.

'If I don't know anything of the world,' she replied quietly, 'it's time I began to learn, considering I have to live in it.'

'And may I ask how you are going to begin? Do you think you can capture the world in a week?'

'No, mother. I am not quite mad. I am going to the Hardings; they will help me.'

'Oh, I see. They know too.' All traces of tears now left Alice. Henceforth she was frozen.

'Yes, I wrote to them. They think I can get on. The world is different from what it was when you tried. Mother, do see that. Do understand. Everybody helps women today. And it's nothing for a girl to earn her own living.'

'Oh, isn't it? You don't know anythig about life and men. You don't know what girls have to put up with, especially when they look like you. You don't know yourself, or how clever men can fool you, and lie to you.'

'A good many women seem to survive it, mother. I don't see why I shouldn't. I'm not afraid, and if I make mistakes I will learn. I'm not going to the devil.'

Her proud self-confidence angered her mother.

'How little you know what you are talking about. You've lived a sheltered life here. You've had no chance to learn what men can be, or how you yourself can feel.'

A curious smile flitted across Asia's eyes. Getting up suddenly, she walked to the window and looked out into the darkness. Her 'sheltered life'! She smiled as she thought of it: of crude, rapidly arrested scenes with Sonny Shoreman; of staggeringly sudden and unexpected caresses on the part of various men, a Kaiwaka curate, a surveyor, an English derelict working on the gum-fields, and others! And of her own adolescent passion for David Bruce, not yet out of her system.

All this Asia saw again as she stood by the window, and she felt that if there was anything she did not know about men it could only be something unexpectedly agreeable.

As she turned back to the fire Alice saw in her face that arrogant cocksureness of youth that so irritates the wisdom of age.

'If I am ever to marry, mother,' she said, sitting down, 'it seems to me I might as well know something about myself and men. Or perhaps you have me pigeon-holed as an old maid.' She did not mean to be scornful, but her mother resented her tone.

'Oh, well, it's useless my saying anything, I know. But you will learn.' She could not avoid superiority.

'That's what I'm going for, mother. For God's sake, understand. You must have realised that I would go some day. Why do you put me in the wrong like this?'

But Alice was suffering too much now to unbend. All she wanted was the hard cold fact.

'How are you going to get the money to begin?'

'Uncle David is lending it to me.'

This was the unkindest cut of all. It looked like treachery.

'I see. And when do you go?'

'By the next boat, mother.'

Alice rose abruptly, her face turned to stone. Ignoring Asia's appealing gesture, she walked proudly into her bedroom, and shut and locked the door. She never undressed or slept, or wept all night.

Asia sat on, slow tears dripping from her cheeks. After a while she stole out into the back garden, but as if powerless to move any further she leaned against the wash-house and sobbed helplessly.

As a late moon rose over Pukekaroro she walked to the side gate and leaned upon it looking at the mountain. He reminded her of the nights and early mornings, of the moonrises and the dawns when she and her mother, watching by sick or dying babies, had turned their faces together towards his inscrutable calm. She remembered the other things they had shared: how together they had looked for the spring's first golden glory on the kowhai trees; how together they had listened for the first tui's song, and rejoiced over the first violet; how together they had watched many red suns go down beyond the river gap; how together they had played and loved Beethoven.

And she knew that she more than anyone else had always been there, like the impossible friend in the melodrama, always on the spot to share the good and the bad. And why could she not have kept on doing it for ever?

Why? Why?

MAKERETI

Hinemoa

Hinemoa was the daughter of a great chief called Umukaria, and her mother was Hinemaru, also a great rangatira. When she was born, Hinemoa was made a puhi (she was made tapu), and a husband had to be chosen by her hapu when she grew up. She was very beautiful, and her fame spread far and wide. People came from distances to see her and ask for her hand in marriage. She lived with her parents and people on the edge of Lake Rotorua at a kainga called Owhata.

On an island called Mokoia which stands in the middle of Lake Rotorua lived another great chief called Whakaue, who had a family of five sons and one daughter. The three eldest sons were Tawakeheimoa, Ngararanui, and Tuteataiti, the younger were Tutanekai and Kopako, and the daughter, the youngest, was Tupa. When the eldest brothers heard of Hinemoa, each thought that he would like her for his wife.

Every year chiefs and members of various hapu living round Lake Rotorua and Rotoiti gathered together to hold a hui at Owhata to discuss matters of state regarding the tribe. At these meetings many young chiefs saw Hinemoa and fell in love with her. She was all that they had heard of, and of course a great rangatira. Many asked for her hand, and among them Whakaue's eldest sons. But the people had not yet chosen a husband for her.

Hinemoa lived in a whare belonging to her father, with her handmaidens who looked after her and waited upon her. She was not allowed to do anything in the way of work.

When the hui took place each year, Whakaue and his sons attended these gatherings, including Tutanekai, a younger son of whom he was very fond. At these meetings Hinemoa and Tutanekai saw each other, and although they never spoke, knew and felt that they were in love. When the different hapu danced the haka (posture dances) and war dances, Tutanekai excelled, as he did in all the games. He was also good to look at, well-built and strong. The hui often lasted many days, and Hinemoa saw Tutanekai each day from a distance on her father's marae (plaza). She thought him the most wonderful man she had ever seen, and her love for him grew until it filled her whole being. Tutanekai would glance at her and wonder if Hinemoa, a puhi, and a great rangatira, would deign to look at him when his elder brothers sought her hand also. He loved Hinemoa, but his love could only be sent by a glance and a look from his eyes.

When the hui ended, Whakaue and his sons returned to Mokoia. Tutanekai built himself an atamira (high stand) on a rise behind his father's house. He told his father that he wanted Hinemoa, and that his love was returned, and, every evening, he and his friend Tiki took their pu (flutes), Tiki the torino, and Tutanekai the koauau, and sitting on the atamiro, played. On a quiet evening the sound of the music floated across the water to Owhata where Hinemoa lived, and she knew that it was her lover playing, and conveying his messages of love through his koauau. Each evening she sat and listened to her lover's music, and felt that she really loved Tutanekai, and could not marry anyone else.

Her people began to suspect this, and thinking that she would go across to Mokoia, dragged the canoes up each evening so that she could not paddle across. But one evening as she listened to the koauau, she could almost hear the message asking her to go across, and felt that she could not live any longer while Tutanekai was eating his heart away on his island home. As the canoes were well guarded, there was only one thing that she could do, and that was to swim across. 'E kore ranei au e whiti ki te kau hoe?' Cannot I get across by swimming?

She then told her maidens that she was going to the whare tapere, the house where dances were performed and games were played, but instead of doing so, she went into a wharau (cooking house), and took six calabashes. She then rested on a rock called Iri iri kapua, which is there to this day, and after that went to the beach to Wairerewai, where she took off her clothes and left them before slipping into the water of Lake Rotorua with the six empty calabashes tied together, three under each arm. It was growing dark when she got into the water, but the sound of the flute gave her the direction of the island. After swimming for a time, she came to a tumu, a stump in the lake, called Hinewhata, which her father Umukaria used for tying his tanga (long fishing nets) on, and a bunch of fern to which the small fish toitoi and the koura (crayfish) stuck. She held on to the tumu and rested, as she was beginning to feel the strain. When the tired feeling left her shoulders, she started swimming again, guided by the sound of her lover's music in the darkness, which took her across to Waikimihia, a warm bath on the edge of Mokoia Island by the lake. Hinemoa knew that above Waikimihia was Tutanekai's home. She got into the warm pool, for she was shivering with cold. She also shivered through being whakama, wondering how Tutanekai would look on her action. She also realised that she had no clothes, and this made her very whakama indeed.

Now about the same time that Hinemoa was sitting in the waiariki (warm bath), it happened that Tutanekai felt thirsty, and sent his taurekareka (slave) with a calabash, saying, 'Tikina he wai moku,' Go and get me water to drink. His taurekareka went to get the water, and had to pass the bath where Hinemoa sat. She asked in a gruff voice, 'Mo wai te wai?' For whom is the water? The taurekareka answered, 'Mo Tutanekai,' It is for Tutanekai. Hinemoa then said, 'Homai ki ahau,' Give it to me. The calabash was handed to her, and after drinking the water she wanted, she broke the calabash. The slave asked her reason for doing this, but she gave him no answer. He returned to Tutanekai, who asked where the water was which he was sent to fetch. The slave replied, 'The calabash is broken.' Tutanekai asked, 'Na wai i wahi?' Who broke it? The reply came, 'Some man did it.' Tutanekai asked him to take another calabash, and get him the water. When the taurekareka filled the second calabash with water, and turned to return with it to his master, Hinemoa asked again in a gruff voice whom the water was for, and the reply was that it was for Tutanekai. She asked him, still in a gruff voice, to hand her the calabash, which he did. Hinemoa again drank some water, and then broke the calabash by knocking it on the stone formation by the side of the pool. The taurekareka returned and told Tutanekai what had happened, and Tutanekai asked who had done this thing. The slave replied that he did not know the man, and that he must be a stranger. This made Tutanekai very angry, as the stranger knew that the water was for him, yet had dared to insult him by breaking his two calabashes.

He then dressed himself in his rapaki with a kahakaha cloak round his shoulders, and a tawaru cloak outside that, and with a patu pounamu (short-handled weapon) in his right hand, went forward to fight the stranger who had dared to break his calabashes.

When he reached the bath, he cried, 'Kei whea te tangata i wahi nei i aku kiaka?' Where is the man who has dared to break my calabashes? Hinemoa knew the voice to be that of the love of her heart, and moved under an overhanging ledge of rock, for she did not want to be seen yet. She rejoiced within her heart to think that what she had done had brought out her lover to her, without her having to go to his house, having no clothes. Tutanekai felt round the edge of the bath until at last he caught her dripping hair and pulled her from under the ledge of rock, saying, 'Ko wai tenei?' Who is this? Hinemoa answered, 'Ko ahau, Tutanekai.' It is I, Tutanekai. Tutanekai said, 'Ko wai koe?' Who are you? She answered, 'Ko au ko, Hinemoa,' It is I, Hinemoa. Tutanekai exclaimed, 'E! E! Hoake taua ki te whare,' Come, let us go home. She replied, 'Ae,' Yes.

He took her hand and led her out of the bath. He saw how very beautiful she was. Her skin was like the tapukoraki, and when she stood out of the water she was like a kotuku*. Tutanekai then took

---

* She was fair and graceful. Tapukoraki is the name of a bird; te kotuku is the white heron.

one of his cloaks and covered her with it, and they walked to his house and slept there. This to the Maori signified marriage.

In the morning early the people rose to work and get ready the hangi to cook their food. After their food they missed Tutanekai, for he was still in his whare. His father said, 'Katahi a te ata o Tutanekai, i moe roa ae,' This is the first time that Tutanekai has slept so long. Perhaps my child is ill; go and call Tutanekai, that he may have some food.

A messenger went to call him. He slid the pihanga, that is the small wooden window, of the house, and looked in. He saw that Tutanekai had a companion, and wondered who it was, and hurried to tell Whakaue, who sent him back to make sure that he had not made a mistake. The messenger returned to Tutanekai's whare, and saw and recognised Hinemoa, and with that shouted, 'Ko Hinemoa, ko Hinemoa te hoa o Tutanekai,' Hinemoa, it is Hinemoa with Tutanekai!

When his elder brothers heard this, they would not believe it, and said, 'He hori, he hori,' for they were very jealous of Tutanekai.

Just then, Tutanekai came forth from his whare, with Hinemoa beside him. His people could hardly believe their own eyes, but when they looked across the lake, they saw several war canoes coming from the direction of Owhata. They knew it was Umukaria, Hinemoa's father, with his people, coming across, as they thought, to take Hinemoa away. They expected war, but when Umukaria and his people came, instead of war, there was great rejoicing, and peace was made.

Hinemoa and Tutanekai lived happily ever after, and many of the people who live in and around Rotorua and the near lakes are descended from them.

EDITH SEARLE GROSSMANN

Husband and wife

Hermione's dearest friends had scarcely predicted for her an unclouded future. Yet the early days of her marriage were bright enough. Bradley Carlisle was by no means a born villain. He had plenty of natural affection, and this had been growing up towards Hermione together with his passion. If he had expressed his opinion of himself it would have been that he was no fool, but neither was he a bad sort of fellow as the world goes. Hermione's sentimentality, as he called it to himself, rather gratified him, since it was in a right direction, i.e. the direction of loving him. He was still young enough not to be utterly unsusceptible to new influences, though his character was of too sensual and sceptical a type for the purer elements to make a deep impression. He meant to be kind to his wife; he was certainly not miserly, and he did not consider himself a bully. Of course he meant to have the upper hand; he despised all men who did not.

But at first he had no need to urge his claims. Her own love granted them freely, and he was brought away from the fast young men, the jockeys and sharpers of Brooklyn, into the closest companionship with a pure-minded, simple-hearted girl, whose entire ignorance of life made her take his word rather than her own instincts of right and wrong. For the tragic centre of Hermione's life was that at times all the elements of her nature were subordinated to one ruling passion. From the very day that she was married she had stifled within her heart every idea of wrong in his words and deeds. In her love she found a Lethe for his faults. Her girlish devotion had been made by her marriage a religious duty. She believed, or persuaded herself into believing, that it was right she should silence every doubt of his perfection, and the elements of passion and duty were strangely mingled within her.

He was really kind to her, and very generous. What touched her heart more than his presents to herself was his offer of settling on her father land and money that would keep him in comfort for the rest of his life. Howard declined the offer, but Hermione was not the less grateful. All her wishes he spared neither expense nor trouble to gratify, unless, of course, they were 'absurd'. As she had no money of her own, everything she had was his present. It was not till they were at Moorabool that he gave her a settled amount, and then he required so much that she often had to exceed it. She was completely dependent on him. Now that they were alone she felt that in him centred all her happiness, all her affections. 'I have only you with me to love,' she said to him once.

In those early days of marriage the two natures acted and reacted on each other strangely. He began to have some perception that the girl he had married was really purer and nobler than the women he had met before. Her sensitive delicacy made up for the lack of coquetry. What laid a restraint upon him more than anything else was the fact that the girl loved him not only with warm affection, but with idolatry. As long as that continued he was not willing to lower himself in her eyes, though very soon the inducement to inflict on her a species of light torture by ridiculing what she held sacred proved too much for him. Unprotected innocence is to such minds as his an irresistible temptation. This kind of humorous cruelty was one of the features of his character.

But she was willing to believe him rather than herself, to persuade herself that she was over-sensitive and foolish. Moreover he had this advantage over her, that she knew herself to be totally inexperienced, whilst he prided himself on his knowledge of 'the world', i.e., of frivolity and vice. Besides, on account of her youth, her character was much less formed than his.

So she was happy, and had no fear for the future. Nor was the sudden change from comparative poverty to wealth a matter of indifference. At present she was willing to be thus, for ever owing and only giving back such loving service as she could. All her ambition and noble dreams, as yet undefined and vague, had taken their flight before this new intense reality. She was willing to bend her nature to his, or rather to what she believed to be his.

Even he was sometimes touched by her love. He had gone out on to the verandah to smoke a cigar while she was undressing, and on coming into the room saw her kneeling down with closed eyes and clasped hands. He threw himself into an armchair with a half-amused, half-inquiring look, then when she rose, said —

'Come here, Beauty. What were you praying for, darling?'

'I had rather not tell you, Bradley.'

'But I want to know.'

He had taken both her hands in his, and for a moment she looked straight at him with her clear, truthful eyes; then the lids dropped as she answered —

'That I might be a good and true wife to you, and make you happy.'

He looked at her and saw the colour rising slowly in her downcast face, yet there was pride in her humility.

'You are a good girl, Hermione,' he said, more seriously than usual, kissed her, and then went on to the verandah.

The girl was a complete mystery to him. He had not expected this perfect submission from what he had seen at Miss Howard's. He sometimes wondered now if her aunt's temper had not been in fault rather than her own.

But after the first week came some of those jarring incidents which, trivial as they seemed, told keenly on Hermione. For when Bradley Carlisle saw that she was his wife, and submitting utterly to him, left him nothing he could win from her, he naturally became more careless in security. After all a man tires sooner of one who is completely his own than of one who has a separate existence. He began to find it interesting to go to concerts and parties, not only that he might show off the beauty of his new acquisition, but that he might meet other girls.

A fortnight after marriage they were staying at Albury. Bradley had accepted an invitation for the evening, but Hermione had a bad headache. He would have liked the Hares to see his pretty young wife, but then there were compensations for her absence. Young Hare was a good hand at billiards, and Hermione had such absurd notions about gambling.

'I will go if you want me to, dear,' she said.

'No, I won't have you ill, Beauty. However did you manage to get a headache, though?'

'I suppose it was the change and going about too much. But I shall be quite well again tomorrow,' she answered, rather anxiously, for he looked vexed. When he came back she was still lying on the sofa, half-asleep, but she got up to meet him.

'How is the headache, darling?' he asked, as he took her in his arms; 'you should have gone to bed before.'

Then he rang for lights, and putting her into a chair a little way from him, examined her critically. He was comparing her to Connie Lake and the Hares' beautiful cousin, young Mrs Montague, who rouged, and pencilled her eyebrows, and pinched in her waist.

'She's worth the lot of them,' he said to himself. Aloud he remarked, 'I wish, Beauty, you would talk more to people. They think you such a queer child, and stupid.'

'I am so sorry if I vex you,' she said, sadly.

'And you will not find it so pleasant for yourself, child. You will be very lonely when we go home; you won't have a single friend.'

She came to him and knelt down by his side. The tears were in her eyes as she said, in a low tone —

'Yes, I will; I shall have you, and I don't want anyone else.'

He laughed a little, well-pleased, as he put his hand caressingly on her hair.

'But I want you to be friends with some people, Mavourneen. You can keep them at a distance if you like.'

For himself he was King of Brooklyn by a well-recognised title, and he liked to be on terms of easy familiarity with everyone. But it rather increased his sense of importance that his wife should be unapproachable, and it certainly flattered his personal vanity.

In the morning Hermione woke early, and with characteristic restlessness began to think over her travels. Where would they be going tomorrow? Ah, she remembered — Beechworth. That was where Bradley's two married sisters, Moll and Kathleen, were.

'Bradley!' she began, energetically.

'Well?' he answered, in a sleepy tone.

'Are you going to see Mollie?'

'I don't know.'

There was quiet for a little time, and she began to think again. He would be certain to go if his mother were there.

'Bradley!'

'Confound you! Can't you let me sleep?'

She lay still in dismay, dreadfully pained, then following her first impulse, got up softly, dressed herself, and left the hotel. The morning sky was still grey and misty, and the dew was on the grass, though the sun had risen. Her old love of roaming came over her, and she abandoned herself to the delight of new scenes till she came to the river. She sat down on a log, and, taking off her hat, looked over the yellow stream to the dusty slopes, interspersed with gum trees and vine-clad cottages, of her new land. Half in shadow and half in sunlight her eye was caught by a rough old boat of unpainted wood, in which were sitting two sun-bronzed men with wide-awake hats and open shirts, showing their brown, hairy chests. They had been fishing, and the sun shone on the silver scales of the panting creatures at the bottom of the boat. But now they were moving off to the further bend of the river. The dip, dip of their oars lazily in the water had a delightful sound to Hermione, to whom all inhabitants of unfamiliar places were of necessity picturesque and deeply interesting.

When Bradley Carlisle got up his wife was nowhere to be found, so he asked the hotel people.

The lady had gone out for a walk; they did not know where. The breakfast he had ordered, expecting to find her in the garden, was ready and would get cold.

'What a precious little fool she is,' he said to himself, with something like an oath.

He walked towards the river, and found her sitting there. She saw him, and ran to him with some eagerness.

'So there you are! What on earth have you been doing?' he said, taking her arm.

'I was thinking,' she began, slowly, her enthusiasm rather checked.

'Couldn't you think at the hotel, pray, or after breakfast?' he asked, sharply.

'Oh, Bradley, don't let us have any breakfast this morning. Let us ask one of those men to take us on the river.'

He stared at her as if he thought her out of her senses.

'No, thank you,' he said, coolly.

'Well, you go back to the hotel and let me go and ask the men. I don't want any breakfast.'

Was ever a man plagued with such a stupid girl while his breakfast was getting spoiled at the hotel? Even Bradley Carlisle felt irritated.

'Confound the men! You shall have breakfast with me when I please, Beauty.'

The defiance of her nature arose at his tone, but the gentleness of her love struggled with it.

'Bradley, I do wish you wouldn't talk like that. You said "confound you" to me this morning.'

'Oh, did I?' he asked carelessly, but half-amused.

'Yes; I don't like it.'

'You will have to take what you get whether you like it or not.'

She drew her arm from his. How could he speak in that way to her?

'Oh, that's right, you're a true woman, Beauty. You will get into a rage now and march into the hotel with an injured look to show people what a beast I am to you.'

It was too much. She put her arm back into his and said —

'Oh, Bradley, don't, don't; I can't bear it,' in a tone more of dread than reproof.

They were nearly at the hotel now, and as the prospect of breakfast grew nearer he felt more amiably disposed, even a little sorry for the child. In their sitting room he placed her chair for her and helped her, but the pork was more than half-cold. After eating his with some expressions of disgust, he glanced up at her; the plate was almost untasted, and her face was pale and sad.

'Don't you touch it, Beauty,' he said, in a kind tone; 'I will get you some of the first grapes of this season — I saw some fine bunches last night.'

'How good you are to me, Bradley.'

'You didn't think so just now, Beauty,' he answered pleasantly.

'I suppose it was my fault,' she said, humbly. 'I never meant to vex you, dear; but I am afraid we don't quite understand each other.'

'Oh, I understand you well enough, Beauty. You are quite a baby in all your ways — you know nothing and care nothing about the world. However,' he went on, more to himself than to her, 'it's pretty tough, and one knows that you are not a made-up thing.' After a few minutes he said, smiling, to her, 'You haven't given me my morning kiss, Beauty.'

He had laughed at her kissing him every morning and evening — kissing by clockwork, he called it.

'I thought you did not want it.'

'Oh, yes, I do. Come along.'

She went to him with a certain shy reserve; he returning her kiss with interest.

'You're a dear child, Beauty. But here are your grapes.'

The beautiful purple and golden clusters were heaped up lavishly among the indented leaves. He took some, then leant back, alternately watching her and the water-colour daub over the mantelpiece.

'I am going to take you on the river. Will I do as well as the fishermen?'

'Oh, Bradley, are you really? Yes, I shall be happy.'

'Well, go and get ready.'

While she was away he thought of her with some amusement. She was a mere child to him, but of course that made him love her all the more, he thought. When he was in a good temper he felt tender towards her, otherwise her youth was a perpetual temptation. A cruel nature feels more, not less, cruel towards a child, especially a sensitive child, than to an equal.

But he was very kind that morning, and rowed her himself and got her to steer; she had a young keen delight in swift motion and novelty. Then she was so proud of his strength and skill. But she had known him such a short time that sometimes as she looked at him, with his coat off and head bare, it seemed almost as if he were a stranger. The feeling that he was her husband made a strange thrill run through her. Her thoughts were interrupted, for he looked up.

'By the way, Beauty, I won't have you going out as you did this morning, not here nor on the station. Now, remember.'

The command shut out so much of her freedom.

'But, Bradley — '

'But — I won't have any of your "buts", Beauty. You must be guided by me.'

She flushed a little, but said, after a pause —

'Very well, I promise you not to go out without your knowing.'

'That's a good girl.'

So the matter concluded. But at night she lay awake with a trouble in her heart. He had been very kind, and yet why did he speak to her as he had done that morning? Why did he order her when he knew she would obey his least wish? 'To love, cherish, and to obey.' Ah, it was very wrong of her to give way to her own fancies and accuse him in her heart. It was her own fault — hers alone.

GRACE MORTON
(As told to Stanley Roche)

A sense of alienation

What do you do without money in a strange country where no one wants the skills you have? Where the very thing that used to be your greatest asset, your voice with privilege and position in its vowel sounds, proves an enemy provoking defensive hostility or contempt or amusement. ('A pom with a plum in his mouth. Hell, they're arrogant! Up themselves.')

Guy found himself a job as a mechanic at General Motors in Lower Hutt. Grace once again stayed behind to tidy away the tag ends of an enterprise. As at Uzhorod, the unpaid bills poured in. But this time there was no way she could settle them — they remained unpaid.

Guy Morton passed into bankruptcy.

He was nearly sixty. Grace looked thirty but her birth-date said that she was in her forty-fifth year.

Laings Road, Lower Hutt. An upstairs flat. Grace with a basket on her arm pirouetting and parading in front of Guy.

'Look at the suburban housewife off to do the shopping!' They both laughed.

But Grace actually putting parcels in her necessary basket thinks, 'Suppose one of my Shanghai friends saw me now!'

'Whatever happened to Grace Botham? That well-dressed, witty woman. The one that was always in demand. Grace Botham the professeur?'

'Oh, Grace! She lives in a dull house in a dull street in a dull suburb in a dull country. She cooks and sweeps and irons her husband's shirts.'

'Not Grace, no, you're thinking of someone else!'

For the first time in her life she lives without a maid. Sweeping and ironing are fairly easily learned though they are never second nature to her as they are to women brought up to them. But cooking is a daily nightmare, a horrible exam that she must sit, unprepared, every night of her life. She buys herself a text but no cookery book is elementary enough. She goes to her neighbours for help — isn't that what you do when you're in trouble?

'It says here to steam it. What does that mean? Do I put it in hot or cold water?'

They laugh at her in shocked disbelief. 'Go on! You do what it says. Steam it.' She never asked them anything again.

With her basket on her arm she visits the butcher's shop, lingering till she is the only customer.

'I don't know anything about buying meat. I want something I can cook tonight for two people.'

He suggests fillet steaks. 'How do I cook them?'

Step by step he tells her. Grace Botham of Shanghai is grateful to a butcher for his sensitive courtesy.

The preparing of the meal takes hours each day. Guy eats what she serves with every sign of enjoyment and asks for more.

'Do you like it, Guy?'

'It would have been all right if you'd . . . if you hadn't . . .'

And when the periodic storms of violence shake him, he yells at her. 'You serve me muck! How can any woman be so stupid?'

Her good mind tells her that she is learning, that the meals she serves are savoury and satisfying, but deep within her a frightened voice agrees with every criticism. Always, all her life, the smell of cooking is to her the smell of failure.

It is all part of her sense of alienation. The sky is strange here, strangely marked and coloured; gross bare hills threaten. The forest (which the natives perversely call the bush) is the wrong shade of green, flowers bloom in winter, and there is a plentiful absence of snow. The very man in the moon is unrecognisable upside-down.

Textures worry her. The memory of the thick woollen socks of the farmers who came to fish at Turangi fills her with a sense of physical repugnance, their scarred and calloused hands horrify. She remembers dancing at the Chateau and noticing that the New Zealand women in the room could be identified by their red, weathered hands.

'They may have to clean and cook and scrub but you'd think they'd have pride enough to conceal it,' thinks Grace, understanding only one brand of pride. She buys rubber gloves and hand-lotion to preserve the pallor of her own.

She listens to the accents around her, vainly trying to classify them as a clue to a social scale more definite and extreme than exists here. She imagines she is complimenting a fourth-generation New Zealander when she says, 'No one would know you were born here.'

But not for nothing is she Nellie Botham's daughter. Her upper lip is outwardly stiff. Already she knows that New Zealanders, in the face of criticism, may reply cruelly, 'If you don't like it, why don't you go home?'

Where is home?

Her nostalgic misery, rammed down into her own bowels — she must keep cheerful for Guy — turns sour there and corrupts. Heart sickness turns into physical lethargy and an unidentifiable, but apparently permanent, sense of bodily distress. She thinks of her old enemy, anaemia. Has it turned pernicious? Or could it be cancer? Reluctantly she tells Guy.

Guy, alarmed and solicitous, takes her to a doctor.

'Not a thing wrong with you,' he says heartily and suggests she take cascara. They score it up, another entry on their slate of sins this country has committed, and look for a specialist.

Guy discovers the admirable and amiable Dr Pacey who examines Grace very carefully.

'Do you really not know what's wrong with you?' She waits for the worst. 'You're pregnant.'

'That's impossible. I can't be!'

'Well, it's either a three-months foetus or a tumour.'

'At my age,' cries Grace, 'let's hope it's a tumour!'

Pregnancy tests are a new and cumbersome technique involving live rabbits and a considerable time lapse. But the results are reliable.

'Firmly positive. And everything seems to be in order. Shall we say December?'

After the first shock the baby rejuvenates them. They are again the adventurous, dashing Mortons. Who else would conceive a child when they total between them more than a century of experience? It also rescues Grace from the horror of cooking in the Laings Road flat. They move to a Wellington boarding-house. Guy has found himself a more congenial and lucrative job in the office of the Wellington branch of Lloyds.

1942. Twice, in June and again in August, the earth stirs and heaves. Precariously perched Wellington shakes alarmingly. In pyjamas and curlers, citizens spill out into the streets. In Customhouse Quay a huge concrete parapet crashes from a building on to and through the pavement below. But it is night time and Customhouse Quay is deserted. No one is hurt. Grace is sitting in the circle of the Majestic Theatre when the second quake comes. Her pregnant woman's instinct for survival gets her down the stairs to the lobby before she is consciously aware of having moved.

All the news from overseas is bad. Singapore falls to the Japanese. They are pressing south towards Australia. Wellington becomes a base for American troops, the streets take on an olive-green tint as marines in their thousands move in. American accents everywhere, Camel cigarettes and Lucky Strikes, condoms in the shop doorways. Coffee shops selling real coffee flower in Willis Street and Lambton Quay.

But Grace, with her private miracle within, is insulated from the stirrings of war. Now that she and Guy have adjusted to the idea of a child they are delighted. 1942 is their late and secret spring.

Standing in a picture theatre for the national anthem, Grace suddenly laughs. It is the eighth month. Dr Pacey has told her that day that the baby has turned with its head well down ready for birth.

'What's the matter with you,' whispers Guy.

'I've just thought — how funny, my son stands on his head for God Save the Queen.'

December, summer, six shopping days to Christmas. On the 17th of the month Grace goes into labour. She has known it will not be easy. To bear a first child at the end of your fruitful years is a dangerous business.

In a private hospital in Willis Street Dr Pacey administers Twilight Sleep to her but her drowsiness is punctuated by huge red throbs of pain so that her body is a drum beaten for three days to a barbaric and mounting rhythm. Over and over again she is moved into the theatre and then out again to make way for yet another swifter queue-jumping birth. Dr Pacey swims into her nightmare and out again. Guy hovers helplessly at the gates of hell. On the 20th her rhythm crashes to a climax. A son is born, vigorous, healthy.

Dr Pacey, triumphant, drives up to Brooklyn himself to tell Guy who after lingering so long has slept throughout the final act.

In the calm aftermath Grace watches from her window a huge magnolia tree. Every morning the great cream flowers open to the sun and, following its passage, droop and die as it sets. Christmas Day. Guy, brimming with goodwill, shares the hospital's festive dinner in Grace's private room. It smells of roses and joy as well as lamb and mint sauce. They are never to be so happy again.

While Grace has been dawdling in the life cycle of the magnolia flowers, Guy has found his family a flat in lovely Oriental Bay and has moved in. The windows overlook the harbour, only the road between them and the beach. As the baby grows, whenever Wellington weather is kind, Grace spends whole days with him on the sand running back to the flat only to fetch his bottle or orange juice or sieved vegetables.

He grows satisfactorily, this miraculous baby, but not in unruffled calm. He is delicate. With the autumn cold he develops asthma. Night after night Grace sits by his bed till daylight, gently pushing to expel the air from his choking lungs. She feels for the first time the full weight of her years. So, apparently, does Guy.

The old problems — housework, money, Guy's moodiness, reassert themselves and dominate lives worn thin by fatigue.

To both Grace and Guy it is unthinkable that a house should not be clean and neat in every particular. It is the nature of houses to be so and, if they are not, then clearly there is somewhere a dereliction of duty.

Tired, Grace cannot meet her own standards or Guy's. There are no maids or chars in New Zealand but there is an occupation that to an outsider looks the same, called 'Help in the House'. It may be a local euphemism so that New Zealanders can have what they in theory deplore, or it may be that by changing the name they hope to expel the sad social connotations of domestic work.

Grace acquires a woman to help in the house. She has already discovered that in the topsy-turvy antipodean social structure doctors occupy the top position. It is mildly surprising to find that her help is a doctor's sister. When one of Grace's friends drops in, the help serves a beautiful afternoon tea then pours herself a cup and sits down with the ladies to drink it and chat. Grace thinks wistfully of unobtrusive Humpty and Juji, but is more amused than annoyed.

It is Guy who upsets the delicate balance by complaining that the bathroom floor has not been adequately polished, nor the shelf where he keeps his razor wiped down.

'I'm not a charwoman, Mr Morton,' says the help and, taking her coat from the peg by the front door, leaves never to return. The difference is apparently not just one of nomenclature.

Money and rage are more basic problems.

To Guy, money is not the measure of man's worth but it is the outward manifestation of that worth. To look poor and act poor is more humiliation than he can stand especially in a country that has, he thinks, nothing else to judge by. He carries his image proudly — a free-spending gentleman — and there is little of his salary left over for such mundane stuff as meat and groceries and the power bill. He is happy to live in debt, it's a gentlemanly failing. Grace, with the missionary ethic behind her, loathes it.

Their money troubles are rocks that surface regularly. The sudden squalls from nowhere are a worse threat.

They are no less violent now than they have always been. Grace, who can look before and after, knows she will weather them. But how can you explain away a shouting violent adult to a terrified toddler?

Friday evening. Guy is breaking glasses against the kitchen door. David is screaming, beside himself with fear. Grace picks him up and carries him, hysterical, through to the bedroom. And while she walks the floor with him, calming and comforting, acknowledges at last that this is unendurable and must stop.

As residents, they avoid the beach in summer weekends when Wellingtonians crowd there to swim and sunbathe. But the next fine Sunday Grace lures Guy out for a walk and knowing she is safe from physical attack with a couple of hundred witnesses around, she issues her ultimatum. 'Either you control yourself or I take David and go. I still love you and you can say what you like and I'll forget it, but I can't take any more violence.'

Guy, as much a victim of his own destructive cycle as any of them, is sad and contrite. 'I don't know why I'm like that. I do love you both so much. I swear I'll never let it happen again.'

And for five weeks it doesn't. He is loving, kindly Guy. Grace begins to relax. Then inevitably the eruption comes, the worse for having been bottled up so long.

Grace has already seen a lawyer who has told her she has grounds for divorce. Guy's lawyer advised legal separation. Very quietly at the end, with much sadness, they part.

MARGARET SUTHERLAND

An easy companionship

Between ten o'clock and eleven in the morning, doors stood open and the concrete driveways of Pleasantdowns came alive with domestic traffic. These intervals provided the staple communication within the suburb. Women arranged themselves on sunny backyard steps in summer and hitched their skirts and dried their rollered hair. Winter kept them inside to emerge a half hour later in a scuttle of wind and rain. While they ate of social interchange, their children munched biscuits and trundled clacking toys on strings. Such periods were invested with an air of time stolen; the daily business of broom and wash-tub thus earning some importance.

On such an outing Pauline Jury marched erect, attuned to some internal clock. She wheeled a pram; her toddlers trailed behind.

'Hard at it, Kate? I only wish I had the time.'

Pauline looked tired which was not surprising as she worked very hard to maintain hospital standards at home. Her children were dismissed to the back yard after breakfast and allowed inside for lunch and the afternoon nap. Time spent in the Jury kitchen (the front room being reserved for special occasions, a custom Kate had thought extinct) left Kate mute and inwardly aggressive. Pauline's conversation was a matter of statement on codes of moral and suburban behaviour, enduring which Kate would feel censured and lose the thread of the talk. She went to see Pauline as seldom as diplomacy required.

Pauline scanned the flowerbeds. 'Father Flynn stopped by just now. I think it's to their credit that they visit members of the parish . . . did Father Ell call on you?'

'I saw him as he passed.'

'He didn't stay? They're such busy men . . . other stops to make. I wonder what they think of some of the places they see . . .'

For there were as many varieties of that religion as Catholics in the street. Pauline's attitude to those who failed to meet her standards was one of determined charity in that, while judging them lazy if they stayed in bed on Sundays or misguided if they questioned, she was infused with the certainty of their salvation. Either they would see or be made to see their error. Pauline's God was the Hound of Heaven, pursuing sinners' souls down the days and nights of Comfrey. She prayed for these stray sheep, a charity for which she would hardly have been thanked.

Both Pauline and her husband Ray bore public witness to their faith. Their parish involvement was displayed rather like the framed Papal blessing hung opposite their front door. The Jurys attended lay conferences, took on church business, privately believed an unfair share of parish work was passed over to them; and would have been offended had it been otherwise. They did not say to each other that the other Catholics in the street were not suitable for responsibility. The common denominator of religion did not stop Kate Goodman from being a mixed marriage and Mrs Bolt a disgrace; and if Tom Vodanovich the fish-shop proprietor was not quite the man to handle parish accounts, and if Bethany Moore never went to Holy Communion, these matters were tacit. Pauline and Ray accepted with a kind of spiritual squaring of the shoulders that some were called to give more than others. A hint of such acceptance marked Pauline's expression more clearly than she could have guessed. People respected her standards and kept their confidences for less armoured hearts.

'I have a matter to discuss with Trixie,' murmured Pauline, passing on. This was very much a Pauline way of saying 'morning tea'. Matters to discuss, business to attend to; she carved her everyday activities in such substance as though seeking promotion above the average rank of housewife.

Trixie Lovatt, amiable at the next-door window and anxious to dispense egalitarian hospitality, tapped just then upon the glass. Kate stood up, brushed her knees and went inside to wash her hands.

Small children in Trixie's back yard were attacking the playthings and each other. Andrew left Kate and ran jubilant to hurl himself on Pauline's son. Pauline made disturbed sorties to the top of the steps.

'You must *share*, Gerard.'

And when Gerard would not, descended herself to prise free the toy and give it to Andrew; who dropped it and ran in search of new mischief. Gerard threw himself down.

'It wasn't . . .' said Kate, 'it was Andrew.'

'Gerard has to learn to share.'

Pauline withdrew. She loved her children. Much of what others thought was hardness (she knew, sensed in silences, looks) was the denying of maternal fondness in favour of character development. To deny a natural instinct could bring pain. It was the pain that gave her strength to mete out judgement and she nurtured it as saints might witness the marks of their penances. Only in the brief span of their babyhood would she allow herself to show affection. Ignoring Gerard's screams now, she lifted the drowsing baby from his pram and held him, taking comfort from his scent. Perplexed lines scored her brow above the nose. She hated the lines, rubbed them every night with lanoline but it did no good.

She was twenty-four, the age of Trixie Lovatt and two years more than Kate.

Trixie, token Anglican, passed pikelets.

'Bethany called yesterday when you were out, Kate. I happened to notice, at the window.'

'Yes?' said Kate.

'I was going to call out to her; but then I didn't like to. I guessed you'd see each other soon.'

'Yes,' said Kate.

There were times when the street's uncompleted schemes of fence and hedge were a handicap to privacy. People watched one another's comings and goings and the net curtains could harbour jealousy; for these were girls closer to their schooldays than any claim on maturity.

'It must be nice for her,' said Trixie, 'to think you've become such friends. She never seemed to want to mix.'

Kate stayed silent. Gossip, that admission price to a community, was permissible when it turned on strangers. Then it might flesh out the figures glimpsed hurrying from bus-stop or garage; it created involvement in other lives much as television characters might take on a spurious familiarity. Her refusal to discuss her friend now indicated Bethany's claim on her loyalty. They had been friends less than a year and every week Kate valued the warmth more. Friendship in the real sense was a rare enough experience; she was not likely to share it with her neighbours who, sensing her reserve, began to talk together of another neighbour not known by Kate. She sat excluded, remembering how she had come home from a routine shopping expedition the day before and found the small parcel propped against the doorstep. Inside the wrapping of a city music store was a seldom-heard operatic aria, one she had chanced to hear with Bethany some weeks before. The small black disc implied thought and phone calls . . . perhaps a special trip to town. The bond between the two had a similar guessed value beyond the definable reasons why people call each other friends.

'It's the children,' Kate overheard; 'the children I feel sorry for.' And Pauline sounded it, sounded really sorry, as though for two pins she would drag them from the street to scrub and soap and spruce them up and send them home sparking her disapproval of their careless mother. Soap and water were high in Pauline's armoury against wrong-doing. She had used it once to wash out Gerard's mouth, hearing him blaspheme.

Kate, who knew of Daphne Bolt only from hearsay, did not join in this discussion. She had heard of the family's marital spats, of stray children brought home in police cars; stories transmitted less with malice than as an antidote to the clean windows and healthy ambitions of Pleasantdowners. Daphne Bolt no doubt had her own access to this kind of bush telegraph . . . in one community drums, smoke signals; in another, teacups.

Their talk passed on to general interests of prices, bargains, milestones, the measles epidemic. They talked of their husbands. They talked of their children. Their loyalty one to the other extended just as far as these bonds. Each girl kept intact some private area, and these were the same areas about which they might speculate, apart. Thus Pauline's rectitude or Kate and Bethany's closeness might be disrespectfully analysed in their absence. The rules of the street were definitive, and those who stayed separate did so at their own risk.

Pauline set her baby down to sleep and took up knitting; a complex Aran pattern for her husband Ray. Her hands were always busy, chasing off devils or the threat of meditation. Even her leisure time was gainfully spent. Visitors did not surprise her in her dressing-gown, or munching cake. She was not a candidate for such comforting breakdown in suburban schedule. Callers were made to wait, never quite sure of their welcome and reminded uneasily of days as culprits awaiting the head teacher's pleasure. Yet Pauline was aware of constant foot traffic to other doors and wondered, standing with her solitary lunch sandwich at the bench, why so few people came to see her.

She told others she had no time for endless morning teas. Now she worked two rows exactly, stabbed her needles through the bundled wool and took her leave. There was always formality about her comings and goings. While other wives popped in or just happened to be passing, Pauline's visits were arrivals and departures. She summoned her children, thanked Trixie for the coffee, nodded to Kate and wheeled away the pram. The other girls lingered in the sunshine. Andrew and Mary, Trixie's daughter, played in solemn and contented ritual. In Mary's three-year-old attitude there was already a maternal note; you could look at her and see the woman. Order and responsibility seemed to matter. She arranged pegs in lines and according to their colour, and howled when Andrew kicked them down. Five minutes later Andrew was beside her docile and the pegs were being returned to their ranks.

'I ought to go,' said Kate. 'It's Thursday.'

'Of course,' said Trixie. 'Your mother's day.'

Yet they continued to enjoy the sun. Theirs was an easy companionship defined by domestic boundaries. Their present roles rather than any real empathy drew them together. Trixie, gentle and fair, her hair bound above her head like a ballerina's, was an antidote to the uneasy tide in Kate. Time spent with her could send Kate home to wash down windowsills, not even minding. When Kate was restless she went to Trixie and came away soothed. There was comfort in Trixie's unquestioning acceptance, and Kate could then believe that life was just as it was meant to be, and would take the children on her knee and chant them nonsense rhymes. Kate's baby girl stirred and chuckled in her pram. Trixie smiled; and sighed.

'Sally's such a good baby. I do envy you, Kate, you're so lucky.' She rocked the pram and the child, startled by shafting sunlight, blinked. Trixie gathered her up and there began that intimate exchange of two beings exclusively delighted in each other, and comprised of bouncings, ticklings, chucklings which left Kate excluded in guilt. She coud not understand Trixie's indiscriminate mothering. The sight of little babies not her own produced in her particular relief that someone else must endure the crying bouts, clean the messes, hang every night drowsing over a drowsy infant unwilling to yield up its wind. For Kate was reacting like many women who, having satisfied the pressing maternal urge, can afford to wallow in the drawbacks of the state.

Trixie spoke. 'I don't know why, Kate. The doctor said there's no reason why not. We try and try, and nothing happens.'

'Perhaps you try too hard.' For, thought Kate, she and Rex had hardly tried at all.

Trixie's eyes above the baby's furry crown of hair met hers, a conflict of reticence and sadness reflected there. She looked, thought Kate, not like Trixie Lovatt, friend wife mother neighbour, at all. Because she was not at ease with this other person she changed the subject.

'Merry's coming to play.'

A small silence descended. For while everybody agreed that Meredith Evans was different and deserved a separate consideration from other children, everybody hoped that Meredith Evans would choose some other yard to play in. Games ended in tears and tales when Merry came to play. Scratches and bites had to be comforted with plasters and sympathy. Children were sent back to their games with the advice that, next time, they should choose somebody nice to share their play. And Merry would wander on, lonely; calling for acceptance with pathetic obscenities that made mothers shake their heads, some in pity, others in disgust.

'Run along, Merry dear,' called Trixie.

The child stood watching. Mary and Andrew went on placing the pegs.

'Off you go now.' And Trixie, baby on her hip, walked a few paces as if to reinforce her dismissal.

The child, not speaking, dawdled on; the two friends witnesses as she squatted to lower her shorts and defaecate in the gutter. Kate, heir to a puritanical properness, looked away. Trixie's face was a confusion of pinkness. Unkindness was foreign enough in her nature to make her guilty when she transgressed.

'She always causes trouble. And she's not a good influence. She won't do as she's told. And really, Kate,' (honesty welling, almost in spite) 'I can't be bothered with her. I know I'm awful.'

'You'd never think, to see her, that she's old enough for school next year.'

'I was talking to her mother in the shop last week; she mentioned a child specialist.'

'My child would have seen one years ago.'

'And mine.'

Blame averted in this way to a woman neither girl knew well, the friends turned back to their own perfect offspring who fought over a tricycle while a second stood unused nearby. Trixie's arbitration was a model of tact. Her motherliness, thought Kate, was ample for half a dozen children. The knowledge could reassure Kate who, arrived less by choice than chance at her present state in life and without experience or maturity to moderate her moods, needed the certainty of people such as Trixie. Her contentment soothed, dependent as it was on no personal aim but rather on the relationships founded upon herself. She should have children, Kate agreed. She was even a prototype of the mother Kate might have chosen to have . . . forgetting that when Trixie's limitations bored she could go home. For Kate's bond with her own mother was less a fondness than an irritation; a battle equivalent to the one Mrs Hope had waged against life.

'It's Thursday,' Kate remembered, 'I ought to go.'

'Oh yes,' said Trixie. 'Your mother.'

YVONNE DU FRESNE

The River

The summer must soon end — but no — people looked out every morning on a whole new summer day, as it used to be, in the days when they had had louise cake and kiss cakes and a sponge and plain biscuits full of uncooked nuts and raisins for our health's sake. No, Eleanor thought, even that memory was starting to be bad, soured. Her summer, now, was like all the summers of the war; dresses with no fullness and lockets and signet rings worn by all the country girls like her, rosy from hot baths taken on blazing afternoons and Old Lavender talcum powder. They had worn their best dresses made from curtain net, hailstoned in red and blue, and Deanna Durbin straw hats, and ridden their spidery, carefully preserved bikes through the dangerous gravel to the Scout hall, to the Bible Class party held in the afternoon. The lovely summer was not to be enjoyed but mixed with Japs, mud and death, and air raid practice in the pony paddock. Now, said Eleanor, if there would just be an alert, danger, to make everyone see through the blandishment of this one summer and steel themselves, as she had had to. She stared at her father's cabbages in the dry crumbling clods of dirt, at the plums in the fowlyard tree, showing their sudden size behind the worn-out lacy leaves.

When, when had there been a safe time? She probed carefully in her mind and longed to rest in a green shade, somewhere, long ago. Then she saw the very old summers — the 1930 summers — the summers of the celluloid years, the grainy newspapers and pictures of men in soft hats who all looked like gangsters, the Mickey Mouse she had had with mad rolling eyes and legs like a fuzzy black spider. She felt the smooth varnish of the Japanese sunshade, thundering on its fragile whirling spikes across the concrete in the great spring gales. Caught, its red poppies suddenly glowed in silent heat on the oiled paper as she looked up through it at the sun.

When she met Pete, at last, she told him everything that had been here when he was away, at the war. He had sat and listened, his eyes flickering from time to time from the impact of the best words she had chosen, reciting those past years, putting in his hands the exact stripes on a tulip, the exact way an orange comb on a window-sill lit up a dark bathroom, when she was three and beginning to see these things.

The lawn and the water and the dried-out January creek had all been there, summer after summer — only waiting to be described, brought out like a lump of crystal for Pete's fingers to close around. Warm and contained, he had listened as she gave him the exact splinter of pond ice to burn his hand, the call of farewell in winter paddocks.

'Yes,' he would say, 'that's it.'

She had climbed to the top of the hill one afternoon, at the back of the farm, when she was twelve, and turned around three times and faced the point on the horizon where her future husband was, at that moment. It was to the north, she remembered.

'What were you doing in 1941?' she demanded.

'Feeling scared,' he said. 'Mucking around Alex later on. No — no — I saw some things — I saw what the guide called the Styx that year — the muddiest ditch and six feet deep . . .'

'Did you hear me in 1941, from that hill?' she persisted.

'Yes,' he said, suddenly sober. 'Yes — I think I did.'

Standing by a river, she thought, after taking to the boats from that other savage island, creeping around the Aegean with his heart in his mouth. And then, coming home, down to her from the ancient world, from the eye of the sun, bringing with him a presence of leaping dolphins, and the bitter smell of the furze that grew on the islands where he had sheltered.

What had she been doing that year? She saw again the few, scattered farmhouses not far from the coast, the endless burning summers, the unpainted wooden hall for the district, that stood at the crossroads where there was nothing else but the roads parting and winding off into the lupin and sand-starved paddocks.

She suddenly noticed her mother coming down the path, looking absorbed in every leaf and flower by the path, showing her shyness in the face of Eleanor's grief. She came up and stooped over a dead flower head to pull it off.

'I wouldn't worry, dear — not at all,' she said. 'They know best — just a break for you — they can always ring . . .' Her voice trailed off — suddenly aware of what the ring would mean.

'If I could just *feel* calm — it's surely all right — after all this time, he's held his own.'

'The Intensive Care people know what they're doing at *that* hospital,' said her mother loudly. 'Why — even five years ago — a heart attack . . .'

'Yes, yes,' repeated Eleanor. Dead in an hour, while I watched him, she heard herself saying, if it had happened five years ago.

'Now, Mrs Crawford,' they had said. 'He's to be here a little longer — perhaps you could have one or two days away — it's been such a strain for you.' Yes, she had said, I will. To my mother's. And had felt the link snap — the thread to the sun they both held in their hands.

'Now,' said her mother, firmly plucking off the withered stalk, 'we thought, Father and I — a little picnic by the river. Mrs Latimer might come, a little brightness for us.'

Yes, she said, feeling the old summers again, the slightly warm water in the taps, in the creek, and, brown and heady, in the river when she swam, kicking great clouds of mud from the chunks of bank that had fallen in.

So they went. She sat in the back of the car, driven carefully as if it was the 1930 Dodge, with celluloid curtains flapping in the wind, winding under a dust cloud over the endless shimmering gravel roads that wound through the lupined hills to the river mouth. The cake-tins and the teapot safely in the boot, they moved into the farmland that announced sand country — long hills shaped like burial mounds, holding the bones of the old people, in their thin old print dresses and limp shirts, underneath the gold wires of summer grass. She felt the dangerous black sand glinting again in its Oklahoma patches, killing the trusting dairy paddock that had started to grow.

Mrs Latimer leaned delicately towards her. 'You'll remember all this part, dear,' she said to Eleanor.

Eleanor smiled, scarcely turning her head.

'You used to come down here — didn't you — Sheila and all of you — on your bicycles?' she breathed.

Eleanor looked at her, and smiled gently back, as if they were both too fragile in Fate's hand to do anything energetically. They passed the same roads running away to nowhere, the same houses with silvered wood, flashing like polished bones in the sun. Then the valley broadened out like a hand upturned in resignation. There was the river, the distant lightening of the sky that said, the sea is here. They bumped and wound over the sparse road, by the gorse bushes, over the flat bitten turf, making the few fat sheep run, and stand panting.

They turned neatly in at one of the sheltered places on the bank, warm, away from the wind. Eleanor closed her eyes in case the bank gave way, sucked away under the car's wheels by last year's floods, but they stayed upright. She opened her eyes — they had stopped — and she started to feel the slow rhythm of the river riding quietly by them, licking the bank in quick curving rushes, and swirling into midstream again, hurrying on to the river mouth. Mica glittered on the sandbanks, wet and exposed by the swiftly dropping tide; the last soft cicadas of late summer chirped like their own ghosts.

'Now,' said Mother, brisk with the manner of the old picnics, the screaming children sliding down the one sandhill on the river bank.

'It was better on *this* side of the gorse,' said Mrs Latimer.

'Yes, oh, yes,' agreed Mother. 'Father — you . . .' But it was clearly useless. There he sat in the front seat, like stone, hat on, gazing through the windscreen at the river. Never mind, they said in lowered voices to each other, scrambling out and around to the boot of the car.

'Eleanor,' said Mother, ever so gently, 'would you like to sit on the bank, dear? Or take the tins from Mrs Latimer?' ('Take her mind off it,' she murmured.) Eleanor, turned into the schoolgirl at home for the holidays, turned and went to the boot.

'Perhaps something to do — would do you good,' said Mother, trailing off. Mrs Latimer looked at the ground.

'Don't worry, Mum,' she said, getting out the round and the square cake-tins.

'It's good to have something to do,' said Mrs Latimer in a warm rush, 'takes your mind . . .'

'Yes,' said Eleanor firmly, feeling the safe schoolgirl world gone. She gazed at the round cake-tin, the slightly faded Queen smiling on its lid. She saw it on the draining board in her mother's house, half full of louise cake, since 1953. And before, she thought, holding the tin for a moment, ah, yes, before then — down a tunnel back to the thirties. The picnics had been at the creek, not far from here. The others had bounced in on a Ford truck, lurching straight down, through the green streaming willow trees. Once there, the children shouted, scrambled down, and then became silent and absorbed in limping over the stones, shoulders hunched, threadbare towels draped over them. The water was secret, black, weed on slippery stone before the first of the stones they threw gulped in. They could swim two strokes one way, three strokes the other. The women sat, big and soft under wide straw hats, on travelling rugs, and opened the cake-tins with the faint lacy pictures on the lids of a green and yellow King George and Queen Elizabeth. Louise cakes, rich fruit-cakes she remembered, and little flour-bag pants on her friends, Mavis and Pat, two little girls with long bobby pins in their thin hair.

Putting the tins in place on the rug, Eleanor strayed to the edge of the bank by the front of the car where Father sat, and gazed at two motorboats that roared around the bend of the river, and arched in, to sink and sputter into silence in the frothing water rocking the reeds.

'No cocky could afford those in the old days,' said Father, in the silence.

'No,' she said.

'Now, they could,' said Father. The wave from the boats slapped secretly, persistently on the mud bank, just under the fringed rug and the cups and the saucers.

'Mind out!' cried Mrs Latimer, leaning back, laughing.

'One of them's Charlie Wood's son,' said Mother.

'It never is,' said Mrs Latimer, sitting up on her heels and looking. 'They could never keep anything in the old days — not even a car.'

The speedboats roared away up the river, turned, started to race each other again, turned aimlessly and sank back flat on the surface, their motors complaining. There was really nowhere to go.

'Now, Rose!' called Mrs Latimer to Mother. 'Let's see how it comes, dear!' And Mother, arching her plump powdered arm in its good blue sleeve, poured out a perfect amber arch from the teapot, neatly tucked into its sitting-room cosy. The wind blew the tea cold in their shallow flowered cups.

'We used to play French cricket there,' murmured Mrs Latimer, pointing to a swirl of water around drowned hummocks of land. 'It's gone now.'

'Oh, it was a busy place, once,' said Mother.

But now only the two motorboats, trapped in their reedy basin, cut the afternoon silence with their idling motors.

Eleanor took her cup and her cake and walked over to the edge of the brown water. River, she said, there you are — flat to the horizon — ditches, pools of flood water in the winter, lit by wild sunsets. Here, soon, you reach the sea, hear it breathing in and out, like a woman slowly knitting and thinking, in the late afternoon sun. I know you, she said, but I have no strength, no strength; I cannot save him, I can only go home to my mother for a little rest. But the shape of the stones in the river mud, the toughness of the pine roots binding the bank further up, the ivy on the dark tree trunks by the fence, crept into her mind.

Now it was flat calm. The river had fallen away with the salt tide from the sea hidden at its mouth. Sand glittered, the edges of the round river stones sharpened in the harsh light — a faint bird's call beat like a pulse of water dripping on to stone. Patiently, slowly, she felt her whole lifetime of these plains and the river in her body; her hair blew in the wind like summer grass, her eyes were the flat blue of the sky over the river.

Pete, it is I who come down into the dark to find you, she said, with a sop for Cerebus in my hand — Eurydice leading Orpheus back to the light, to the sun that he had given her. I do not say with the grieving Greek women long ago, 'Weep, for the young horse is gone from the meadow, the bay leaf gone with him into the dark.' I say, here is a piece of tough river rush to hold in your hand, here are the mud and the stones whose reality is as strong as your body, that will make you live. Soon the tide will turn, the light fall more gently on the water, the thread to the sun in our hands once more.

Motherhood

MARY FINDLAY

Desperate remedies

On Sunday morning Stan and Bill rode over to mow the grass on the tennis court. They took a cut lunch and two bottles of beer. With the men out of it, May and I set to work to fill the tins with cookies against the arrival of the mill on Tuesday. The thermometer was already ninety in the shade and the kitchen was as hot as a furnace. Suddenly May drew a chair up to the table, sat down and covered her face with her hands.

'What's the matter, May dear? Are you all right?'

She took her hands away and I saw that her eyes were screwed up and her forehead wrinkled.

'No, I'm not all right. I'm going to need your help. I'm sorry you won't be able to go to tennis or the Browns' for tea.'

'What's up? You look awful.'

'Sit down, Mary, and I'll tell you.' She spoke slowly and with deliberation. 'I think, and I hope, I'm going to have a miscarriage.'

'You're pregnant?'

'Three and a half months.' She clasped her belly as another spasm of pain showed on her face.

'Shall I ring the doctor?'

'No, don't do that for goodness sake! He'll try to stop things. When it's over you can tell him.'

'What about Stan? Do you want me to get him?'

'No, not unless things go wrong. I'd sooner he was out of it if you can help me.'

I was thoroughly frightened but tried to sound reassuring.

'I don't know anything, but I'll do what you tell me to.'

'There's nothing to worry about, nature does the job. I've had other miscarriages. It takes a few hours and it's a bloody business, but it should all be over before milking.'

She got up, then leaned over the table, beads of sweat forming on her contracted brow.

'I'm sorry to let you in for this, Mary. You see, Stan and I slipped up. I'm forty-six. We don't want another child, it's too late in life and we couldn't keep this job if I had a baby, so I had to do something about it and this is what happens.'

How calm and matter-of-fact she was about it. I wished I could feel the same. Fear of the unknown was gripping me, and I was horribly aware of my inexperience and incompetence. How would I know if things went wrong?

'Tell me what to expect and what to do.'

'I'll be in pain for a few hours. The pains will get worse as time goes on. When they get bad I may cry out — it'll mean I'm near the end of labour. I'll bleed and a tiny mannikin will come out. Then you'll press my tummy to get rid of the afterbirth. Do you think you'll be able to manage?'

I felt sick at the thought. It must have shown on my face. May put her hand on mine.

'Will you try? You can call the doctor as soon as it's over.'

'Yes, of course, May. I'll do my best.' But if things go wrong? How would I know? May was holding the door as another pain gripped her.

'Keep the kettle boiling,' she said. 'Then get some old sheets and lots of newspaper and bring them into my room.'

May was calmly stripping her bed when I returned with the newspaper and rags. I had butterflies in my stomach and my brain was full of questions. Why didn't she want the doctor? Why didn't she want Stan? Shouldn't I at least get a neighbour? Would I be able to manage later when the pain got worse? Supposing — supposing things did go wrong? Would May know? Would I know?

'We'll just get the bed fixed, Mary, then I'll explain a bit better. Go out to the barn and see if there's a piece of canvas there and bring it here and we'll need more newspaper, there's some in the washhouse by the copper. You poor kid, don't worry, I'll be all right.'

Glad of the activity I quickly located the canvas and the paper and brought them into the bedroom. May was sitting in a chair, bent over. She straightened and stood up. The spasm was over.

'Put the canvas over the mattress, then spread all the newspapers over it. After that, two old sheets, then fold another into a square and put it in the middle of the bed. Oh, and we'll need a good-sized enamel basin and some Jeyes Fluid.'

Between us we made up the bed. May was putting on her nightdress while I went for the basin and disinfectant. By the time I came back, she was lying in bed and smiling. Astonishing woman!

'A good hot cup of tea is what we need now, Mary.'

'I've been trying to think of first things first,' she said, as I handed her the tea. 'You must remind Stan to kill a sheep tonight or there'll be no meat for the mill. This is what's really worrying me, you'll have to manage as best you can when the men come. The doctor will make me stay in bed for a week, I know. Breakfast will be at five o'clock in the morning, milking is done by lamplight earlier, and the evening meal won't be till after dark. Tomorrow I'll ring up and see if one of the McNulty girls can come and give you a hand, but we can't rely on it. Eight men come with the mill and Stan has four others lined up, so it means cooking for sixteen and they eat like cannibals. Hang on a minute, till this one goes.' She arched her body and covered her face. 'That was a strong one — maybe it won't be long now.'

I marvelled at her strength of mind. To be planning for Tuesday's meals while in the middle of a miscarriage! And worrying about me! Tentatively I laid my hand on her shoulder.

'I'll manage the cooking all right, if I have to stay up all night to do it. Forget Tuesday and think of yourself. Are you sure you don't want me to get Stan?'

'How could you get him except on foot? You can't ride and you can't drive and it's six miles. I need you here. Stan knows nothing about this, I haven't even told him I'm pregnant. You see, he's a Catholic and would disapprove. No, he doesn't go to church but I want you to keep this secret. He'll think it's accidental, like the others were. You won't tell him, will you Mary?'

'Of course I won't. But he doesn't even know you're pregnant?'

'I didn't tell him for two reasons. The main one is that things aren't going too well on the farm and unless the figures at the end of March are better, some of us'll have to go. It may be Stan and me or it may be Judith and Johnnie, it could even be you. Stan was worried enough without this happening. *Ouch!*' She waited for the pain to pass, then went on, 'I didn't think it would go so far. I tried all the usual things, Epsom salts, hot baths, jumping off chairs, quinine and ergot. Nothing worked. Then I got desperate and used a knitting needle. Desperate situations sometimes need desperate remedies. I hated doing it because I love babies, but Stan's nearly sixty and he'll find it hard to get another job like this. We may have to go anyhow, but if I had a young baby we'd certainly have to leave. The conditions of our job here are for a married couple with no children.'

It was all a bit beyond me. Then I had an idea.

'What about Judith? Couldn't I get her? It's not far.'

'Judith's gone to Dunedin and Johnnie's in the back country. You'd better see to the fire.'

I went back to the kitchen. I must control my distress. Poor, poor May. How on earth must she feel, in pain and with only an ignorant girl to help her? I went back to the bedroom.

'How is it?'

She was red in the face, her hair damp and rumpled. 'Soon, I think. Tear up that other sheet and make big sanitary pads out of it.'

Silently, keeping my eyes on the bed, I did as she asked. The pains seemed to be continuous now. I glanced at the clock, half-past three. Milking was at five. May groaned.

'Hold my hand, Mary. No, could you rub my back? That's it, the small of the back. *O-o-o-h*,' she gasped. She turned on her side, her face away from me.

'It's coming.'
She pushed back the bedclothes and grunted.
There was a lot of blood.
'The basin, Mary.'
It was as she had said, a bloody business. There was the blood and there was a tiny figure, the size of a kewpie doll. Without warning, I quickly vomited, covering it. May lay still, gasping. I held the basin. I was weak at the knees. She turned towards me.
'Is it there?'
'Yes.'
'Thank God. Get rid of it down the dunny.'
It was cooler outside. I felt better. I emptied the basin and returned. May was on her back. She looked awful, but was smiling. 'Put the basin between my legs. Then press my tummy hard.'
I tried.
'No, *really* hard. To expel the afterbirth.' She yelled with pain. More blood came out. 'Keep going.' She set her teeth.
The afterbirth came away.
'Give me a pad and empty the basin.'
Like a robot, I obeyed.
May smiled. 'Pull up the bedclothes, Mary and thanks. You were wonderful.' She put out her hand and pulled me to her. Without words we embraced. We looked at each other, bound by an experience we both could have done without. She put her finger to her lips. 'You'll keep my secret?'
I nodded.
'Now you'd better ring the doctor.'

The mill arrived on Monday night. May was sitting up in bed, perky as you like. The doctor had come the previous night and done whatever it was he had to do. He patted my shoulder and said, 'Good girl. You'll be a fine woman one day. Not many could keep their heads in an ordeal like that.'
'It was Mrs Cameron, she told me what to do.'
'And you did it. Have you ever thought of nursing as a career?'
'Yes, but I'm not old enough.'
'When you are, think again. I'll write you a reference.'
Stan was less articulate. Poor man, tears were in his eyes as he put his arms around me. 'Thanks, Mary. Christ! Thanks for everything.'
But the country calendar waits for nothing. Here it was, Monday night and the kitchen full of men. The big black kettle boiled, the big enamel teapot held tea for sixteen. The talk was of the weather prospects and the job to be started in the morning. For the second time, but for a different purpose, I carried newspapers into May's room.

'Just spread them out and give me the spuds,' she directed. A kerosene tin of spuds had to be peeled each day. Sitting up in bed, she made a start on them.

'Has Stan butchered the sheep?' she enquired.

'Well, he's cut it in half.'

'Into sides?'

'I suppose that's it.'

'Bring it in here and I'll show you what to do. Bring the chopper as well.'

Under May's instructions I spread the paper on the floor and, with chopper and knife, separated forequarter, loin and leg.

'Now, chop the chops.'

I giggled and not very skilfully chopped the chops. It seemed an awful lot of meat.

'You've got two days' supply there. Cook a forequarter and a leg each night. The chops'll do for breakfasts. You may or may not have some cold meat for lunches, but you'd better order ten pounds of corned beef and ten pounds of sausages from the butcher. Stan'll have to kill again tomorrow. Did Bill pick the peas?'

'I don't think so.'

'Well ask him. If he hasn't, he'd better do it now while it's still light. I'll shell them later. You hop out and pick peaches — enough to fill the two big pots. Cook them tonight and make some custard to go with them. You'll have to keep ahead. Too bad Jean sprained her ankle, but we'll manage. Jessie Brown and Maggie Holmes are baking for us, so you won't have that to worry about. Now go and see to the peas and peaches while I finish these spuds.'

For eight days, in the sweltering heat, I cooked and washed dishes. There was no let-up. No sooner was one meal consumed and the dishes washed then it was time to start the next one. I enjoyed it. It was a challenge. The men joked and laughed and teased me. They did full justice to my cooking and I had a sense of satisfaction. Tired as I was, it was no trouble to get up in the morning — it was cool then and I would partly cook the joints while getting the breakfast. This saved stoking up in the midday heat.

May was marvellous. In addition to the nightly preparation of vegetables she mixed puddings and rolled pastry from her bed. Towards the end of the time she joined us for dinner and the men cheered. The outside work went well, the sun shone and no rain threatened. Stan was pleased. The successful harvest meant no winter worries and would strengthen his position at the end of the financial year, when he would have to justify his stewardship.

On the last day the men finished early. We ate at six instead of eight-thirty. I was putting away the last dish when I heard the skirl of bagpipes, *A hundred pipers and all and all*. At this signal the men emerged from their quarters, each carrying a bottle. They formed a procession towards the kitchen, where the corks popped. Later, wives and girl friends arrived and we had an impromptu dance. I didn't drink any beer, not caring for its taste, but someone offered me apple cider and in my innocence I thought it was some kind of soft drink. I had only the one glass, but it was a big one. The next thing I remember was Stan and May standing by my bed with a cup of tea and saying, 'Wake up, Mary, it's morning.'

It was ten o'clock.

PATRICIA GRACE

Between Earth and Sky

I walked out of the house this morning and stretched my arms out wide. Look, I said to myself. Because I was alone except for you. I don't think you heard me.
    Look at the sky, I said.
    Look at the green earth.
    How could it be that I felt so good? So free? So full of the sort of day it was? How?
    And at that moment, when I stepped from my house, there was no sound. No sound at all. No bird call, or tractor grind. No fire crackle or twig snap. As though the moment had been held quiet, for me only, as I stepped out into the morning. Why the good feeling, with a lightness in me causing my arms to stretch out and out? How blue, how green, I said into the quiet of the moment. But why, with the sharp nick of bone deep in my back and the band of flesh tightening across my belly?
    All alone. Julie and Tamati behind me in the house, asleep, and the others over at the swamp catching eels. Riki two paddocks away cutting up a tree he'd felled last autumn.
    I started over the paddocks towards him then, slowly, on these heavy knotted legs. Hugely across the paddocks I went almost singing. Not singing because of needing every breath, but with the feeling of singing. Why, with the deep twist and pull far down in my back and cramping between the legs? Why the feeling of singing?
    How strong and well he looked. How alive and strong, stooping over the trunk steadying the saw. I'd hated him for days, and now suddenly I loved him again but didn't know why. The saw cracked through the tree setting little splinters of warm wood hopping. Balls of mauve smoke lifted into the air. When he looked up I put my hands to my back and saw him understand me over the skirl of the saw. He switched off, the sound fluttered away.
    I'll get them, he said.
    We could see them from there, leaning into the swamp, feeling for eel holes. Three long whistles and they looked up and started towards us, wondering why, walking reluctantly.
    Mummy's going, he said.
    We nearly got one, Turei said. Ay, Jimmy, ay, Patsy, ay, Reuben?
    Yes, they said.

Where? said Danny.

I began to tell him again, but he skipped away after the others. It was good to watch them running and shouting through the grass. Yesterday their activity and noise had angered me, but today I was happy to see them leaping and shouting through the long grass with the swamp mud drying and caking on their legs and arms.

Let Dad get it out, Reuben turned, was calling. He can get the lambs out. Bang! Ay, Mum, ay?

Julie and Tamati had woken. They were coming to meet us, dragging a rug.

Not you again, they said taking my bag from his hand.

Not you two again, I said. Rawhiti and Jones.

Don't you have it at two o'clock.

We go off at two.

Your boyfriends can wait.

Our sleep can't.

I put my cheek to his and felt his arm about my shoulders.

Look after my wife, he was grinning at them.

Course, what else.

Go on. Get home and milk your cows, next time you see her she'll be in two pieces.

I kissed all the faces poking from the car windows then stood back on the step waving. Waving till they'd gone. Then turning felt the rush of water.

Quick, I said. The water.

Water my foot; that's piddle.

What you want to piddle in our neat corridor for? Sit down. Have a ride.

Helped into a wheelchair and away, careering over the brown lino.

Stop. I'll be good. Stop I'll tell Sister.

Sister's busy.

No wonder you two are getting smart. Stop . . .

That's it, missus, you'll be back in your bikini by summer. Dr McIndoe.

And we'll go water-skiing together. Me.

Right you are. Well, see you both in the morning.

The doors bump and swing.

Sister follows.

Finish off girls. Maitland'll be over soon.

All right, Sister.

Yes, Sister. Reverently.

The doors bump and swing.

You are at the end of the table, wet and grey. Blood stains your

pulsing head. Your arms flail in these new dimensions and your mouth is a circle that opens and closes as you scream for air. All head and shoulders and wide mouth screaming. They have clamped the few inches of cord which is all that is left of your old life now. They draw mucous and bathe your head.
    Leave it alone and give it here, I say.
    What for? Haven't you got enough kids already?
    Course. Doesn't mean you can boss that one around.
    We should let you clean your own kid up?
    Think she'd be pleased after that neat ride we gave her. Look at the little hoha. God he can scream.
    They wrap you in linen and put you here with me.
    Well anyway, here you are. He's all fixed, you're all done. We'll blow. And we'll get them to bring you a cuppa. Be good.
    The doors swing open.
    She's ready for a cuppa Freeman.
    The doors bump shut.

Now. You and I. I'll tell you. I went out this morning. Look, I said, but didn't know why. Why the good feeling. Why, with the nick and press of bone deep inside. But now I know. Now I'll tell you and I don't think you'll mind. It wasn't the thought of knowing you, and having you here close to me that gave me this glad feeling, that made me look upwards and all about as I stepped out this morning. The gladness was because at last I was to be free. Free from that great hump that was you, free from the aching limbs and swelling that was you. That was why this morning each stretching of flesh made me glad.

And freedom from the envy I'd felt, watching him these past days, stepping over the paddocks whole and strong. Unable to match his step. Envying his bright striding. But I could love him again this morning.

These were the reasons each gnarling of flesh made me glad as I came out into that cradled moment. Look at the sky, look at the earth, I said. See how blue, how green. But I gave no thought to you.

And now. You sleep. How quickly you have learned this quiet and rhythmic breathing. Soon they'll come and put a cup in my hand and take you away.

You sleep, and I too am tired, after our work. We worked hard you and I and now we'll sleep. Be close. We'll sleep a little while, ay, you and I.

ROBIN HYDE

I have this infant

In the bracken I lay face downwards, pressed against the earth, watching the dewy bramble-leaves, the jewel-red leaves. I couldn't write — wrote nothing all the time except the free-lancing thirty shillings' worth for the Wanganui paper, which kept me, and one poem to a dead man whom I had loved a number of years before — but I was not unhappy. That earth was too quiescent, its skin was like my own; brown skin against white skin, and the high-stalked bracken watching. I thought it would not be bad for my child. From the beginning I had made up my mind, since I was going to have this infant, to want it. In the dream, this was not very difficult. I planned for a daughter, Jennifer, though other absurdly fanciful names came into my head; names suitable for waterfalls and mountains and small towns, but certainly not for human beings. I thought once, if Jennifer were a boy, of calling him Tane, after the dead god of Maori forests; but a dead god seemed not the best of patrons, and besides, everybody would pronounce it Taine.

Lonnie had sent nearly all the money for nursing home and doctor, and a good deal it was. There was a green room with white lace curtains, and kindliness, and cleanliness. I was going to have those. Lonnie wrote, with fitful cheeriness or fitful grief, saying how he had lost or won at the races, and this fiver would be a bit of a hurdle. I let him take his hurdles. Afterwards, when I went back to my lucrative job, Lonnie could be my friend and on no account send me fivers, and for Jennifer, in a cottage, I could install an ancient nurse, perhaps with whiskers on her chin and china-blue eyes.

I let Annie Cresley collect my mail for me one night. That was hasty. Mrs Cresley was sullen for a day afterwards. Then she came upstairs to the room where the flames were, and asked me to leave. She said, her eyes blazing, 'You're a wicked woman, that's what you are. A wicked woman.' I cried, not to her, but to the doctor I had chosen. There were two, one who believed in anaesthetics, one who held by good old nature. The one who held by good old nature was out . . . He stroked his chin, 'Is that all?' and recommended another boarding-house, where, by the way, I played chess with an Archdeacon.

It was at Mrs Cresley's that I met (and liked) a tall thin grey-haired aunt of Katherine Mansfield's, one of the Anakiwa aunts. She was very friendly. I showed her some poems, without telling her they were mine, and she liked them. 'But they're too sad,' she said soberly. 'I think the girl who wrote them must have had her sweetheart killed in the war.' Crushing comment from the modernist critic's viewpoint: not only mournful, but also dated.

Funny little triplet-tragedies. First Mrs Cresley, though that was comedy except that it is always bad when two women are at loggerheads. The second was running into a woman who had known my family for ages; I had been to her wedding, when she married, in her thirties, a farmer somewhere in the Sounds region, but I had never even thought of her since. There was only one thing to do — lie, and lie again. I told her I had married an unemployed boy, and would lose my own job if anything were known; I swore her to secrecy, and, her grey eyes round with excitement and importance, she sped away by launch, whence she had come. So far as I know, she kept her promise. I might even have been honest with her. But, caught in the door, can you or dare you be honest with anyone? Only in the last resort, when honesty is Antony's sword and Cleopatra's asp.

Then a note from my paper in Wanganui. They were sorry, but . . . well, there was no lucrative job to go back to, no job of any kind at all. They made no allegations, but I guessed one of Trixie's girlfriends or boy-friends had gossiped a little. I wrote and asked them for a month's notice money. Got it. Wrote to Lonnie, who was politely frantic. 'My Dear Girl, I can't imagine anything more disastrous . . . But I know you'll keep your promise.'

The baby, making no bones about the matter, was keeping its promise to arrive in the world in about a fortnight's time. The boarding-house where I was staying was too full, other guests were coming . . . So I found a third and last place, with a Jersey Island woman, who was blessedly fat and rubicund, little silver-grizzly curls fringing her harvest moon of a face. All her other lodgers were either men or boys. I don't think the sight of a woman near her time, going in and out among them, distressed them in the least. They probably made broad jokes about me, and Mrs Jarne certainly did; also prescribed for indigestion, and then served up enormous, sumptuous meals of home-cooked things that would have sent Lucullus happy enough to bed. All her lodgers were treated as her boys, and when they wanted to bring their girls for a weekend from Blenheim, she found room somewhere . . . but no goings-on, mind you.

Nevertheless I was glad to be in hospital. White and green and clean. Curtains and quiet, babies like funny little milk-full pink puppies. You're being so wonderful, Mrs Challis. Then, rather to everybody's distress and astonishment, Mrs Challis was not being at all so wonderful; but the doctor coped with that.

Then there was this red-visaged little creature, with solemn blind slate-blue eyes, done up in white clothes, and streaks of sovereign-coloured hair all over its head. I was rather proud of that. Gwen's baby stayed bald for a month.

'Oh — he's rather a nice little baby, isn't he, Doctor?'

'He's a *very* nice little baby.' Professional reproach.

I couldn't feed the creature, but gave it its bottles, and rolled it up and down the bed like a doll. It took everything lying down. They said, 'That baby of yours doesn't cry half enough.' Personally I thought every baby cried twice too much. The baby and I had three visitors — one invisible, an old author who lived down in the Sounds and sent me a huge basket of flowers, the other the wife of a local chemist, who said decidedly, 'Well, I think he should be called John. I'm going to call him John.' (My most respectable man friend was called John, and wouldn't have liked it at all.) The third was the — does one say vicereine, when it's a Dominion, not an Empire like India? Governor-General's wife sounds ridiculous, Governor-Generaless worse. She was on a tour of inspection. 'Oh,' she said, smiling uncertainly into the room, whose white natty curtains were blowing back and forth, 'is this your baby? *Nice* little baby . . .' Not being in a position to curtsey, I smiled, and we parted. Her hair was almost the same red-gold as Derek's, but not so fresh from the mint.

Lonnie telegraphed that he was glad I was alive and well. But in his next letter he regretted he had lost heavily at the races 'something which would have seen us through all our troubles'. For that matter, it might easily have been true. He had a patient, elf-faced, wistful trust in horses, and, as they did for myself, the damned things invariably went dog on him. Lonnie had only to back a horse, and it threw its jockey, or was doped, or developed spavins.

'Job,' I thought, in a hard little rhythm, 'job, job, job.' I was well, though shaky. The babies slept in their cots, with parasols to shade their august small cheeks from reddening like apples in the sunshine. Derek was a good sleeper, a decently-behaved and unprotesting child, though they insisted he should have cried more.

I went to Blenheim to register his birth. Somehow I couldn't bear, in the last instance, to say to the doctor and nurses, 'I have a past. I have a present. I have this infant, and this infant, by the look of things, has me.' Going to Blenheim was only putting off the evil hour — slinking out — because, in any case, the hospital would receive communication. And in the second place, I don't suppose for a moment that they would have cared how immoral I was. I paid cash, Lonnie's cash.

At the last moment, in Blenheim, I had a spasm of vertigo. There seemed to be something unspeakable in registering a child as illegitimate. I went to a lawyer's office, and there made another mistake, for he happened to be an old man with a beard, who had seen me in Wellington scores of times, though he hadn't met me. As soon as I asked him whether I would be sent to prison for registering Derek as legitimate, he became nauseating, in the hand-patting, we've-heard-it-all-before manner of speaking. I went downstairs to the Registrar's Office, which was in the same building, crying as if my tear-ducts would break if not my heart, and registered Derek. I gave him the Forest of Arden's name for a second title, and my alias for a third — not that any one of them was precisely a way out of the wood.

What I was going to do with him next I hadn't the faintest idea, except that we must immediately leave for a city, and there I must immediately find a job. The first stop was Wellington. Certainly I couldn't take Derek to my home and family. I had written informing them that I hadn't a job any more, and already they were furious. Derek would be a different thing, an act of violent cruelty, not on their part but on mine. They were not caught in the jamb of the door, they were on the other side: all their associations, love, friendship, building-up of sound life from life of poverty, were on that other side. To disturb them with a baby would have been a crime: and besides, I'd been enough of a trouble to them already.

Derek was to be smuggled. I had bought him, for a cradle, a dress-basket, wherein he lay quite complacently, sleeping most of the time. He was a baby with character. He had an elf face, at first faintly like his father's, and that red-gold hair, and large unwinking eyes. Inopportunely he had developed a rash. The Sister told me it was only red gum, and that nearly all babies take it, but it did not improve his appearance. Where he was not slate-blue eyes and red-gold hair, he was large pink spots. The smuggling was arranged in Wellington by a doctor whom I had told about his coming with joy and pride (pompous words); a doctor who had known me as a sick and nerve-torn child, years ago, and who was quite pleased, though vaguely harassed, that I should take to myself some sort of happiness, unorthodox or not.

'You'll look back,' said the little dark Sister, 'and think of these hospital days as the happiest of your life.' For a long time she was not so far out. But I mustn't think of that. I mustn't think of that.

Dress-basket, Derek and I went aboard the *Tamahine* in fair weather, and the sunshine was steeping the no-less-gold of the laburnums, which had touched my hands every day I walked down from the hospital beneath their dripping fringes, trying to find my feet again. This, to the day, was three weeks after Derek was born.

On the ship, our adventure was very nearly sunk with all hands. We had taken a cabin below decks. Strolling on the deck I saw the creamy-haired, black-sticked figure of a Wellington artist, old 'Dolla' Richmond, who knew me moderately well, though my family not at all. Still, to have explained to her that she mustn't mention to anyone I was travelling with a new baby and a dress-basket seemed to me, at the time, an undertaking of which I was quite incapable. I fled down to Derek, and looked at him in his basket. He was wide awake. I had a bottle handy, ready to shove into his mouth and say, 'Here, take this.' He gave me a rather dirty look; I suppose he blamed me for the pink blotches all over his face and neck, and the way the *Tamahine* rolled.

'Don't cry,' I implored him, 'please don't cry.'

It was not a mother's imagination. The steady slate-blue look was replaced by one of elfish understanding. Derek, all the voyage, lay staring at the cabin ceiling like a Buddhist at his navel. He sucked steadily at his bottle when I administered it, hiccuped, but did not cry. Again I thought of the madness of those nurses who had wanted him to cry more. They couldn't have understood the situation. He never let a peep out of him.

I imagined buying for the Sister, who was dark, a long necklace of lapis lazuli. For Nurse Burch, amber, not the reddish but the thick yellow sort: she was very fair. For the two other young ones, carnelian, and if I could get it that crushed turquoise which is made in flat beads, neither green nor blue. The nursing home where, owing to Dr Sidney's intervention, they were able to take Derek as a boarder at two guineas a week, was a good place but not to be counted on for long, because mostly it took straight-out maternity cases. Of Lonnie's money and mine I had about £20 left. There should have been more — the hospital gave me a discount for cash, which I hadn't reckoned on — but I mentioned I was a bad spender, and it had gone on a mail-order trousseau for Derek, gone unaccountably, just leaked away. I suppose I should have felt apologetic towards him: but whenever his slate-blue eyes stared at me, they seemed perfectly wise and understanding.

PATTI BAKER
(As told to Joss Shawyer)

She hadn't died

They gave her to me to hold. That's right, I remember it. And I was so *embarrassed*. I just wished they'd take her away, because I didn't know what to say. I didn't know what to say to the baby. I knew what I would have liked to have said. But she wasn't my baby to say it to. All those people hanging around. I was embarrassed even looking at her. Well, I didn't know how to behave in that sort of circumstance. If she'd been my baby I would have known what to say. What I said to my two, my next two. I don't know that I said anything out loud to them, but I said a lot of things in my mind. Oh, I told them how much I loved them. And how beautiful they were and how glad I was that they were healthy and all the hopes that I had that they would be happy, and I would try hard for them. But I couldn't say any of those things. I didn't say anything. I just lay there, feeling embarrassed. Waiting for them to take her away. Not ashamed at all, but she just wasn't mine. She was a stranger. If someone lay me down and gave me somebody else's baby to hold, I'd feel the same way. Except that all these people were expecting me to react somehow. If it was somebody else's baby they wouldn't expect a reaction, but they expected one of me. It's strange, that although they treated me so impersonally, they didn't expect me to have any emotions when I was in labour. Once the baby was born, they expected me to trot out with all the old ones. I don't know why they gave her to me anyway. I remember that just after she was born the doctor said, 'It's a girl and I'm going to call her Joanna.' That just brought home to me that my baby had died and the baby that he delivered was their baby. And my mother wasn't allowed to be there — the Matron was there instead, because that was her prize.

When I first got pregnant, I thought Jim and I were going to be married. He loved children. He was so excited. He planned all the things we were going to do. We really wanted to be good parents and we were really going to enjoy having a baby. We thought of all the possibilities; taking it to the beach, playing games with it, teaching it football, and then suddenly, when I wasn't going to marry him any longer, the possibilities that I could offer the baby on my own seemed so limited. I wanted such big things for it, I'd promised it such big things, and all of a sudden I couldn't go through with it any more. I didn't know what financial assistance would be given to me if I kept the baby. People told me that one could be given some sort of a Benefit. But nobody told me how much. And they always led me to believe that it was impossible, virtually impossible, to raise a baby simply on that Benefit, without any outside help. I assumed that I would have to go out to work. And I couldn't possibly go out to work and leave my new-born baby. And also, I would have to find somewhere to live, and then I wouldn't see my parents very often. Yes, I did need them. My confidence in myself was practically nil at that stage. Nobody ever said I could manage alone. As far as I recall, there were only two people, apart from my parents, with whom the topic ever came up, and that was with the Matron, who had always let it be known in no uncertain terms that a single girl was no fit mother for a child, and a Social Worker I met at an ante-natal trip to the hospital, who made me seem like a very sensible, mature, well-adjusted girl in realising that no mother could cope with a baby by herself. And my parents made it plain that it would be by myself, although they never actually discussed the subject with me. Strangely, people didn't want to talk about the alternatives. They made it clear what their stand was, but they wouldn't discuss the alternative with me. Now, it horrifies me when I know the Benefit that I could have received. When I know my parents well enough to realise that they wouldn't have let me go off on my own with the baby. And I'd been on my own for so long, anyway, that I couldn't have felt any more on my own than I did then. But I couldn't see that at the time.

I was so much more on my own when the baby was gone, when she was born, than I'd ever been before then. I was so sure in my own mind that she was only my baby till she was born, that for the next weeks and even months, I thought of her as she was when I was pregnant. I didn't think of her very much as she was away from me, in her new place. I thought of it sometimes, but generally I thought about my being pregnant with her, when she belonged to me. And then after about a year, I started to realise what had happened. That she was my baby and that I didn't have to give her up. And that she hadn't died! When she really needed me most, I just hadn't been strong enough to really think what was in her best interests. I guess it's all very easy to look back over the past and realise when you're fairly detached what you should — could have done. Well, I'm detached by reason of my responsibility now. But I'm very much involved by way of my feelings. I don't know whether I feel guilty or not. I just feel that I wasn't in possession of myself and that if I had been, if I'd been given support, I could very easily have reached another decision. No, it wasn't mine. There was never any decision involved.

I remember going to the Social Welfare Department on the North

Shore and filling out a form. I remember being asked my preferences of adoptive parents. They made it quite clear to me that it would be very difficult to adopt a part-Maori child, particularly if it was a boy. I thought, God! How damned fussy can people be? This is my very own baby, my beautiful, beautiful baby, and they're almost grading it as if it were meat. Giving it a red stripe or a green stripe or a blue stripe. It wasn't even born, it hadn't even formed its character or anything, and already it was fairly undesirable in certain ways. There were so many things that I couldn't understand, I couldn't rationalise. But I just accepted that I wasn't in a fit state, I wasn't mature enough, and that other people were better equipped to handle it. I just had a zero estimation of myself. And even if something did seem irrational or illogical to me, I realised that it was just my screwed up version of events and that no doubt things were different, there was bound to be some adult around who would tell me what was logical and rational. No belief in myself. I drove myself to the Social Welfare Department. I filled in papers. I think the woman filled them in for me. She asked questions and then wrote down things. I saw her twice. Once when I was applying for a Benefit from Jim for my expenses during pregnancy, and then once, I think, about the adoption. Over the adoption she asked whether I preferred Maori or Pakeha parents, which religion I preferred — any belief, that sort of thing. But making it quite plain that I should just be damn lucky if anyone wanted the baby. I can't remember that I put down any particular qualification. For all I know, she could have gone to parents who, even though there were two of them, weren't as capable or qualified to look after her as I was. Because she was an undesirable baby, being so-called half-caste. I suppose that she would have gone to anyone who showed any interest. Maybe to people who applied for Pakeha babies, but missed out, so had to take a half-caste instead.

You know we were talking before about how I felt embarrassed when she was born? I told the people at the hospital that I didn't wish to breast-feed her and they said that was a good idea. And I wasn't too sure if I wanted to see her or not. One day the hospital Social Worker came to my room when my mother was visiting, and asked if we'd like to see the baby. My mother, of course, was dying to see her because it was her first grandchild, among other things. So we were taken to another corridor and into a room and there was a baby lying in a bassinet. And it was my baby, although it was just as if someone had taken me round a nursery and said, 'Ah — oh, that's your baby.' Just pointing to any one because it didn't matter. I didn't know any more than that. And my mother immediately rushed over to it and picked it up in her arms and talked to her and told her who she looked like and she even smiled. And Mum went into raptures about her smiling. And Mum just talked to her so naturally and then she passed her to me and I didn't really want to hold her. And I felt so *embarrassed* all over again, as if I was holding the Social Worker's baby. Because people were expecting me to say things to her and do things and behave in a certain way, when all along they'd make it quite clear that it wasn't going to be my child any more, once it was born. I think they were prepared to accept that I would have to give my baby up, but they weren't prepared to hold the responsibility of denying me any emotional attachment to my own child. I really think that's what it was. They realised, when I couldn't respond to it, that they'd denied me that attachment, and they wanted me to show some signs of emotion, because it hurt them too much to see the contrast with that and a so-called real birth.

After the birth, people kept coming out with hearty things like, 'Oh, it's all for the best and now you've got your whole life ahead of you.' And they wouldn't look back on any of the bad parts, they were just looking into the future and justifying everything that had happened. Wasn't I glad that they'd decided that I couldn't have my baby? And wasn't I glad that I didn't have it at home? And wasn't I glad that none of my friends knew that I'd been pregnant? Showing me all the marvellous advantages of my accepting their way out. I realise now how bad they must have felt about it at varying times. They knew what was right in the circumstances, but what they knew was right didn't *feel* right. They grovelled for my reassurance. Now lots of people say they admire me. It's the same thing. I didn't associate signing the adoption papers with the baby that I had been carrying. That was my baby, and my baby was dead. In fact, I've thought about this family that she was going into. I think the father was a Maori. I'd been told that he was an electrician, that she was an ex-schoolteacher, that they had already adopted one part-Maori boy who was about three years old, and I thought how nice it was going to be for them and they'll be pleased that this is all cleared up and they can take her home and get on with life. I didn't really associate my baby with the baby that they were taking home. It was a different baby. When my baby was born, she belonged to everyone that had been telling me what to do all the time. She belonged to everybody else. And my baby was still inside me. So it didn't hurt to sign the papers . . .

Sometimes in the months after that my mother would say, 'She really did smile at me.' Or, 'She really is going to look quite like you.' And she'd talk about her as if she was her grandchild! I don't know how my mother felt about her. I really don't. In a way I think that she really loves her. She has her name written at the front of the family Bible and her birth date, along with all the other children. But she never told my youngest brother and I've never been able to tell him. I respected her wishes. She didn't want him to know. And so I couldn't tell him. Also, my middle brother's wife doesn't know. The Bible's locked away. I don't think it's written with all the other names. I think it's written on the second page in. I've seen it. I can't remember, but I know that it's done in such a way that no questions would be asked. One thing that really upset me last year when we were talking about the baby, which we quite often do now, was when my mother mentioned that if I had wished it, I could have brought the baby home. And do you know, she'd never ever given any intimation of that. In fact, she always intimated completely the opposite, although, as I've said, we never actually talked about it. It was just always understood that I could never bring the baby home. And now I feel that she's trying to justify herself. But I can't believe now that all those people could feel guilty. That's the hardest part at the moment in my acceptance of the whole thing, because most of my decisions had been made to please all these people because they were so well qualified to know what was right and what was wrong, and I can't accept now that they're feeling guilty, because it implies that they feel they *weren't* right, that maybe what *I* wanted was right. And each time I see them feeling guilty, it makes me feel yet again that I did the wrong thing.

AMIRIA MANUTAHI STIRLING
(As told to Anne Salmond)

Hoki kino mai ra ki ahau
(This is a bad home-coming)

George did very well at Ruakura, but he was always thinking about coming home and that's why he bought this motor-bike. He thought he wouldn't have to spend his money on bus-fares, he could just hop on his bike and come home. One time he wrote to me and asked me to come to Auckland for a holiday, because he was planning to spend a weekend there and he wanted to see me. I went to stay with my brother-in-law Herbert Wright at Remuera — he'd been married to Ani, my half sister, before she died; and George came up on his bike. I wanted to go home after that but George asked me to stay another week, he'd be back the next weekend.

When he got back to Ruakura he went one night that week to an indoor basketball match, and he took one of his mates behind him on the motorbike. It happened to be raining and misty that evening, it was wintertime. They came to a bridge near Hamilton and that's where it happened. They couldn't see very well with all the mist, and a truck was parked on the wrong side of the road just beyond the bridge with no lights on . . . They crashed into it, and George was killed.

Afterwards we sued the man who owned the truck for doing that to our son. He said in court that he'd just gone a little way from his own place when he realised he'd left his wallet at home, so he thought he might as well leave the truck there and rush home and get it. He left that truck on the wrong side of the road with no lights on, and that slight mistake of his caused our son's death. The boys crashed into it, and George was killed.

A policeman came to Herbert's place in Remuera soon afterwards and told him about the accident; then Herbert woke me up and told me that George was dead. From that day, everything changed with me . . .

We took the body home from Hamilton and the people from Ruatoria came with us. A man called George Grace who used to live with us on the farm made up a beautiful lament for our son:

   Nga iwi, karanga ra!   Call, the tribes!
   Mo taku mate, taukuri e   For my dead, alas,

Hinga mai nei i runga o	Fallen upon
Nga mania o Hamutana	The plains of Hamilton.
Toro atu aku ringa	I put out my hands
Hei piriti mai ki ahau	A bridge for you to come to me
Aue! Hori e,	Alas! George,
Moumou ra koe, i tenei ra	You are wasted, this day.
Hori e, e tama e	George, child
Hoki kino mai ra ki ahau	This is a bad home-coming
Ki te kore koe i Hamutana	If you hadn't gone to Hamilton
Ara kei Te Reinga	You would not now be dead
Toro atu aku ringa	I throw out my hands
Hei piriti mai ki ahau	A bridge for you to come to me
Aue! Hori e!	Alas! George
Moumou ra koe, i tenei ra	You are wasted, this day.

When we arrived at the marae all the women started wailing; it was the most heart-breaking sound I've heard in my life. There was a dog howling in the background and it was Pete, tied up at the back of the marae, jumping at his chain and crying his heart out. The body was put on the porch of the meeting-house, and all the people kept coming to tangi for George. In the end somebody let Pete loose and he came racing to the meeting-house and tried to jump on the coffin — I could hardly bear to see that dog. The people kept coming for days, and then George was buried. They shovelled dirt on to his coffin and I cried out,

'Oh son, the violets and freesias are blooming now — where are you . . . ?'

That night the dog broke loose from his chain. Someone heard him howling in the cemetery, and they found Pete digging at the graveside, trying to find George, so they took him home and tied him up again. Later on the family told me that on the night George was killed, Pete had suddenly started to howl at about midnight and he cried for the rest of the night, they couldn't make him stop. Early the next morning the news about the accident came to Otaimina.

That's how our son George lost his life.

After George died I just couldn't bear the place, everything was too much a memory of him to me. Even the dogs and the horses in the paddock and the fruit trees, they all made me feel sick. I started to get low in my mind and I didn't feel hungry and in the end I grew very weak. One day I collapsed in the house and it started to play up with me like that. They sent me to the doctor in Opotiki and he said that I had TB, I'd have to go to Waipukurau to get better.

Then I started to worry about the family; I knew I'd have to leave them for Eruera to look after and he already had the cows to milk and everything, and that made me feel worse.

One morning I was lying in the bed while the girls were doing the housework, and they must have all gone outside because it was very quiet. I fell off to sleep and I had a funny dream — I dreamt I was on a mountain. When I looked up it looked like Hikurangi with all the snow on top, but when I looked down it was black, as though it was floating in mid-air. I was about halfway down that mountain and I was slipping, you could see the marks where I'd been. I knew that if I wasn't careful I'd fall right off and that would be death, because it was black all around and the mountain was just standing there in the middle of a great big hole. I slipped a little way and I prayed to God in my heart that he'd give me strength to climb up again, but the grass was slippery and every time I put my foot on it I'd slide down again. I struggled to get back to the top of that mountain but I kept on slipping, and in the end I fell off. When I was falling I knew I was dead, so I called out, 'Dear Lord, help me to get back, I want to stay with my family!'

A rock broke my fall, it was protruding from the side of the mountain and I knew that was the Rock of Ages from the song, 'Rock of Ages, cleft for me . . .' I started to sing this in my heart, and there I was, hanging on to this rock. When I looked down — oh, it was jet-black down there. I knew that only Almighty God could save me now; if he wanted me to be saved, that rock would stay firm. I made one last struggle to climb up and the rock fell away. I thought, well I'm gone. I had a tangi to my family and I could feel myself going, I was lost and finished.

The next thing I heard the birds twittering, and that brought me back to myself. When I looked around I could see these birds singing in the air, and they seemed to be following me. I was flying too, I had big wings and I was flying in the air beneath the mountain. I looked up and saw the snow on the mountain, and I knew it was this world of ours; when I looked down I could see the sun shining onto dried grass, and that was the other world.

I still wanted to stay with my family so I tried to fly back, but the harder I flew the further the mountain went from me, and in the end I got tired of trying. I thought, well it's no use Amiria, you're for the other world now; you'd better fold your wings and start to walk. As soon as I folded my wings, I landed in a tree; I could see the other birds still flying around, and when I looked down I saw this beach — I'd never seen a beach like that before! The sand was like iron-sand and it was all mixed in with the water, so that when the waves dashed up there was more sand in them than water. I said to myself,

'E hika! Where am I now? I've never seen a beach like this before, even in Ruatoria, Tuparoa or the Bay of Plenty, I've never seen a beach like this.'

'Ko te kainga tuturu tenei . . .'

I heard this voice talking and I looked up.

'What was that?'
'This is the last home; the place where people truly love one another. This is the final resting-place.'
'The final resting-place?'
'Yes.'
'Oh . . . Do you know an old lady called Mereana Mokikiwa?'
'I know her well.'
'And what about my mother, Ani — how is she?'
'She's well, we are all well here.'
'Where is this place?'
'This is the Rerenga Wairua.'

I thought, I'm going to get out of here! I tried to fly but I could only go around in circles so I thought, it's no use, I'll have to go down there on the ground. When I put my wings together, huh! I was on the ground, walking. I could hear people talking but I couldn't see them, and just then a pakeha woman called out to some children and I felt one of them brush past my legs.

'Hurry up, dears — come along!'

I looked around but I still couldn't see them, so I followed the sound of their voices and the next thing I saw this tiny little gate. Every now and again the gate would slam — bang! and after a while — bang! I thought I might as well go through that gate but when I tried it was too small for me.

I kept on trying, and in the end I turned sideways and managed to slip through. I heard these people still in front of me, and then I saw the church. I thought oh! — this is the first thing you've got to do, you've got to go to church; I must be really there now. The people were going in so I started to climb up the steps, and just as I was about to put my head inside I heard the minister start up a hymn. When I heard his voice I knew it was Te Aperahama Tatai Koko, a minister who used to be in Tuparoa — he had such a beautiful singing voice. I wanted to go in and listen, but the next thing.

'Moo . . . oo . . . oo!!'

One of the working steers made a big noise and he woke me up. I looked out of the window and it was Reddy, he was leaning over the fence crying out to the cows in the milking-shed; he couldn't get to them because the gate was shut. I thought, oh Reddy, good on you, you've brought me back! If you hadn't called out, I might have been stuck in that other world forever.

After that dream of mine I got very low down, I couldn't eat and I couldn't sleep at night — cough, cough, cough, cough! I thought I'd have to go to the sanatorium in Waipukurau, but one day Eruera said,

'No, Mum, I want you to go to Auckland first.'
'Auckland?'
'Yes, you'd better see a specialist up there.'

I came to Auckland and stayed with my brother-in-law Herbert Wright. He said,

'Amy, I'm going to take you to see Dr Richard. He's the best doctor we've got here in Remuera — I'll take you there tomorrow.'

The next day Dr Richard examined me.

'What did the doctor tell you in Opotiki, Mrs Stirling?'

'He said I had TB, so I had to go to the TB hospital in Waipukurau.'

'Have you got any TB in your family?'

'No, nothing.'

'Well . . . I don't know. You'd better go to Auckland Hospital and have an X-ray.'

I went there and had an X-ray, and a few days later Dr Richard rang me. When I went back to his office he examined me again.

'You haven't got TB, Mrs Stirling — there's your X-ray, look at it! Your trouble is you've strained your heart, and that's why you're coughing. Every time you cough it relieves the heart a bit, but that's not the real trouble . . . Now tell me — what is it that's been worrying you?'

I had to tell him the whole story.

'All right, Mrs Stirling, you listen to me. From now on you have to try and forget what's happened. I'll give you some pills for three months, and in three months I can cure you, but you have to keep away from tangis, anything that depresses your mind. Keep that weight down and do the things that you enjoy, and I can make you better.'

He made me shake hands with him and promise.

I came away and I tried, but I just couldn't manage it. I kept worrying about my family at home, and how Dad was getting on, and how we could get Tama to College, and Kepa, and Kiwa and Lily . . . When I went back for another check Dr Richard said,

'No . . . no, you haven't kept your promise, Mrs Stirling.'

I decided that the only thing to do was to go home and ask my husband to lease Otaimina, so we could bring the family to Auckland; because if I went home and looked at hills and started thinking about George, it would all come back to me again.

When I asked Eruera to leave the farm, he agreed, but he said,

'What about our son? We'd better get his stone finished, then we can leave everything behind us.'

That's how we hurried the unveiling of George's stone, and it was at the unveiling that I had my last blackout. We started to get the meeting-house ready, and when I looked at the mattresses they were all dirty, so I went to get some ticking from Waihau. On the way home I stopped in at the marae and told the girls to get on with our work, while I went home to sew up the ticking. They didn't like the idea much because we had fifteen fowls to stuff, but I said,

'You don't have to worry about that. Just get the stuffing ready and when I get back, I'll fix it all up.'

I went back home and cut up the ticking, then I put the machine on and I must have collapsed. When I came to myself I was lying on the floor, and when I looked at the clock it was four in the afternoon — I'd started to sew at eleven. I couldn't stand up so I crawled out onto the verandah, and the cream-truck came along. Maani Waititi was driving, so I called out to him to send one of my kids from the marae to catch my horse, it was running around in the paddock with the saddle on and everything. He thought I was just sitting there and having a rest.

'Why don't you go and catch it yourself, Amiria?'

'Maani, please send . . .'

'Oh! Get on your feet!'

After a while he realised I wasn't well, so he went to the marae and sent the kids home to Otaimina. I managed to finish my sewing, then I got on my horse and went back to the marae. When I arrived they told me off.

'Oh — Good gracious! Fancy, you went home and had a sleep, I suppose.'

I told them I'd had a blackout but they didn't believe me, so I thought never mind about that. When I looked at the chickens, none of them were done although it was getting quite late. I said to them,

'You could have done these chickens yourselves — see. It's simple, you don't have to sew them up; you just put the stuffing in then fold the top through the point of the tail like this . . .'

They'd never seen that before; I suppose in the country they didn't know how to cut chickens that way, but I'd learned it all in Auckland. In the end we managed to get everything ready, and the unveiling turned out very well. All the people came from Ruakura, it was one of the biggest unveilings at Raukokore in those years. One of George's professors, Dr McMeekan, came out from England to unveil the stone, and afterwards we had a big evening at the marae.

It was two or three years later when Roy Gallagher arrived at Raukokore. He had come back from America with his wife, and the first thing he wanted to do was to come and see George. When his parents told him that George had passed on he couldn't believe it, so he found out where Raukokore was and came there in his car.

It just happened that we were staying at the old people's place, and I was in the kitchen looking out of the window when this couple came walking up the path — I'd never seen them before. The old lady was sitting on the verandah and they talked to her, then she called out to me,

'Amiria, te pakeha nei e pirangi ana ki te kite i a korua — this pakeha wants to see you . . .'

I stepped out on the verandah, and when I shook hands with this man, he was crying. He said,

'Mrs Stirling, I'm Roy Gallagher, and I was one of George's best friends at college — but I've been away in America.'

He told me how he and George had shook hands and promised each other that whichever one of them got married first had to bring his wife to the other one's place. When I told him that George was dead he said that he had heard that, but he didn't want to believe it; anyway, he wanted to keep his vow. The old lady and I took them down to the cemetery, and we've still got a photo at home of Roy Gallagher and his wife standing beside George's grave.

Before we came away to Auckland, our youngest son Kingi came to live with us at Otaimina. You see, when George was killed and I was sitting beside his body at the tangi, one of the women told me that my sister-in-law Edie had given birth to a baby the day before George's accident. I asked her,

'What is the baby?'

'It's a boy.'

When I heard that I felt my son George had come back again, and all through the tangi I was hoping that I could get this baby; I knew it would help me to forget what had happened. When Edie came to Stirling Castle with the baby not long after, I asked her to call the baby after George, and she agreed. Then I said,

'I would like to take the baby, Edie — you give that baby to me and I'll look after him.'

'Oh no, no! You leave the baby with me, but it's all right, I will name him Kingi George, after George.'

Kingi George was the name given to our son by Mrs Williams. He was born on June 3rd, and when Mrs Williams heard about it she said,

'Fancy that — June 3rd is King George's birthday! I'm going to ring Amy up and ask her to call the baby King George.'

She rang me up about it and I said,

'I'm very sorry, Mrs Williams, but this baby has already been named. The old lady has called him Te Ariki-tapu-ki-waho, after one of her ancestors.'

'Well, you can give him this name too, because he was born on King George's birthday.'

Just to make her happy I agreed, and our son was christened Kingi George Te Ariki-tapu-ki-waho.

Anyhow, Edie said she would call her son Kingi George too, but she said,

'I want to keep this baby, Amy. Later on maybe, when he's running around and you can feed him on kumara it might be all right, but while he's a baby, I think I'd better look after him.'

'It doesn't matter about the feeding, Edie; I fed my own babies with a bottle, I can look after him.'

'Oh never mind, Amy, leave it, leave it . . .'

I didn't bother her again while I was sick, but when I came back from Auckland I really started to think about this baby. One day somebody said to me,

'Did you know that Edie's gone to Te Puia?'

'What for?'

'Oh, she's going to have another baby.'

'Is she? Who's looking after the baby?'

'Her eldest daughter, Maru.'

I thought, here goes, I'm going to get that baby now. I rang Frank Walker and told him that I wanted a taxi to Te Araroa.

'All right, Amy — when?'

'Right now, today!'

He came and picked me up, and away we went to Te Araroa. When we got there I walked into Edie's house.

'Hello, Maru, how's everybody?'

'Oh, all right, Auntie. Mum just had her baby the other day you know, she's still in the home.'

'Where's Kingi now?'

'There he is, under the table.'

The baby was crawling around and trying to stand up under the table so I grabbed hold of him and picked him up.

'Where are his clothes, Maru?'

'In the room. Auntie . . . what are you going to do?'

'I'm going to take this blanket and look after him. Just give me his clothes and a blanket.'

She gave me all the baby's clothes and I wrapped him up in the blanket, and got in the taxi and went back to Otaimina.

When Edie came back from Te Puia, she couldn't see Kingi anywhere.

'Maru, where's Kingi?'

'Oh, Auntie Amy came here and took him away.'

'Did she now!'

As soon as she was free Edie came to Raukokore and told me off for stealing her baby.

'But I *told* you Edie, I wanted that baby. If you'd had a trouble like mine and lost a dear son, you'd need some comfort too. I feel better now, because I've got someone to talk to when the kids are away at school . . . So you look after your baby and I'll look after mine, and we'll both be all right.'

Edie wasn't very happy about it but she went away, and left Kingi at home with me at Otaimina.

FIONA KIDMAN

Puff Adder

I thought I saw Annabel Sherwin in the Pink Gallery viewing the antiques at Dunbar's annual Trentham sale. Afterwards, I had bad dreams.

I had not gone to buy antiques for I could not afford them. But every now and then I am drawn to look at these beautiful objects despite the vulgarity of some of the would-be buyers. Indeed, I think I go to look at them too, for in their way, they are curios of another kind.

The woman I took to be Annabel was standing in front of the Persian rugs. Item 781, to be exact: Shirvan rug with three medallions and stylised birds 1473×1118 cm, according to the catalogue.

My eyes were full of tears at the time because Ross was with me, and he had complained at the price of the catalogue which he said we did not need if we had not come to buy. But it seemed to me that if we were going to look at the antiques it would be helpful to know what we were looking at and so we had quarrelled like tired foolish children. Ross had bought a catalogue and that had seemed as bad to me as him not buying one. Then he had stood near the door, refusing to look at anything at all.

In January it is very hot in the Pink Gallery. We should probably never have gone. We do not usually behave like that these days. We have come a long way; that is why it was suddenly painful, and I was so close to weeping.

I looked studiously at every item then, as if I was making the best possible use of the catalogue, even though I would have given a lot just to have walked out. I was sick of the whole thing, and sorry for myself too. And because of this careful scrutiny of the catalogue I did know that it was item 781 that Annabel, if it was her, was looking at, and that the Shirvan would have looked exactly right in her long low elegant house in Weyville, the town where we had all lived once, long ago, and where no doubt she did still. It was the house where I believe her son once violated my child, and from which I had been excluded, and which, after a period of general humiliation and social ostracism, I had begun to visit again, until I left the town of Weyville.

I wanted to go over to Ross at once and say, 'Hey, is that Annabel Sherwin over there?'

Of course, as we were not speaking to each other, I didn't.
Besides, on reflection, it is something about which we have nothing more to say to each other.
I walked out of the gallery and caught up with him, already heading back to the car. The sun was harsh and bright.
He took my arm and said, 'Come on, Ellen, I'll buy you a drink. Very cold.' It was nice of him and I was grateful.
Still, I couldn't help wondering if he had seen her too.

I cannot imagine Annabel living anywhere else but Weyville; she had a niche there. She had been the queen of our new subdivision many years ago, amongst all the young matrons. Her coffee parties had been at once larger and more exclusive than anybody else's. Larger, because she knew so many people from all over Weyville, not just our suburb; and exclusive because she knew the right people. Living near to Annabel did not always mean that you would be invited, even if you had minded her children for her the Sunday morning before, when she and Martin went out for drinks. She had subtle ways of implementing segregation — like telling you that there was measles around, or a new kind of flu, which everyone, or their children, had had but you.

Martin, Annabel's husband, was not a doctor, or a dentist, or a lawyer, like the husbands of most of her friends. He was, in fact, quite an ordinary clerk in the office of an engineerig firm, although Annabel could make it sound as if he was the managing director.

It was Annabel's father who held the key to her good breeding. He had made a fortune out of lavatory pans during the Depression, and now that the industrial magnate's manufacturing days were over the family lived back in Hawke's Bay where their forbears had first settled. I cannot remember who told me about the crap catchers, because it wasn't Annabel, or any of her friends. Still, it was something that everyone somehow knew. She did tell me about Hawke's Bay though. As I got to know her better, she told me more often. I had no doubt that she was well connected. Annabel told me she was, and though it may seem surprising, she was a person who was always believable in her way. Besides, the evidence was in her favour.

Her money didn't bother me, as such. Some people have it, and some don't — in those days my expectations were small. Neither did Annabel herself as a rule, though I was susceptible to hurt. But mostly Ross and I used to joke about her and the silly things she said.

She was exceptionally plain, but she talked about her good looks with such authority that you came to believe in them like everything else about her.

'After I came to Weyville I went for my very first medical to Roland — ' (she always spoke of doctors by their first name) 'and I took off my dress,' she would say — for she told this story often — 'and there I was in my lovely white satin slip with my boobs swelling up above, and poor Roland took a deep breath and simply didn't know where to look. "Annabel," he told me afterwards, "I get so many *slags* in here."'

Roland and his wife used to have dinner with Annabel from time to time over the years that followed. I find it difficult to say Annabel and Martin, even though they were such a devoted couple. Thinking back, it is hard not to think of Martin as the live-in handyman and not much else in that household, although he could be self-opinionated and pinched bottoms at parties and held forth a lot about what nowadays we call morals campaigning.

I think we would also, fashionably, describe him as holding double standards.

Annabel would clean her already spotless house for nearly a week before one of these dinner parties, polish silver, organise clothes, set open fires ready for quick combustion, arrange flowers, marinate meat, make sauces, all according to a list that had been made for at least a fortnight before the event. She would also practise smoking, at which she was not accomplished, before her parties. It was still considered smart.

I used to think she looked like a puff adder then, or what I thought a puff adder might look like. I had read that it was 'a deadly snake that blows up the top part of its body when it is excited'. She would puff and blow, filling her plump cheeks with smoke and emitting it in little blue spurts, trying not to cough. At the same time she would attempt to tell racy, sexually titillating, though never explicit stories.

All of this would be a rehearsal for Roland's coming. I think it unlikely that they ever slept together. In fact I doubt that Annabel ever slept with anybody in those days, though she is the sort of woman who is probably coming to it in older age when others of us have learned to care for ourselves.

I return to bad dreams.

When I was a small child I started to have nightmares about snakes. I think they began when my parents taught me how to play snakes and ladders.

In my dreams I would be standing on an island which was only the size of my feet, in the middle of a river. The river would not be of water, but of snakes.

I carried this dream into adolescence, and although it left me then, the terror of snakes did not. Everything that I disliked I equated with snakes or rats, creatures that slithered near the ground. It is only recently that I have been able to look at snakes on television and only then with the utmost effort of will, and at that, since the day in an Australian zoo where I had gone for the express purpose of looking at snakes. I walked round and round the snakehouse for nearly an hour that day while school parties of children laughed and shrieked and knocked on the glass at the snakes, before I could bring myself to go up and look at them.

There was an adder with its face pressed against the glass and its eye was open and malevolent, pushed between the soft flesh of its folded body, and the pane which parted us. Sick and revolted, I had put my hand against the glass, covering its eye.

I will beat you, I thought then. I will never allow you to terrorise me in my sleep again the way you have all my life.

I thought also, that if there had been an earthquake and the glass had broken, then the snake would have had a chance to win. But the earth was quiet and my luck held, and I do not dream of snakes.

If you asked me, I would say that I looked them in the eye.

Yet I have not stopped dreaming dreams of one kind or another. Maybe it was better when there was a shape, these amorphous shapeless forms are not pleasant either.

Did I see Annabel in the Pink Gallery?

I keep moving away from the point of all this. It is not intentional.

Annabel and Martin had three sons. They were very proud of them. You couldn't blame them for that. They were good-looking kids, all dark skinned with blue eyes and thick eyebrows — I believe Martin's mother was middle-European, though just what was never specified. The boys were very charming in their manner. The older two had been trained to wait on table when there were guests, which their friends thought delightful. They freshened up people's drinks, and even complimented Annabel's women friends on their appearance. Their names were Thomas and Humphrey, and the youngest was Adam.

It was a little surprising that Thomas and Humphrey were not at boarding school, but the young people of Weyville were generally cost-conscious and, as well, I suspect that around that time Annabel's brothers had been making demands on the lavatory pan magnate. Besides, between them, most of their friends managed to comprise the local high school board of governors and the school was being run pretty much as they wanted it. They had zoning worked out to suit themselves very well, and most of the Maori kids went to a different school. They had a say in whom the school employed and, as they said, theirs had a good tone. The principal was reputed to be a Christian, practising that is, for Annabel's friends were professed if not always visible ones.

As for us, we occupied a curious geographical position in relation to the Sherwin's house. Several houses were grouped around a park, so that although we were neighbours in the same subdivision, we faced different ways. The Sherwins had been there much longer than we had, and their property had many trees, some old ones which had been left when the division of the land had taken place, others fast growing birches and silver dollars. Their place looked old and established, ours looked new and raw.

And our children, two small girls, were much younger. One was a baby and the other only three, so that there were quite natural barriers to a regular relationship. Indeed, if Adam had not been Annabel and Martin's afterthought, and only four at the time, Annabel and I might have gone month in and month out with nothing more than a wave over the back fence when we were putting out the washing. As it was, Annabel often needed someone to look after Adam during the day, and when I agreed to take him once or twice she offered to take my daughter in return.

I suppose I was grateful. I found suburbia difficult, I never felt that I did it well, I was not good at preserving or bottling, or making the children's clothes. I had started to work on a part-time basis in the evenings which was frowned upon, but gave me a little freedom that saved my sanity. If I was grateful to Annabel, it may even have been for her sillinesses and excesses. I think I found them more amusing than I cared to admit. And although I have dwelt on the ridiculous and pretentious side of her nature, there were times when she seemed kind, even sensible.

I remember us talking about child molestation one day. 'Ellen,' she said, 'If anyone touched one of my boys I would kill them with my bare hands.'

I was impressed, she spoke with such passion.

I looked at my little girls, and I thought, yes that is exactly how I feel, it is good to have a friend who feels the same way as I do.

Another day, she looked after my three-year-old. She might have to slip out and pick Adam up from afternoon kindergarten, but Humphrey would be home that day, because he had sprained his ankle, and would I mind if he were to keep an eye on my daughter for twenty minutes? He was fifteen after all.

Naturally, I said that I did not mind.

My small solemn child was quiet when she came home that day.

The same night she woke crying and I could not comfort her. It took me a long time to understand what she was trying to tell me. At last I did. That afternoon Humphrey had taken her to the gardening shed.

My child was not visibly damaged or hurt, not in the sense of being able to present some evidence. But I do know she was hurt in some other and terrible way. I know that as she grew up her adolescence was blighted by an unnatural reserve, and that though she began to see young men she sometimes appeared to be afraid of them.

Perhaps I interpret events too much in the light of this childhood incident. There may have been the perfidies and quarrels of her parents, a dozen reasons preferably but not easily forgotten, that made her uneasy. Three-year-olds have short memories you may say. But she says she remembers, and I, who have always claimed early childhood recall for myself, see no reason to deny her the same. The fact is, that for a long time she was unhappy and it is as hard for me, as it has been for her, to see past Humphrey.

And there is more to it than this. There is what we did and didn't do, Ross and I.

For a start, we pretended to our daughter that it had not happened, that it was some figment of her imagination, better forgotten. That was a terrible lie, and it is one of which I am ashamed.

Nor did we at once go to Annabel and Martin. Instead, Ross took time away from his job at the radio station one afternoon, visited the school which Humphrey attended, and saw the headmaster. It seemed to be the easiest way. We did not want trouble in the neighbourhood, somehow we felt vaguely ashamed of what had happened, as if in some mysterious way we were to blame. We were afraid that we were wrong or would be shown to be wrong, and that that would disturb our careful neighbourly relationship.

Yes, that is the truth, we were more afraid that our way of life would be disturbed than we were determined at getting at the whole truth. To each other we called it 'saving Humphrey's face', or 'saving Annabel and Martin'. We did not say 'saving ourselves'.

The principal was ingratiating to Ross, the worst kind of Christian. He said, yes, he would handle it, he would speak to Humphrey.

Soon after, for the boy's sake, as it was told to us, he also saw Roland who was on the board of governors. He felt it should be shared with someone who knew the lad, who would help Humphrey, someone who would put him on the right track.

Roland of course told Annabel. I think back, and know that was as it was intended. I suppose that it was correct that she should know. She should not have been told this way. That is something that Ross and I did not do well.

If I have a word of defence for my own and Ross's behaviour, it is simply this: Annabel would never have believed whoever told her.

We became, overnight, the neighbourhood outcasts. We were liars and filth-mongers. Humphrey's charm was recounted by every indignant matron who had ever enjoyed Annabel's hospitality. Before long no one spoke to me in the supermarket. I changed where I shopped, and was sent a written bill for a loaf of bread that I had put on the slate before the storm.

One evening Annabel rang. Her tone was as cold as the frost on the wires. 'Martin and I have been thinking,' she began. Her voice, beneath its coldness, held the trace of a lisp. I had never noticed it before.

I clung to the phone, my tongue paralysed.

'We really cannot let this situation go on, Ellen,' she was saying. 'We should like to come and see you.'

I thought at first that she was offering to reinstate our friendship.

'There are some things that really ought to be sorted out. You should know where we stand. We're not at all pleased you know.'

This was a long time ago, twenty years. What does it say of me, of my failures, of my inability to assert myself, of my capitulations, that I went away that night?

Ross suggested that I go to the pictures, and I agreed, though at first I was doubtful. I said, 'It was me she asked you know.'

'But I was the one who went to the school,' said Ross. 'I should sort it out, if that's what they want.'

I was reassured. Confrontations were other people's business. Men's work. Ross would make it all right, and perhaps we would still be friends again.

When I came home that night it had been agreed that our child had made the story up. It was perfectly clear, someone had *talked dirty* — that's what they called it, *talking dirty*, to her and she had rearranged a fiction to fit Humphrey. Our clever little child.

In return, it seemed life would return to normal, we could go on as we had before, we could all forget. I could belong again.

Nearly, but not quite. It was me that Annabel had wanted the evening she came to visit. Some women seek to punish other people, provided they are never men.

She invited me for coffee a few mornings later. I accepted, and although I was timid when I walked up to her door, I was pleased that she had asked me.

She was practising smoking that morning. Puffing and spurting and erupting in her little clouds of smoke, her prominent eyes glittering.

'You'll have to be careful of that child,' she observed, over our second cup of coffee. 'I could tell she was bad from the moment she was born.'

'There are some things she couldn't have known, Annabel,' I ventured.

'Some children are born with dirty minds,' she pronounced. 'Still, if you get on to it early enough you might be able to do something about it.'

I felt humble. She pressed her advantage. 'There had better be no more of this,' she said. 'We can do something about Ross's job, I wouldn't hesitate to go to the top if anything like this comes up again.'

She did not exaggerate; she knew the right people and she could have jeopardised Ross's job. That is how it was then, and maybe still is in Weyville.

I do not know whether it was Annabel in the Pink Gallery. I didn't approach this woman. The chances are, that if I had I would have been civil and charming. That is how people are when they have lived in Weyville and meet years later in the Pink Gallery.

I was sitting in the sun by the sea in a town called Chanea in Greece. The sky was a most exquisite and tender blue. From where I was sitting I could see the old sea wall which surrounds the town, jutting out into the sea. A fisherman was laying his nets. Red poppies bloomed in the grass which led to the sand. They were like Flanders poppies which are part of New Zealand folklore, symbolising death in war; people sell replicas made out of rolled up red cotton on street corners in April. This was April and the poppies were real.

I was not sure whether the place where I was sitting was on private property or not. It appeared to be the foundations of an old building but it was bare and exposed to the elements, except for the remnants of a thatched roof. It was rather like a derelict pavilion. Alongside of it, and running down to the beach were steps which also led to a poor house which stood out on stilts across the water. I knew that it was inhabited for clothes hung outside, but it is difficult to tell whether buildings are being put up or pulled down in Greece. I sat on a concrete ledge and set about writing to my daughter. The poppies at my feet stirred. I thought it was a breeze moving amongst them but when I looked, they were alive with rats, foraging in the grass where rubbish had been left. I drew my feet up around me.

'My dear daughter' I wrote, and stopped. I told myself that it was the sun which made me drowsy, that it was easier just to sit and think of her. I like to think about her. She has turned out now, funny and clever, tough and wise. She seems not to have suffered a permanent kind of damage. That is what I told myself, sitting in the sun in Greece.

I think I may have gone to sleep, for I did not see the young man come, though he may have passed along the steps beside me, in order to be sitting so close to me, or he may have come from the house below. He was sitting on a rush chair which had been piled in the corner. The chair looked as if it might break under his weight.

'Kalimera,' he said.

'Kalimera,' I responded, without warmth.

He smiled, he had bad teeth. I knew that he was thinking that a middle-aged foreign woman sitting alone by the sea in Greece awaited his invitation. Although in New Zealand there are certain Greeks whom I love, in Greece I was uneasy in the presence of local men. I was not afraid the young man would inflict himself on me in a physical way; I mean to say of course that I was not afraid of rape. But I did not wish to have the morning spoiled by his proposition nor bear his displeasure when I refused him.

I tore up the page I had been writing on and started again, in a busy way. 'My dear daughter, my beloved child, there is a language we learn very young, the language of submission, abnegation, guilt, remorse, it is only when we are older that we learn the language of choice — '

Only of course I did not write it — she would have thought that jet lag and loneliness in foreign countries was sending me mad. Besides, she has already learned and unlearned this language, and others that I will never know.

How could it have been that Annabel made me feel responsible for what Humphrey did to my child?

There was another young man, after I left Chanea. In London, I was going to lunch at the Grosvenor.

I caught a Victoria Line tube to Green Park, and as I was coming through the subway, a young man died before my eyes. He had already lain down to die as I arrived at the top of the escalator, and two men were beside him. I stood for a few moments and watched his death. One of the men who had been kneeling by him went for help. I did not like to stand and stare, the young man seemed too dead to be looked at any more.

When I was outside the station I thought that I should have given mouth-to-mouth resuscitation or heart massage. I sat down on a bench and wondered what to do, whether I should go back inside and offer, but so much time had elapsed by then, that the situation would certainly have been irretrievable.

I was shocked that I had done nothing. If I had been in New Zealand, I said to myself, I would have done more, I would have been involved. It is all this Britishness that has undone me. That is what I told myself as I went to the Grosvenor for lunch. But I couldn't be certain about it.

When I came home I told my priest this story. 'Ah,' he said, 'you have discovered that you are not a universal person.' It was a pleasant and priestly way of saying that I had failed to do well enough.

I think he is right. It is easy to make excuses about the circumstances we find ourselves in, and how we react. We can say it was our age, or the times in which we lived, or the place in which we found ourselves. We can perform good acts to expiate the things we did or did not do when we were younger, but there is still something we cannot calculate which is, who we really are, and what we will do when something special is required of us.

Annabel was stronger than me. She had said that she would kill anyone who touched a hair of her children's heads.

She had managed a good deal of damage and embarrassment at our expense which was perhaps a satisfactory equivalent for Annabel. Whereas, I had done nothing about killing Humphrey. Thinking back, it would have been a small thing to do. But leaving even that aside (for, to some, it may seem irrational and extreme), there was a point at which I could, simply, have stopped agreeing with Annabel. It would have been the very least I could have done for my child.

Work

'EMILY MORGAN'
(SANDRA CONEY)

I Wanted Honey

It's warm in bed in the early morning with the heat of a whole night trapped under the blankets. Opening my eyes for a moment I can see the early morning sun slanting (between the slats on the venetians) onto the floor. They need dusting. I shut my eyes and snuggle into the blankets. If I'm lucky I'll manage a few more minutes sleep before Christopher starts screaming for his first bottle and Katy and Linda want to come into bed with us.

My husband presses his big heavy body against my back and before I know it his fingers have insinuated themselves between my legs and are fiddling with the soft folds at the opening of my vagina. I try and shrug myself away but he isn't deterred and then I feel his erection pushing against me. I think about diaphragms in bathroom cupboards and jellies and crouching with my leg up on the lavatory seat in the cold bathroom with my eyes still full of sleep and I think about my warm bed, mentally cross my fingers and do nothing. It all happens at once. Christopher shrieks from his cot, the girls tear through the bedroom door and he comes (I hope outside of me).

Breakfast is barely controlled chaos. It's bitterly cold in the kitchen even with the heater on and I can see the cows on the mountain stumbling round in the frosty grass, their breath hanging like clouds above them. He wants a clean shirt and then when I've ironed it he says he wanted a coloured one not a white one today (who's he trying to impress!). I say I haven't got time to iron two shirts in the mornings so if he wants another one he'll have to do it himself and he says you know I can't iron a shirt! And why don't you iron a shirt the day before for God's sake: what the hell do you do all day anyway? The kids are fighting over breakfast. Katy says 'Why have I got jam on my toast. I said I wanted honey! I said I WANTED HONEY!' We have a spilled cup of milk and jam on Linda's clean jersey (which has to be hand-washed) and she starts to cry because when I go to get her lunch-box out of her school bag she's lost her drink bottle — the third one in a month — and I tell her she'll have to go without. I clean yesterday's rotten pear and sandwich crusts out of the lunch-box, I put bacon and eggs in front of my husband and sit down with a cup of tea.

'Let me have a piece of the paper,' I say to my husband.

'You know I don't like breaking the paper up,' he looks at me sternly over the top of the paper.

'You've got all day to look at it,' he says. He twitches one nostril: 'I think Christopher's done something in his pants.' Christopher smiles delightedly back at us from his highchair. If I was there on my own I'd leave him sitting there in it, he doesn't mind. Although I'd shift the highchair further away from the table. But I can't impose that on my husband in his city suit and grey shirt and polished shoes, so I take Christopher off into the bedroom and gag as I deal with it there.

After the goodbyes and the dishes, the beds and the nappies I get Christopher into his pushchair and we set off up the road to do some shopping. Trundling down an aisle in the food market with Christopher perched in the wire basket, I catch sight of the immaculate Mrs Whiting from No.10. She *always* makes me feel so inadequate. Her children always have socks that stay up at the knees and their jerseys never look thin at the elbows. She's always neat and fashionable: always made up, always looks as if she's just had a blow wave. O enviable Mrs W. As she sees me she smiles weakly and says Hello. Good God, she's been crying! Her eyes are swollen and red. She hurries past looking intently at the shelves to avoid my astonished gaze. Later when I'm looking at the prices of toothpastes, I hear her over the other side of the stand. 'Leave that alone!' she says in a panicky voice. There's silence, then a crack, then a wail from Jonathon. 'I told you I'd smack you if you touched another thing,' she hisses to her child. Can mothers hate their children?

The afternoon is peaceful enough, at least until the children come home from school. I take Christopher outside and put him on some blankets on a big sheet of plastic on the ground. He rolls around wrapped up in his woollies. The ground is cold but I'd much rather freeze outside than in. There are bulbs just starting to come up and leaves to be raked into piles and weeds grow no matter what time of year. Then I notice Christopher's pants steaming so I take him inside for a change and while we're there the kids come home from school and want sandwiches and toast and biscuits. Linda's got a long story about a boy who pushed her over on the way home from school. It's the third time in the week she's complained about that so I suppose I'll have to go up to the school and see what I can do about it. Otherwise I'll have to walk up to the school every day and pick the kids up. If only I could have the car but he says he needs it for work. A bit later I start thinking about dinner. I make custard and stewed apples and decide a stew with baked potatoes would be good and nourishing. Except! I forgot to get some more potatoes up the road and can't face the thought of dragging all the children up the road and back just for that. I can't just cook rice. He says it's not real food, only fit for

Chinese. I decide to ring him at work and get him to get some potatoes at the dairy on the way home.

I get his secretary. 'He's in a board meeting,' she says 'Is there some way I can help?' Some way she can help! She knows it's me. She knows I only ring when I've run out of potatoes or the plumber's intimidating me or when Linda's tooth has fallen out. I am very tempted to say:

'Well as a matter of fact I was just ringing to see if Mr Bryant will be in Buenos Aires checking up on the political situation there next week. Or will he be in London checking up on British Sterling or Rarotonga arranging more banana imports or do you think there's the slightest chance we might see him at the matrimonial property within the next few hours.' I say none of these things but leave a message for him to ring me when he comes out of his meeting. About an hour later he does. Would he get some potatoes on the way home?

'Look, I'm sorry dear. I'm terribly busy, there's still a lot to do here before I can leave. Actually I was going to ring you to say I'd be home late. Probably about 8.30. You'd better keep my dinner warm for me.'

My heart sinks. The next three hours seem to stretch before me like a prison sentence. Well, that solves the problem of potatoes: the kids and I will have rice.

The kids and I have dinner in the kitchen. Christopher sucks on a rusk, then has a bottle, belches quietly and goes off to bed. Linda and Katy watch TV, fight over which bedtime story they're going to have and take what seems like hours to change into their pyjamas. I haven't bathed them. I should have but I'm just too tired to bath them. I'll rub the obvious dirty spots off their arms and legs before they go to school in the morning and hope the teacher doesn't notice. I'll still feel guilty about not having bathed them though, just as I feel guilty that they don't have home baked cakes in their lunch boxes and Christopher hasn't got hand knitted jumpers and guilty that I haven't taken him to Plunket for three months and guilty because I lose my husband's socks and he has to look for them in the dirty washing basket in the mornings and guilty, guilty, guilty because I forgot the potatoes.

I flop in front of the TV, then think that perhaps a sherry would be a good idea. So I sip sherry and watch Coronation Street and think of the ironing I've got to do before I go to bed. And the dishes. I'd forgotten the dishes.

He comes home at nine. He was delayed in his slick city suit and shiny shoes. 'Fancy forgetting the potatoes!' he says. 'You are a muddler.' He ruffles my hair. 'It's just as well you haven't got a job like mine. Where would they be if I just forgot things?'

Before he goes to bed, he looks at the children, soft and asleep. He smiles at them and turns the light out. Then it's my turn. I've got my diaphragm in and I'm all ready. I'm tired but I am awake. He gets into bed in his clean pyjamas, taken from the pile where they sit in the drawer, neatly folded in pairs, tops and bottoms matched. I nestle up to him, twisting my leg between his and nuzzling my face into the smooth part of neck where it joins his shoulder. His body warms mine. I put my mouth on his in the dark.

'Don't do that. I've got to get plenty of sleep. I've got an extremely busy day tomorrow and I've got to be in top-notch form.'

He pecks me kindly on the cheek. I turn over and go to sleep.

MARY FINDLAY

An experienced cook-general

'Yes, Miss?'
Don't stammer.
'You have a job in the window?'
'Yes, for an experienced cook-general.'
A long shrewd look.
'You are experienced and have references?'
Didn't think of that one. Look her in the eye.
'Yes, I'm experienced.'
'How old are you?'
'Eighteen.' (Has she forgotten the references — what will I say if she asks again?)
Opportune diversion — the telephone. 'Excuse me.'
I'll tell her I have references, but have left them at home.
She puts down the receiver, all smiles.
'Well Miss, I have a nice lady on the books and she works with the help, so it won't be a hard place. Would you like to go and see her? It'll be two and sixpence for the address, refundable if you don't suit.'
(Oh God, why was I so green — two and sixpence!)
'Well, Miss?'
'I haven't any money.'
Silence. Then — 'You could pay it from your first week's wages. I'll ask the lady to withhold it and send it to us.'
'Oh yes!'
Out into the street with the precious address — Upland Road, Kelburn. From the Quay to Kelburn, a fair walk, time to think, cablecars are for the solvent.
Wish I were experienced — not just jobwise, but worldwise. Lucky about the references, but what if the employer asks for them? You'll have to think up something before you get there. Never asked about the pay or the hours of work either — panicked over the references. How will you manage for clothes? Can't work in a gymfrock but that's all you've got.
On the Terrace now, look the other way, there are some classmates on the other side of the road. They look nice in their holiday clothes, the day is warm for May, too hot for a coat, but it hides the gym. Two weeks to earn and then back to school. Later, with luck, the three weeks of the August holidays should produce another job. At around

ten shillings a week for five weeks, two pound ten shillings. But two and sixpence to the Agency means five shillings for the two jobs. Can't spend a penny of it, though.

How to get a reference? One would do. How to get a dress? One would do. Looking down on Wellington and opposite the university now — that's where you'll sit the exam and, if you pass, you'll be qualified to enter. Perhaps Aunt Elsie would lend you a dress, be a bit old for you, it's a nuisance being big, Cousin Claire's wouldn't fit. Shall I go and get it first? No, her place in Karori is too far. Worse, the Agency might send another applicant. So, just remember to hold coat closed over knees. Kelburn Parade now, getting nearer and getting hot on this hill.

I have it! Tell the employer you have a reference at home, but it's from Palmerston North, where you worked for the past two years. If you get the job, go home and write one yourself with a fictitious name and address. Maybe, if she likes the look of you, she won't bother to ask.

Upland Road and a seat in the sun. Sit down and collect your wits. My mother raised me to 'Tell the truth and shame the devil.' She hated lies and so do I — but she is dead, dead, dead. And my father — but I shan't think about him now. His drinking, his mad rages, the beatings . . . I try to push them out of my mind, remembering the neighbour I'd tried to talk to, just to tell someone — and the way she'd made me feel . . . 'Mary, you foul your own nest by talking like that. It's a poor bird that fouls its own nest.' All right so I won't talk, not to anyone, and I'll try not to think.

My mother is dead. I wish my father were dead. But I am alive and must go on living. Honesty doesn't pay. This is 1930 and who will give me a job if I say I am fifteen and want a job for only two weeks? They would say, 'My dear girl, there are plenty of people older and more experienced wanting permanent positions.'

Stifle the guilt feelings, they rob you of confidence — the rotten gymfrock is enough to cope with. Nearly there. What will the 'lady' be like? I've got to put myself across. Golly, what is a 'cook-general'? Cook, yes, but general? Let her do the talking — bosses all like to talk and you just answer the questions.

It's a really big and beautiful house, two storeyed and gabled. People who live in houses like this must have a lot of money. Still I don't suppose I'll get more than ten shillings a week, that's all they pay. I've pushed the bell too hard in my nervousness, should have been more discreet. Footsteps, the woman is big and unbeautiful.

'Yes?' Peremptorily.

'I'm from the agency.'

'Come in.'

Wide hall, carpeted. Curved staircase at the end. I follow her into

the drawing-room. Through the windows, Wellington Harbour, inviting in the sunshine. Inside, brass. Brass tables, brass candlesticks, brass ornaments, catching the light.
'Sit down.'
Fold the coat at the knees. Sit up straight.
'I am Mrs Burgess. You are Mary Wilkinson?'
'Yes.'
She looks me up and down and I take the opportunity to do the same. I am frightened, she is pale as putty, fat as a barrel, red hair horribly dyed, pudgy hands and feet. That face, with its piggy eyes and nose like a beacon of light in a sea of skimmed milk . . .
I can yet escape. The door is shut but I can open it and run. I feel revolted and trapped. My guilt has gone, evicted by this new fear — surely this woman is mean — can I stick it? I don't know. The small mouth above the several chins opens.
'Where was your last place?'
She must mean where I worked last.
'In Palmerston North.'
'How long were you there?'
'Two years.'
'Why did you leave?'
The answer comes pat. I am committed. The two-guinea goal is the thing.
'I wanted to come to Wellington.'
'Why?'
'It's a big city.'
'Hmm!'
My fingers feel cramped with holding my coat and she is staring at me. I feel uncomfortable and look out the window.
'How old are you?'
'Eighteen.'
'When could you start?'
This sounds like business. No mention of references, thank goodness. I don't like it, but if she'll take me, I'll give it a go.
'Immediately.'
'Can you cook plain meals?'
'Yes.'
'This is a big house and I like to help the girl with her work.'
The mean mouth stretches into what is intended as a smile. The fat hand fiddles with a watch.
'It's four o'clock now. Could you move in tonight about seven?'
'Yes — thank you, Mrs Burgess.'
'Very well, Mary. We'll see you at the back door at seven.'
Out the door, down the steps, out the gate, around the corner — whew!

Off with the coat. The erstwhile navy gymfrock, now purple with age, flies in the breeze.

What did she say — oh yes, the *back* door — servant's entrance, that's it. It's only for two weeks, but she doesn't know it, and what's two weeks if it means that exam fee — or two fifths of it? Get up to Karori and borrow that dress and put your books in a suitcase, you've no clothes to worry about.

Aunt Elsie was cooperative and gave me a dress — albeit the hem put up with small gold safetypins. (You can fix it in your spare time.) She produced a pair of shoes which pinched only a little and would 'work in' if I wore them in the rain. Sound idea. My only pair had cardboard over the holes in the soles and rain does predictable things to cardboard. Best of all, she gave me a good dinner. That really helped. I felt quite brave when at five to seven I reached the gate in Upland Road. Just in time I remembered — the *back* door.

My tummy doesn't feel so good — I'm for it now — I'm a servant — a lower type of being, who must always go around to the back.

This time no drawing-room. I follow my mistress to the kitchen and am told to wait, but not invited to sit, while she gets Mr Burgess. I put my case down and remain standing.

'Arthur, this is Mary, the new girl. This is Mr Burgess, Mary.'

'How do you do, Mary?'

'Very well, thank you, Mr Burgess.'

'Well Arthur, I'll just give Mary a few instructions for the morning and show her her room.' Over her shoulder, she says, 'I'll be back in a minute.'

So that's the master. Already I'm developing the thinking habits of the menial (skivvy's the word, isn't it?) Tall, gaunt man with hollow eyes — he's her boss, though, not mine. The kitchen is huge and there is only one window, so it will be dark by day. An electric stove, how do they work — the same as gas I hope. She's coming back.

'Now Mary, you will rise at half-past five and sweep and scrub the yard. You will endeavour to be quiet about it. Our bedroom is just above and I don't wish you to wake Mr Burgess. He is an accountant and often works late at night. Here is the broom, bucket, brush and sandsoap.'

She opens the back door and, switching on the light, shows me a concrete yard about twelve feet by twelve feet. She must be mad — sweep and scrub a concrete yard at 5.30 a.m.!

Returning, she adds, 'You will then bring the master and myself a morning tray at half-past six. I will show you how to set it now.' She does.

'If you have any spare time after the yard and before the tea, you are to start sweeping and dusting the dining-room, which in any case must be finished before breakfast at eight.'

(Heavens!)

She continues, 'Breakfast will be porridge and bacon and eggs. I have soaked the oatmeal, here it is. Cook it slowly for about one hour — no lumps, mind. We like our bacon crisp and don't make the toast till last. You'll find the table cloth and cutlery in the sideboard. Do you follow?'

'Yes, Mrs Burgess.'

(Follow — yes, all too well — but achieve all this by 8 a.m.? Well, she hasn't asked if I can. So what?)

'After breakfast, we'll go into the daily routine and I'll tell you what we want for dinner. Oh yes, I forgot, we have two friends of the family staying with us, Mr Richardson and Mr Evans — they take their tea at seven. My son and daughter are away at present, but will be back on Sunday night.'

(That's six adults to cook for. God help me! Ask her what the pay is and what time off you get. Missed the bus, she's away again.)

'Now I'll show you your room.'

She opens a door off the kitchen.

'I expect the girl to keep her room as clean as the rest of the house. I'll say "goodnight" now.' With a roll and a rumble, she is gone.

Where in the name of all that's holy did they get it? Perhaps it was inherited, but the tip seems more logical. An iron bed, rusty; grey army blankets (perhaps a quartermaster in the family pinched them from the store); sheets, dubious colour, well patched; flock mattress, lumpy; ancient wire, well down in the middle. What's this — a note under the pillow? 'To the next girl. Don't let the old bitch kill you — no one stays more than a month — ask the milkman and don't rub her back. Good luck!'

Bless her! I *will* ask the milkman. What does she mean, 'Don't rub her back'? Perhaps she means scratch — don't crawl to her. Bed is hard up against the wall on three sides and there is a three-drawer chest with an alarm clock on it. Chest is also hard up against the remaining wall. Floor space, four feet by three feet — less when the door is open. The door won't shut — lock gone — the floor is bare. There's a holland blind at the small window — no curtains — window won't open. Door won't shut, window won't open — three grey blankets — put the coat on the bed — a fine May day but a frost tonight.

OK, it's a thoroughly horrible little room — no, don't cry, there's no one to cry to. Think of something funny — maybe the milkman will give you the glad-eye. Maybe Mrs Burgess will melt if she stands by the fire. Maybe she'll choke on a lump of porridge (no, that's tomorrow's problem). Maybe you'd better get some sleep. Five-thirty will come soon enough.

The uneasy combination of a lumpy bed and a fearful mind resulted in an awakening ahead of the alarm. Down on my knees on the cold concrete, I warmed myself with the exertion. I worked fast, afraid of the time factor and of the work involved. Wet the ground, round and round with brush and sandsoap, mop it up, wipe it dry. Hurry! There's the teas and the dining-room and breakfast waiting for you! With energy, spurred by fear, these duties were accomplished. The porridge free of lumps and the only casualty, a broken cup, carefully stored in the rubbish tin. The thing was to get on with it and look forward to the end of it.

One can usually find something to look forward to, and in my case it was Friday — *pay day*. Keeping this firmly in mind, I found the monotonous days passed. Mrs Burgess's countenance became a little more unbeautiful as each morning she gave me the drill — and sometimes, the works.

'Mary, did you scrub the yard this morning?'

'Yes, Mrs Burgess.'

'The scrubbing brush is dry. I do not care for liars. I like to see that concrete *white*. Plenty of sandsoap and elbowgrease are needed. I cannot keep a girl who is lazy and tells lies.'

'I'm sorry, Mrs Burgess — it was the porridge boiling over and then it was time for your tea.'

'No excuse.'

I hang my head, suitably intimidated.

'Well now, today is drawing-room and ironing day. We will have stuffed chickens, potatoes, baked and boiled, pumpkin and peas tonight. The sweet will be apple pie.'

(Time she re-dyed her hair; I can see the grey at the roots.)

'When you have finished the house, and turned out the drawing-room, hall and stairs, let me know, and I'll inspect your work. Pay particular attention to the corners.'

'Yes, Mrs Burgess.'

'Oh, and have you a little black frock?'

'No, Mrs Burgess.'

'Well, you will need to get one. I like the girl to look smart to answer the door in the afternoons. I supply the caps and aprons, which you'll find in that drawer. Put them on after lunch today.'

Thank God she's finished and I can get on with the drill — daily routine, as she calls it. As if the daily sweeping, dusting, cooking and dishwashing weren't enough, each day brings its extra tasks — one for the morning and one for the afternoon.

The Legend printed on the wall in the kitchen reads:

MON.	A.M. Kitchen and dining-room
	P.M. Washing
TUE.	A.M. Drawing-room, hall and stairs
	P.M. Ironing

WED.	A.M.	Master bedroom and Miss June's bedroom
	P.M.	Afternoon off duty
THURS.	A.M.	Mr John's room, Mr Richardson's room and Mr Evan's room
	P.M.	Brass
FRI.	A.M.	Bathroom and laundry
	P.M.	Silver
SAT.	A.M.	Windows upstairs
	P.M.	Windows downstairs
SUN.		No extra duties
		Alternate Sunday afternoons off duty.

There it is, compiled either by an incurable optimist or the operator of a ten-horsepower automaton. Still, I've survived so far.

The Master is heavily henpecked and beyond a 'Good-morning, Mary', doesn't interfere with me in any way. I don't like the daughter, June, but she scarcely needs my regard — she's so much in love with herself. She looks like her father, but I suspect she's her mother's daughter. I wouldn't mind some of her clothes though, and her dressing-table is covered with all kinds of exciting make-up. Wouldn't mind borrowing some for my afternoon off.

Her brother John ignored me at first, but last night he smiled sweetly at me and said. 'You've a stunning figure, Mary.' Then he pinched my behind. Luckily he heard his mother coming and went quickly out the front door. I'll have to be careful of that young man.

The 'friends of the family', Mr Evans and Mr Richardson, are boarders, I've discovered. I read an unfinished letter in Mr Richardson's room. It had a bit about me. 'Mrs B. has a new maid. She's a well-built girl, plenty of bosom and hips. I don't think she'll last long — none of them do. She's a bit bouncy and servants should be unobtrusive. I hope to be out of here myself soon, I can't stand much more of Mrs B.'

Valuable, but hardly complimentary information, and reading letters on the sly won't get my work done and today is Tuesday and we're having guests for dinner. Think about tomorrow, Wednesday, half a day out of this prison and soon there'll be Friday. *Pay Day*. After that, only a week to go and it'll be all over.

It looks at the moment as if it's going to be all over all too soon. I've lost the chooks! Old Queen Elizabeth (that's what I call her — I must have seen a picture of the aged queen somewhere) put them out on the bench for me, and covered them with a teatowel. Her idea of 'helping the girl'. Here's the teatowel on the floor, there's the plate on the bench. But no chooks! She's gone out, so I can't ask her. Frantic opening of all the cupboards and then the safe reveals no chooks. Perhaps the milkman pinched them — no, he came before she put them out. Panic — despair. Noise outside — a nasty yapping little dog

— what's he got in his mouth? A chicken! Christopher Columbus! I'll wring his neck like a chicken when I get him.

He doesn't respond to my intimidation. I'm puffed out with chasing him and now the rotten animal has crawled under the house, complete with chicken.

The tears fall as I lie on my belly and peer among the piles at Mrs Nextdoor's pedigree pekinese — in my opinion the mangiest cur ever whelped.

'Here boy! Good boy! Come on, good dog, nice doggie. Come here.' Translate: 'Bloody mongrel — come here and I'll kill you.' He doesn't move and the chicken lies before him. He wags his tail.

'Good dog, here boy, come on.'

The so-and-so doesn't budge.

And then the incredible happens. Another dog, of vague ancestry, appears with No. 2 chicken in his mouth. He lifts his head, sniffs and drops the chicken, then nose down proceeds to the vicinity of No. 1 dog. Hastily I retrieve the bird — Vague Ancestry is no longer interested in it. 'Yap, yap, yap.' They're both at it — Pekinese rushes out and a good old rough and tumble ensues. Lovely! Under the house goes Mary the maid — victory!

My cosmetic skill on those dead bodies would be the envy of any undertaker. The dinner was cooked to perfection and served with triumph. However, when the bell rang for me to collect my plate to eat in the solitude of the kitchen, it contained no chicken. Oh well, the inquest will be held in the morning and she'll have her theory — but she'll never know the truth.

Pay day was a bitter disappointment. I should have been prepared. The preliminary lecture did nothing to sweeten the hour.

'Good morning, Mary.'

'Good morning, Mrs Burgess.'

'You have been with us one week now, and you are proving to be not entirely satisfactory. The yard is discoloured, showing that you haven't scrubbed it thoroughly; there are traces of egg stains on the forks, it looks as if you skimped on their cleaning; Mr John tells me that yesterday he found crumbs in his bed, which indicates that you just pulled it up instead of stripping it. In short, your work attitude is not good. On the other hand, your cooking is passable and on this count I am prepared to give you another week's trial, during which time I hope to see a considerable improvement.

'Here's your money, we'll have the corned beef and carrots and cabbage tonight, followed by a steamed pudding.'

With these remarks, she puts some money on the table and departs.

I just look at it. Five miserable bloody bob — made up of small denominations to boot — church money, no doubt. The B.B.! I'm working for an education and I'm learning fast. My school friends get this much a week for pocket money and I've worked from 5.30 a.m. till 7.30 p.m. daily for the same amount. Never understood the Bible. 'Unto every one that hath shall be given, but from him that hath not shall be taken away, even that which he hath.' The understanding has come, but the justice eludes me.

I want to lie on my bed and cry, cry for myself and the home that died with my mother, cry because everyone I know has the love and security I've lost. What's the use, I'm a big girl and nobody cares. That's it! Nobody cares (blub, blub). But *I* care, and am I going to howl once again like a child? Or am I going to face the hard economic facts of life? Wash your face and go and see what you can do about it. She's in the lavatory — wait in the hall — there's the cistern running. Out she comes.

'Mrs Burgess . . .'

Ever imperious, she is not embarrassed.

'Wait, Mary, till I wash my hands.'

The small delay finds my courage ebbing.

'Yes, Mary?'

'My wages, Mrs Burgess, I thought . . .'

She interrupts. 'I left you five shillings, that is correct. You are barely worth seven and sixpence a week. Two and sixpence is, of course, for the agency. As I explained earlier, you'll have to do better in the future if you wish to be retained. Are you clear on this?'

'Yes, Mrs Burgess.'

'Is that all?'

'Yes, Mrs Burgess. Thank you, Mrs Burgess.'

'Well, hurry along with your work now.'

Defeated, disconsolate and dismissed, I return to the sink, forlorn. The dishes stretch before me, inanimate, symbolic.

PAULINE O'REGAN

Above all, simple and joyous

The novitiate lasted for two years. We were to strive to become humble, obedient, prayerful and hard-working, and our Mistress of Novices was there to help us. Printed on the wall in the novitiate room was a list of the virtues that were to be the hallmark of a Sister of Mercy. At the end of the impressive list was written, 'Above all, simple and joyous'. There was great emphasis on simplicity. I had always thought that to be called simple was denigrating, but now, in this new world, with its new values and new language, the word 'simple' was one of high praise. It meant just being who you were — no airs, no playing games. It meant having a readiness to acknowledge one's faults and to cheerfully accept having them pointed out to you. It meant walking the tightrope between acknowledging one's gifts and strengths without being 'vainglorious'. It meant getting praise sometimes, where you least expected it, because you had acted simply. There was a lot to learn . . .

Simplicity might be the most desirable virtue, but it was humility and obedience that were to get the most practice. Mother Aquin believed that humility was best acquired through humiliation. We gave her plenty of ammunition. One thing that all novices did was to break a quite alarming number and variety of objects. Cups slipped through our fingers, plates hit the floor of their own volition, light bulbs expired at our touch, door handles came away in our hands. We carried out most of our duties with a dangerous combination of earnestness and speed and, as much of our time was spent washing dishes, we broke them — endlessly. We whittled away at the convent delft with a saucer today, a cup tomorrow and a plate the next day. Now and again we cleaned out entire dinner sets in one hit. A novice, running against time with a huge armful of plates for the boarders' dining-room, would trip or slip or execute some complex footwork that sent her off-balance, and she'd drop the lot.

Every breakage had to be 'acknowledged' and Mother Aquin would act as though some plot were afoot to ruin the convent and bring it to bankruptcy. You never defended yourself. There was simply no circumstance where it was appropriate to offer an excuse. Our model was Jesus before Pontius Pilate, and the words, 'Jesus was silent' were the ones quoted for our imitation. Needless to say, every breakage was an accident but woe betide the novice who said so. It was customary to 'show up' only one piece from a given breakage and the smallest piece always seemed the best choice. How big was this plate, Sister? There were three of them, Mother.

The other novices were sisters in every sense. The bond created by so much shared experience was deep and loving. We listened to one another's woes, helped one another out in our work, comforted, laughed, cried and gave full vent to our feelings with complete safety. We were never in competition with one another. Ambition was non-existent. There was a minimum of pettiness. We somehow realised that for any one of us to come through that kind of test, we had to have the support and help of others and to give it in return. I've heard men speak in similar terms of the war.

To speak of war is to remember that while all this was happening in my life, there was a war going on. It was the early 1940s and New Zealanders were fighting and dying in North Africa, Italy and the Pacific. We knew nothing of what was going on. We were in a kind of monastic desert cut off from the world. The only reminder we had of the awful presence of war came from the blackout on all the convent windows. The building was three storeys high and had windows everywhere. Each one had to be blacked out every night to wipe Timaru off the map of any passing enemy.

The vow of obedience at that time meant handing over your life in many ways to the direction of a Superior. It was regarded as an act of abandonment of self of the highest spiritual order. From my early days in the novitiate a certain phrase had captured my imagination. It seemed to be spoken of in almost hushed tones, and was known as 'blind obedience'. We heard about it from a book that was read to us at lecture time each day. It was a very old book with thin yellow pages. The author was a Jesuit by the name of Rodriguez and his writings had an enormous effect on generations of religious men and women. It seemed that a Superior could ask anything, no matter how apparently crazy, and the good religious person would carry it out promptly and without question — in other words, with blind obedience. I was fascinated. Each day I prepared myself for the test, quite sure that the Mistress of Novices would 'try' me sooner rather than later. I had no idea then that, while these lofty ideals were constantly held up to us, in practice our Superiors acted with considerable common sense. The example of blind obedience given by Rodriguez was that of a humble lay brother who was planting cabbages when his Superior, to test his obedience, told him to plant them upside-down. He promptly did this and they grew into beautiful large cabbages. I longed with burning zeal to get the opportunity to plant cabbages upside-down.

One day we were all walking down to the orchard to pick fruit at recreation time. Everyone was laughing and talking and I was walking along beside Mother Aquin. Suddenly I heard her say, 'Stand there!' I froze. This was it. There was no reason for the direction. I could make no sense of it. It must mean she was trying me to see if I could practise blind obedience. I stood, rooted to the spot. I could hear the others all talking and laughing as they picked the fruit. Finally, a novice came running back to get more boxes for the apples. She looked at me in amazement. 'I wondered where you were. Whatever are you doing?' I was near to tears. I explained what Mother had said. The novice was quite certain I wasn't supposed to be there, but I wouldn't budge. It was blind obedience or bust. When she joined the others she told Mother Aquin. She says you told her to stand there. It was nonsense! She'd said no such thing! I was sent for immediately. At last she remembered looking across to the back door of the convent and remarking, 'There's a man there.' I didn't always pick up her Irish accent and besides, I was waiting to get a direction that didn't make sense. I tried to explain. She was singularly unimpressed. As she talked, it began to dawn on me that you didn't take everything from the lecture book too literally. Obviously, my Superiors would be satisfied if I managed to do what I was asked with a good grace and as well as I could. I could forget the cabbages.

The vow of chastity was considered to be very personal to the religious and, in those days, we had a very inadequate theology of it. Since the Vatican Council of the 1960s it has been more appropriately termed celibacy, and a full and human theology has been developed of its place in community life. Today I see it as the keystone of religious life, but that understanding came only with the passing of the years. In the 1940s and 1950s it was an individual counsel that the religious lived but spoke little about. The poor theology of the time tended to place this vow in the area of expediency and it was seen as a way of freeing us from family ties so that we could give our whole attention to the work of the church.

In my novitiate years, our mentors had little to say about the vow of chastity, but they suffered no such reticence about the vow of poverty. Poverty was seen as a detachment from all worldly things, and it meant possessing nothing but the bare essentials. We had to be ready to give up, promptly and cheerfully, anything we had at any given moment. Language was very important. For instance, we never used the possessive pronoun. We spoke of 'the pen to my use, the shoes to my use, the singlets to my use'. It was amazing how quickly I began using such idiom quite naturally, and I remembered my sister's startled response when I unconsciously referred to 'the hankie to my use' during a visit.

Twice a year, we had the 'wants'. This meant making a list of things that you needed and submitting it to the Mistress of Novices with the appropriate evidence. Mother Aquin would examine a pair of stockings that I thought had fully expired, comment on the quality of the darning and weigh up whether they could take another darn over the one that had worn through. Mostly, she thought they could. Singlets were darned with white thread until they were too threadbare to support another stitch. New cuffs were knitted for cardigans, veils were patched so well as to defy perception, and habits were repleated to hide the parts that had worn thin. For some nuns this repair work was an art form. Even the less gifted, like me, reached a level of needlework skill that was amazing. The custom of 'wants' lists and collective buying went on until the late 1960s. The professed nuns were not subjected to such stringent examinations as the novices. To some extent the process depended on the Superior concerned — some were generous, some were tight.

Once during novitiate several of us were given a new pair of shoes. They had the dubious merit of being both cheap and from the first batch of shoes ever made in New Zealand. Undoubtedly, the leather had been on the cow's back a month before they were made. It was hard, inflexible and had a distinct greenish tinge. All this could be borne if they had not also had the most extraordinary squeak. We tried to walk on our heels, on the sides of our feet, on our toes. It was no use. Every step we took resulted in a long, drawn-out, embarrassing squee-ee-eek. We rubbed huge amounts of lard into the resisting leather, we packed them with wet newspaper to make them stretch, we bent them back and forth until cracks appeared, we prayed over them! But the squeak seemed to have a life of its own. It did subside eventually, and the shoes did settle down. Meantime, they had served an important function for their wearers. They had promoted our humility — through humiliation.

We were constantly reminded that there was little use in practising poverty if we did not grow in its spirit. It was pointless to voluntarily give up owning things, if we yearned for them or resented not having them. Little by little, we came to experience the serenity and freedom that comes with not caring unduly about material possessions.

I later came to realise that the poverty of the religious life was not as simple as it had seemed. Individual poverty is something that most religious people have practised faithfully and well over the years, but now, in the name of justice, we have been forced to look at the complex and demanding responsibility of corporate poverty. We can no longer easily rationalise that, because personal poverty has been faithfully honoured, there can be a place for collective wealth in the church and religious orders.

The spiritual exercises that the Sisters did each day comprised: celebration of Mass, forty minutes meditation, saying the Office, reciting the Rosary, making the Stations of the Cross and doing personal spiritual reading. There was also an exercise called 'particular examen'. This was commonly called the 'quarter' because it took quarter of an hour. You took one fault or weakness that you had perceived in yourself, or that someone else had pointed out, and you examined your day accordingly. You prayed for help to see yourself honestly, noted where you had failed, repented of it, expressed regret and worked out how you could, with God's help, deal with it in the next twenty-four hours. When this was done, the remainder of the quarter was spent in prayer.

Most of our days were governed by silence. It was a novitiate rule that, even on a recreation day, there had to be three novices present before you spoke. I have wondered since about the reasoning behind this practice and I think it must have been seen as a way of preventing 'excessive' friendships between any two nuns. We had to be all things to everyone, and it was frowned on to have what in convent language was called a 'particular friendship'. Wherever a special friendship became evident, it was always pointed out to the Sisters concerned. This created guilt, or prevented what could have been good, healthy friendships. It was particularly hard on those who flourished in one-to-one relationships. But, it also prevented any exclusiveness or snobbery and the growth of unhealthy cliques in the community.

There's no doubt that the older, wiser people also knew that lesbianism could enter convent life by subtle paths and some of these rules would have had this in mind. But it was never spoken of. The rule of silence took on a particular importance at night, and the time from the night prayer bell to the call bell next morning, was known as 'the great silence'. It was broken only when absolutely necessary and was seen as a time for deep recollection and prayer.

In the refectory we sat at narrow tables arranged in a U-shape. The Reverend Mother and her Council sat at the top table, with the Sisters facing one another along the sides. Each Sister took it in turn to serve the others at the table. When you were server, you donned a long white apron and put on white cuffs to the elbow. It was your duty to see that the food was served quickly and was accessible to everyone.

Those who served on tables also had to read to the community. Most often we read from books entitled *Annals of the Sisters of Mercy*. I loved these books. They told the story, through letters and essays, of the Sisters of Mercy going to set up the Order in the United States, South and Central America, Canada and England. All these stories, while simple and factual, revealed women of courage, faith and amazing resourcefulness. Most of all, I loved the Annals of Ireland which told of the foundation of the Order itself and of a warm, humorous and highly intelligent woman called Catherine McAuley, who, in spite of all the obstacles that men placed in her path, established the Order of Mercy in Dublin in 1831. Ten years after her death in 1841, the Sisters of Mercy had spread right throughout the United

States, to England, South America, and even Australia and New Zealand. In 1850 the first sisters of Mercy arrived in Auckland to begin life in a raw young colony. My heart used to burn within me as I munched my meals.

On the last Wednesday of every month was an exercise known in the convent simply as 'last Wednesday'. Its more chastening name was 'Chapter of Faults'. The idea was that each Sister acknowledged her faults before the assembled community. In our case, a prie-dieu was placed in the centre of the chapel and each Sister knelt on it and said, 'I accuse myself of all the faults I have committed in the discharge of my duties especially for . . . and I beg pardon of God and the prayers of the Sisters.'

This custom had been practised for centuries in religious orders. In effect it was saying that every Sister, from the oldest to the youngest, from the Reverend Mother to the newest novice, stood in need of the community's forgiveness. We were all sinners, and in this exercise we implicitly assured one another that there were no exceptions. In its original form the Chapter of Faults might well have given the members of a community the opportunity to reveal themselves to those they trusted and it could have brought the healing awareness that everyone has weakness and faults. But such sharing calls for a small, close-knit community. As communities grew to numbers of thirty and forty, this ideal gave way to a formal procedure that did not allow for real sharing.

For me, it was a nightmare. On the last Wednesday we knelt beside Mother Aquin and told her what we wished to acknowledge that evening. There were the times we were late for Grace before meals, for Office, for recreation. There were the neglects of duty: we didn't lock the parlour windows one night, we forgot to collect a sick Sister's tray, we left the lights on in the attics . . . The scope for possible neglects of duty was unbelievably wide. And always, each month, there were the breakages. I was not a scrupulous neophite. On the whole I only mentioned those things that were already public knowledge and which I felt were quite sufficient to convince the community that I was a sinner badly in need of tolerance and forgiveness.

Every day in the novitiate we spent twenty-five minutes reading from the 'Guide'. There was several of these books and they contained guidelines to be observed in our daily duties. They were like large exercise books and had all been hand-written. The writing was of an earlier style and it changed as different writers took it up. As I read, I often wondered who had written those pages for me. Some of them were written forty or fifty years before, and the pages were well-worn and thin. We, in our turn, wrote up pages of the 'Guide' for future generations of novices, copying carefully what had been passed on to us. Typing and photocopying are certainly more efficient, but they do not give the sense of continuity, the sense of being in touch with someone in the past, that those carefully hand-written books did. The assumption was, of course, that things would never change. The guidelines were for Sisters of Mercy in every decade. It was not considered that new guidelines might need to be drawn up for new times. New wineskins for new wine. That disturbing challenge was not to come until the 1960s and the Second Vatican Council of the Catholic church. If Mother McAuley were to return, we were told, she was to recognise the Sister of Mercy by the tone of her voice, the quietness of her step, by her Mercy habit, her spirit of recollection and many other things that had been dear to her. It never occurred to anyone that, while keeping their essential spirit, Mother McAuley would have adapted and changed many of these customs to suit the vastly different times and places that the Sisters now lived in.

COLLEEN BROWN
(As told to Sandra Coney)

A few problems being the only girl

I wouldn't call it a class. It's like I'm an alien and they're the humans. Like I'm from outer space, that's how I'm treated. You know, stupid comments, and I get picked on all the time. There are ten guys and me in Telecom and all the guys stick together. See, when one guy starts the others join in.

Last term some time I was talking about how people shouldn't be racist. There were these two dark guys in my class and they all went against my opinion. Even these guys who were dark themselves, they hated their own race and they wouldn't stick up for me, just because I was a girl. They wanted to stay on the side of their mates because they were boys. I think if I was a boy they'd have stuck up for me.

One day when I was doing work in the library this boy Mike helped me, but when we went back to the classroom, he went back to being horrible again. If a guy does stick up for me and says 'Leave her alone. You're always picking on her', they say, 'Oh, so you love her now. Is she your new girlfriend?' or 'Are you two going to get married?'

When I started to get better marks the guys started calling me a cheat. They don't realise that I swot and do my work and they don't. But then I have to *prove* that I don't cheat. That really got me down. They can't face a woman actually doing better than them and that's why they give me hell.

The things they do to me . . . like I walked into the classroom once and the only seat left was next to Robert, he's a real troublemaker. I thought, I don't want to sit there, but I had to because it was the only seat. Then he said 'What are *you* sitting there for? I don't want you next to me!' and he tried to push me off the chair. So I pushed him back and said 'Fuck off!' Then all the guys said 'We never knew women could use such foul language!' I said 'I use foul language on men who make me mad.' Then they all said 'Go away! We don't want you with us. Women always cause trouble.' So I got up and walked out and I never went to English, and then I got into trouble for not going to English. The teacher wouldn't believe it wasn't my fault.

Last term I was going to pack it in. I couldn't hack it any longer. I had a real big crisis in the classroom. The teacher went out and they really started picking on me, they took my books and were chucking them round the room. I got really mad and upset and walked out of the room and told my course supervisor. He was really pissed off and he went and talked to them. The only time I get respect is from my teachers. But I was still thinking of quitting. I went home and I was looking through the newspaper, looking for just a normal job, when my tutor rang. He said he thought really highly of me and not to give it up. He told me if it happened again to go and tell him. They quietened down a bit after than, but they still give me hell.

Are you with the same boys all day?
In some of the classes I'm with different kids. Like in maths I'm with a different bunch of guys, but they still hassle me. The maths teacher did something wrong and I was trying to tell him and they were saying 'Be quiet! Women don't know anything. Women don't know maths.' They make remarks like that all the time.

In electronics one day my circuit board exploded, it went all black. They all laughed, but it wasn't my fault the thing exploded, the element went out. But they said 'Typical woman!' and 'I told you women can't do this.' I didn't say anything, though I was really mad . . .

Because they'd get at you again . . .
Or they'd give me a hiding. Like one guy was going to give me a hiding once and I was really scared. I disagreed with him about something and he said 'Now you're really asking for it!' and he went like this to me (Colleen screws up the neck of her tee-shirt). I was really scared because all the guys started going against me and saying things like 'Why don't you get out of here. We don't want you in this class.' I feel so much out of place in that class.

So although the teachers are supportive they don't see this going on?
No, they only do it when the teachers aren't there. That's why I started going late to class, then I got told off for being late. But I'd rather come late so the teacher is there.

Is this course something you really looked forward to doing?
My father does electronics and all my life since I was about five, since my mother died, my father used to work under the house on his electronics and we used to get lonely in the house so we'd go and play with it. When I was in the third form I was doing typing and bookkeeping but the other girls said how boring it is sitting and typing in an office all day. I wanted to do something really good and my father said 'Why don't you do electronics?' I thought that sounded good and they told me go to ATI.

When I talked to the man at the ATI he made me feel better because he said they wanted women to come into those courses and he said something about women's rights. I didn't know there was such a thing as women's rights, I didn't know what he was going on about. He said 'I believe in women's lib' and I said 'What's that?' Now I know what he was talking about. He was talking about a girl can do what she wants. I just came and did it and he accepted me because my marks were good enough.

When I started I thought the guys would be more mature, I thought they'd treat me like another class member not a space creature. They're so rude too. I can't tell you what they do, they're really filthy.

Do they try and touch you?
Yeah, all the bloody time. When I'm sitting on a stool they'll come and pinch my backside. I say 'Piss off' because I don't want them to do it to me. They just try to stir me up. They're filthy too. They've got calculators and they can make them say things like . . . I don't know. I can't say it . . . things like 'boobs'. They'll put it in front of me and say 'Read it, Colleen'. And I have to read it. They say to me 'Do you wear a bra, Colleen?' and they come and feel down my back to see if I have one on. Sometimes they feel my leg to see if I've got pants on under my jeans. One day I had a wrap-around skirt on and they undid it. I could feel it all loose. It could have fallen down in the middle of the corridor in front of all the guys.

Are there no other girls in your classes?
There's a girl in English, but she's real quiet. The guys hassle her too and she lets them, she doesn't stick up for herself, even though I can tell she hates it. There was one girl doing civil engineering but she's already left. The guys were also hassling her because she was Maori. She was the only girl and the only dark person. They'd say things that really hurt her inside and now she's gone. We used to get on really good.

Can you talk to your father about what happens?
When I told him about that crisis I had, he went on their side. He said I must be to blame, he said I must eye them up and give them looks. He went mad at *me!* My sister sticks up for me, she's really good. She said 'I could just kill those guys in your class.' She's fifteen. I don't really talk to my brothers, they're so lazy!

They leave me and my sister to do all the housework. I said to one brother 'I do men's work as well as women's work, so why can't you too. You should do the vacuuming.' He just turned around and said 'Are you mad?' It reminded me of the guys in my class. They just get out of everything, me and my sister, we're just like slaves.

Do you think the guys at ATI are really threatened by you?
About four weeks ago I got a letter through the mail from a guy doing Civil Engineering and he threatened me with rape, just before my exams. He's a male chauvinist and he just can't face girls being there. I used to sort of know him and then he kept hassling me and a friend who's doing secretarial. I got pissed off because he called us lesbians in front of all the class. I rang him up at home and said 'Leave me alone, stop hassling me' and then I put down the phone. I wanted nothing more to do with him, but he kept on annoying me. He just wanted me to flunk all my exams so he'd be right that women can't do a man's work. He can't face that I'm doing well in my work. He says there must be something wrong, a woman can't gain marks like that.

I showed the letter to the guys in my class and that's the first time they really respected me. They said 'Colleen, you shouldn't muck around with that, you should take it to the police.' I took it to the police, they said they'd contact me and they haven't, so he's getting away with it. And he said he would rape me, he said it to all the guys too.

Did you see anyone at ATI about it?
I told my course supervisor and he was really mad. He said that guy must be really sick. He said don't worry Colleen, just think about your work. I told the counsellor man but he said he can't make the guy talk to him, the guy's got to come to the counsellor. So they did nothing.

I've felt like quitting all year. Right from the first day when I walked into the classroom and they looked at me in this terrible way. I've decided not to come back next year. I've made an application to Television New Zealand to do a course in Wellington and then when I've done that I could carry on with stage four of Telecom. Then I'd have two qualifications. I felt welcomed when I got the application form from television because it was male or female. A lot of jobs say just male and I think 'Oh, that must not be for me.' I just can't face going back to ATI next year to the same group of guys. It just goes on all day. You see they think hassling me is a joke. Hassling me is one big joke. But it's not for me, it's just horrible.

REBECCA JOHNSTON

Young, Female and Unemployed

The queue took the form of a row about twelve vinyl chairs long. Arranged so they faced the door. Each chair was silently occupied. Some, embarrassed by the enforced eye contact with people passing outside, stared at the floor.

Others scrutinised those who came through the door, and wandered around vaguely till a chair became vacant.

Walking through the door and seeing those chairs like twelve formidable judges, was like passing through a force-field. One that stripped you of any personal characteristics and turned you into just one in the mass of unemployed.

Being in a queue usually gives me a feeling of excitement; waiting before a concert, toying with the idea of not getting in. Or even waiting to go into the pictures and feeling the electric cord of impatience in everyone around me. I think that's what I noticed first when I walked into the Labour Exchange; the familiarity between that queue and waiting to see the dentist. No-one is naive enough to give up her place, but no-one wants to go up to the interview desk from whence waft the nasal tones of the interviewer:

'Well, John, you haven't had a job for six months, and you're — how old did you say?'

It was funny how you never heard the interviewee's reply, but the interviewer was always kind enough to repeat it for us: 'Twenty-three, did you say, John?'

You can pretend you're not listening to the interviewer, but everyone knows that everyone else is listening in case it could give some possible advantage to your own interview.

At this point some of the braver people began to scrutinise the situations vacant columns, although we all knew secretly that no jobs were left by eleven o'clock in the morning. Some of the weaker ones even smoked. Hadn't they considered the interviewer's prominent signs of 'No Smoking'. Now the interviewers would hide all the possible jobs for a nervous wreck at the back of the leather files.

God! I began to search my own mind for some screamingly obvious blotch. I knew my hair was a mess, my trousers too casual. I'd even forgotten to put on a double dose of deodorant that morning, so I'd reek before I made it through those eleven other chairs. I wondered if they have some secret criteria for judging you worthy of employment. 'Anyone under five foot six must be disregarded on the basis of having an inferiority complex.' 'Anyone over six foot three doesn't need help to get a job — they could be anything from a basketball player to a policeman.' Maybe if you looked right, if you were between eighteen and thirty, were between five foot six and six foot two (to be on the safe side), had a muscular or trim physique, excelled at rugby or kept an autographed photo of John Walker next to your bed, you'd be considered as material for being employed.

Where did that leave me, at seventeen and five foot three? I even liked soccer better than rugby, and last but not least of my faults, a Paul McCartney poster is all that's by my bed. It was a wonder, when you think about it, that I was actually allowed to sit in the row.

It was painful in the short term to think like this, but better in the long run, for if I didn't get a job it would be because my outer appearance had rubbed the interviewer up the wrong way. I didn't get the 'Sorry, luv, we've just taken someone on' job because they did not like short or freckled or blue-eyed people. Not actually me, they didn't dislike the me; the real me; they didn't have the chance.

I took a look at the man next to me. He was an average looking man. Brown hair, brown eyes, nothing particularly distinguishing about him. No reason why he shouldn't get a job. He was quite old I suppose to be on the dole, or just unemployed. Most men my father's age seemed to be pretty firmly entangled in their firm's best interests, even to the point of refusing to bow out gracefully at the regulation age of sixty-five. Still, it must be easier when you're older, you have had the experience, you're more confident in your capabilities, you can handle it better emotionally. As if to prove my thoughts, the man about my father's age turned and laughed about the performance of changing seats in the queue. It was as if an invisible string pulled all of our faces into a comical grimace each time we had the inconvenience of standing up, moving to the left a pace, and sitting down again.

Then something unfair happened. Something definitely unfair and highly unacceptable to the brittle frame of mind we in the queue collectively shared. Someone stepped straight through the doorway, passed the surveillance barrier, ignored the brown vinyl seats and sat straight in the interviewee seat.

The man next to me half rose in protest, then sat down realising that the fuss caused wouldn't be worth it. Some of us had waited a whole frustrating hour, but it would only mean a few minutes longer to wait. It didn't really matter . . . or so I thought.

The man about my father's age shifted in his chair, his face showed all the self-doubt and fear unemployment brings. 'You bastard!' he murmured to the air.

Then it hit me. Being unemployed isn't an embarrassing game. It's ruthless. Me against you, and for Christ's sake let me win. Being unemployed is something more than feeling humiliated at waiting in rows, having to fill out uncompromising forms about your qualifications or lack of them, having to lie about your age. It's a gut feeling about your own worth. Those worthy of respect, position and financial reward have jobs. So what does that make me?

I did eventually make it up to the desk, but I think the mole on my left arm put them off because that leather file would not part with a job for me, and I left with a feeling of relief to be out of the queue. I decided to wear high shoes next time.

MARGARET SUTHERLAND

A life's occupation

On wet days the smell of the library was different. Damp air crept among the books and the everyday polish-and-ink essence was overlaid then with another scent, hygienic and faintly woody, like a place where joss-sticks had once burned. It was on wet days that Clodagh imagined herself enclosed in a kind of temple whose silence was enhanced by the sounds of wind and rain outside.

Few subscribers in this ageing district ventured out in bad weather. Those who came seemed to sense the reverent atmosphere and went about the selection of books silently, somehow subdued and in a huddle beneath waterproof blacks and greys. Perhaps they were merely discomforted by the drips they shed on the brown linoleum, but there were few conversations as cards were removed from pockets and books presented for stamping at the desk. On wet days the business was carried out without delay, as though the people, like dutiful church-goers intent on getting their Sunday duty attended to, were anxious to be away to the comfort of homely kitchens and cooking aromas. Coughs would break out and be supressed somewhere in the catacomb-mazes of shelves, and that too served to put Clodagh in mind of a church: though a disused church visited for the service its history could provide, a place where the air of worship lingered but to which the real worshippers no longer came.

Someone before Clodagh's time had made an effort to cheer up the staff-room. The floor was a chessboard of red and white lino tiles, stamped with the twenty-year sum of stiletto heel-blows. When Clodagh came in, Nance Parker and Dorrie Figbody were there already, aligned like fireside chairs beside the fan heater.

'Pull up a chair.' Nance shunted hers, fractionally. 'Blooming cold, that's all I can say. Tea's poured.'

'Mind, dear.' Dorrie came in on cue. 'Yours is the cracked one.' It was established, this Pass-the-Old-Maid game with the cracked cup; common property like the other shared habits of years; the joint Art Union tickets, the cream cakes all round on birthdays. The game might have lost its edge through overplaying. Yet if the authorities had seen fit to issue a replacement set of staff china they would have felt deprived.

'We were trying to decide,' said Dorrie, who always brought

latecomers up to date, perhaps because she rarely said anything that could not be shared, 'which would be worse, cremation or burial. I say being buried; what do you think, Clodagh?'

'Cremation's quicker.' To judge by the brew, Nance was on Teas; which also meant there would be no spare hot water left in the jug.

'I've heard it takes longer than you might think to do the job.' Nance's general knowledge extended to strange subjects, and they could not challenge her for she had a way of sounding incontradictably right.

'I wouldn't fancy that,' Dorrie said. 'How awful. Perhaps the old way's better then. Though I've never liked the idea of coffins. Imagine if you weren't really dead; all the knocking and the knocking, and no-one being able to hear you. At least you'd be sure if you were done the other way.'

'She should write horror stories.' Nance edged a wink in Clodagh's direction. ' "Slowly the knocking began again, and as they watched in the half-light the lid of the coffin suddenly . . ." '

'Oh no, Nance,' cried Dorrie. 'Oh don't.'

'You love it,' Nance suggested. 'I've seen you, when you didn't know anyone was looking, sneaking books out of the Horror section.'

'I don't, do I, Clodagh?' Dorrie appealingly knitted bony hands above the over-long skirt she wore to cover the legacy of poliomyelitis. The days when immunity could be administered by needle had come too late for Dorrie Figbody, who now fast travelling the ageing cycle was compensating by a retreat into the mannerisms of girlhood, which mainly served, like the skirts, to draw attention to the facts they were intended to conceal.

'Anyone doing anything interesting over the weekend?' Nance did not pause for breath, that being one of those questions to which no answer was expected. 'I know my plans anyway; tidy the place, do the washing, and then look forward to the pleasure of my own company. Did you know someone pinched the gear-knob out of my car last night? They make you wonder these days, they really do.'

'Perhaps it was someone who had mislaid their own gear-knob?' ventured Dorrie.

'Very likely,' Nance said. 'It's the sort of thing one loses every day after all.'

Sarcasm withered Dorrie. Clodagh intervened.

'How's your family of cats, Dorrie?'

'Oh dear, Clodagh; we're nine now. Another one arrived yesterday. You'd wonder how they know, wouldn't you? They say animals aren't intelligent, at least some people say so.' Dorrie looked at Nance.

'Saucers of fish are an open invitation, I'd say.'

'But Nance,' said Dorrie earnestly, 'I can't leave them to go hungry. I mean, can I?'

Nance shrugged. 'Apparently not.'

'They keep coming. What can you do? They're so grateful, oh Clodagh, I wish you could see them, the way they put up their little paws as if they're trying to say thank you . . .'

'I believe you,' said Nance. 'How's your young boarder, Clodagh? Still with you?'

'Oh, yes.'

'How's it working out? I thought she was only staying a few days?'

'Slight change of plan. I rather enjoy having someone else around the house actually.'

'And your beau?' Only Dorrie would be able to consider Leo in that light. 'Isn't he jealous?'

'Why should he be?'

'Men are funny,' said Dorrie wisely. 'They like to feel they're the only ones on the home ground.'

'In that case he ought to do something about it,' suggested Nance.

'You mustn't hurry these young men; don't listen to her, Clodagh,' advised Dorrie, most of whose reading matter came not from the Horror section but the Romance Rentals, 'or you'll frighten him away.'

'That's up to Leo,' said Clodagh, with less kindness than she'd intended.

'Give me my bed and a good book.'

'You're only as old as you feel, Nance,' said Dorrie.

'Then I'm a hundred and fifty.' Nance, smiling, looked for a moment less grim.

'Anyway . . .' Dorrie steered the conversation to lines she preferred. 'I think your young man's very nice, Clodagh.'

'Hardly young, Dorrie.'

'Of course he's young!' Youth was an engagement whose deadline Dorrie was willing to extend; she had once spent five minutes talking to Leo on the steps of the library while he waited for Clodagh to finish work, and did not intend to let anyone forget it. 'He's a mere boy!'

Clodagh smiled. She would tell Leo. It would please him.

'Actually,' she said. 'I'm meeting him tomorrow.'

Dorrie, who could be relied on to extract the maximum potential from such a remark, beamed.

'Oh, that is nice! Going anywhere special?'

'I doubt it,' said Clodagh. She had tried to make Leo see that uncertainty was not her way of doing things. He did not often indicate his plans in advance, and that she might have found less annoying if she had had the choice of alternative offers.

Dorrie sighed. 'I do envy you,' she said, quite without envy.

Nance reached into the pocket of her smock.

'Before I forget, girls; there's some petition here. I understand we're expected to sign it. Undesirable literature, some such thing.'

'Who's it from?'

Nance squinted. 'The Society for the Protection of Community Standards. My God.'

'I don't know; someone has to set an example, surely?'

'Why, Dorrie?' Nance looked pleased with herself. 'Why, may I ask?'

'If we in books don't, who will?' Dorrie looked anxiously for support. 'Clodagh, are you signing?'

'I'll see.' For it could be easier to prevaricate. 'Just now I have to do the orders for the adolescent section. Suggestions, anyone?'

'I loved Ethel Turner at that age.' Dorrie, naturally.

'*Lord of the Flies*.' But Nance's cynicism was in part affected; and they knew it.

'I think Clodagh was really meaning fiction, Nance,' Dorrie explained with some care.

Was it a contradiction that, of these three women who had made of books a life's occupation, only Nance (less often as she became older) read anything apart from what was categorised on the library shelves as 'Popular Fiction'? It was rather that like so many, the majority perhaps, each had taken on such work less from choice than expediency; the chance of a job with adequate pay and prospects coinciding with their own freedom to take it up. Now bounded by books, none looked much further than the horizons of those with promising covers and happy endings. Not even writers of popular fiction however are always obliging; and if Clodagh discovered her prejudices and misconceptions gazing from the innocent print like her own reflection returned from a dangerous pool, she would uneasily skip or take the book back to the library unread, later to describe it to prospective borrowers as 'rather heavy going'. Yet she thought of herself as a reader and in a sense did love the books with which she lived, finding in resinous scents of gum and new paper, as she worked at the mending table, a kind of sensuous pleasure.

'Excuse me.' Nance pushed back her chair as though there was no more to be said. 'Who's doing the Story Hour this afternoon?' Nance knew. They all knew. It was another of those possibilities about which they could deliberate, pass time, and finally reach the foregone conclusion. Nance frankly disliked children; Dorrie's quavering Story Hours had the atmosphere of classrooms where the teacher has not showed up.

'I don't mind. Unless anyone else wants to?'

'Your funeral,' said Nance.

'Bless you,' said Dorrie.

When it rained the children came, sidling like part-broken colts, seeking shelter as much as entertainment. Then the library held an earthier scent, of damp clothing and wet hair. Clodagh liked to read to them. For they were outspoken and did not clothe their opinions in misleading dress; and if they were devious, it was transparently so. Clodagh, who was thirty-two and in many ways as reserved as an adolescent, believed them innocent and was drawn, not understanding that she found adult relationships less rewarding because she was wary of emotion. She would certainly have argued, had it been suggested that the self she projected was a selective version made up of what she felt was expected of her rather than what she was. For she had come to believe in that first and safer self, and allowed others to move over the surface of her nature and probe no deeper. That might have been why previous affections, friendships, had failed to grow; for honesty implied an offering, in turn risking rejection, and she would not take such chances. She was unaware of that though, and wondered when her relationships, denied the welding scar-tissue of truth, ceased to go further. But she did feel allied with the children rather than those bright or nondescript, young or ageing mothers who wore their wedding-rings with disregard; who, having seen their offspring into the respectable atmosphere of the Public Library and the hands of the quiet librarian in twin-set and pleated skirt, seldom lingered to listen. It was a source of relief to Clodagh.

She was reading from *The Wonderful Wizard of Oz*; and the children, preparing to enter with her into a place more magic than an old suburb on a wet afternoon, waited. She began to read.

'She's got a way with them,' Nance conceded.

Dorrie was helping her refill the trolley at the desk during the late afternoon lull. Briefly the two women paused under the humming fluorescent lights, drawn in by the thread of an old enchantment:

> Now while the tinsmiths had been at work mending the Woodman himself, another of the Winkies, who was a goldsmith, had made an axe-handle of solid gold and fitted it to the Woodman's axe, instead of the old broken handle. Others polished the blade until all the rust was removed and it glistened like burnished silver.
>
> As soon as he had spoken the Tin Woodman began to chop, and in a short time the tree fell over with a crash, while the scarecrow's clothes fell out of the branches and rolled to the ground. Dorothy picked them up and had the Winkies carry them back to the castle, where they were stuffed with nice clean straw; and behold! there was the Scarecrow, as good as ever, thanking them over and over again for saving him.
>
> Now they were reunited, Dorothy and her friends spent a few happy days at the yellow castle, where they found everything they needed to make them comfortable. But one day the girl thought of Aunt Em, and said:
>
> 'We must go back to Oz, and claim his promise.'

'Yes,' said the Woodman; 'at last I shall get my heart.'
'And I shall get my brains,' added the Scarecrow joyfully.
'And I shall get my courage,' said the Lion thoughtfully.
'And I shall get back to Kansas,' said Dorothy, clapping her hands.
'Oh, let us start for the Emerald City tomorrow!'

'And we'll be getting the sack,' Nance reminded Dorrie. Together they went on sorting the Rentals.

PHYLLIS GANT

Vegetable girls

— Look at you with all your talent
(— What talent?)
— working in a factory.
(— You could do worse than work in a factory.)
— You always used to beat Cassie Hepworth
(— I didn't.)
— at essays and that when you were at school. Yet she's a famous journalist now,
(— She gets a byline.)
— and you, you're just a factory hand.

Roberta's silent war. She is so hard and cold and silent at times that she reduces Ruth to tears or frenzied rage.

— Haven't you got anything to say, then? Ruth would cry.

And the father:

— Edgar Wallace wrote a hundred and fifty novels in twenty years. No one could have started with less. He was an orphan. He was saved from the workhouse by a fish porter who brought him up. He worked as a milk boy and he sold newspapers. And he wrote a hundred and fifty novels in twenty years.

Catch train 6:12 a.m. Out from the station, cross river, enter building. Enter building. Trees and sun and river, goodbye. See you — later. Much later.

Up the stairs; clock on.

Into changing room.

Strip to pants and brassière.

In the compound packed with female bodies, two hundred-odd different kinds of scent and soap or none, clean hair or dirty, armpits deodorised or rank; breath and warmth, suffocating; arms and legs and breasts and backsides.

Clothes stacked neatly or thrown on the benches around the room. Fighting and swearing and grabbing: That's mine!

The two English girls, scarlet, tuck their hankies between their breasts.

— Anyone'd think you had something different from the rest of us! No need to be shy here!

And they laugh at the English girls because they wear singlets even in the Melbourne summer.

And the Jew girl:
— It is like the Nazis.
Push and shove, fight your way to the counter. Everywhere, flesh. You cringe; it touches you, however, unavoidably.

The English girls and Roberta are among the last; they stand back, pressed against the benches, waiting till the worst of it is over.

Pass your clothes and handbag across the counter, under the grille. Watch where they are put in a pigeonhole, receive your uniform and your numbered ticket.

Clamber into the baggy pants (tied at the ankles) and top; put on the unbecoming cap.

There are different coloured uniforms for different classes of jobs; the lowest in the scale, and most numerous, are the greens for the girls on vegetables. Pink for those on canning. Yellow for the forewomen. White for the office girls — dress smocks, however; no baggy pants for them. They speak only to each other, and the bosses.

No talking during working hours; no leaving your place without permission.
— Where are you going?
— I'm going to the lavatory.
— Don't you know you can't go without permission? You come and ask me, and then we'll see about whether you can go or not.

And if you're lucky she scrawls a note, your pass to the dyke. And if she's got it in for you, or it's only half an hour to lunch time, she says you can wait.

The girls hate the forewomen. Hell, they all started off as vegetable girls; they forget awful quick.

Someone, prepared to suffer for it, one day delivers the short answer. When she is asked by one of the bosses to explain herself, she says she wasn't allowed to go the dyke and she couldn't wait, so.

The rule is relaxed a bit; some of the girls even get together there for a smoke and a few yarns.

Five minutes library break each day. You can change your book or just browse or read magazines. And you can take your book on out to morning tea with you and give it to the forewoman when you go back in to work and she puts it in one of the offices till lunch time or when you knock off.

The librarians are good; they help you if you don't know what to read. They talk to you nicely, too. It's a very good library. Roberta reads all her free time: walking from home to the station; riding on the train; even crossing Prince's Bridge in the crowd.

There is a view over city and river from the big windows in the cafeteria; there are roof-top games courts.

A trained nurse is always on duty. Oh, they look after you, all right. The nurse says whether you are sick enough to lie down for a while or should go home, or whether a couple of aspirin is all you need. Or a telling off.

— There's nothing the matter with you. Get back to work.

She sends Marge back on the crayfish when Marge is having a mis. Of course Marge can't say she's having a mis, because she's supposed to be single, so she just says she's got her pain and she feels crook and can she just have a lay down for a bit. Anyway, there is Marge at her bench, clutching at her belly and blood and goo running down into her shoes. They get her off to the sick bay then, all right. Roberta takes the shoes and washes the congealing blood out of them under the tap; someone has to.

There is a bonus system, a reward for good work — threepence, sixpence, ninepence extra in your pay packet. If you are a nice girl to the bosses it can run into shillings. You soon figure it out: it hasn't really got much to do with how good your work is, unless you're a real dud; Roberta knows she works well, she can see that she can keep up with Gina, for instance, who skites about her bonuses; but Roberta never gets more than ninepence — no, once she got a shilling. There is a sort of lucky dip, too, because every now and then someone gets a tenner or even twenty quid bonus in their pay, you just never knew. The instruction is that you are not to disclose the amount of your bonus to fellow workers; bloody artful.

Roberta earns less than half what she was earning before. But it's a good place to work if you don't count the strip show; she was lucky to get in.

Gina never has to go on onions; her lovely eyes are never red from onion tears. Dot says when she's crying from doing onions it makes her think sad thoughts, like having a row with her boy, and supposing she really is preg this time, and she has a real good cry.

And on cray: your hands get torn to pieces, even through the rubber gloves. But you can nibble bits of cray as you work.

Gina yawning her head off. Her Catholic cross lying beside the purpling teeth marks on her neck. Her hoarse whisper. And sudden silences as the forewoman comes around.

— . . . and there I was, Mama said, in the arms of a sailor, with my dress up around my waist and backside bare to the world. Mama dragged me inside and rolled him over to the gutter and left him there. I don't remember a thing. I went to confession yesterday, so I'm right for next Saturday night.

— Does your mother make you go?

— Hell, no. I want to go. That's something you Proddies'll never understand in a hundred years.

And it dawns on Roberta: Catholics accept that they're sinners; in fact, they're quite cheerful about it. Protestants can't get over it; they refuse to believe it's truly a part of themselves.

A union meeting is called after tea break and Sadie, the shop steward, hops up on to a chair and makes a speech. Roberta is amazed. Little Sadie, wiry and pale, standing there, beating a fist into her hand! And talking like a gramophone record. A girl! Roberta is all attention. And gazes at the serious faces. The sensible questions when Sadie asks, Any questions?

The upshot of it is, they're on strike.

— Why did they go on strike? says Ruth when Roberta arrives home at eleven o'clock.

Roberta doesn't know.

— But I thought you said the shop steward made a speech?

— Yes. She did. I don't know what she said, though.

— You *must* have been in a dream.

And, in a dream, Roberta goes off to work next morning, turns in the doorway, about to make her customary bolt up the stairs, and bumps into the picket.

— What the hell are you doing here?

— I've come to work, of course.

— You know we're on strike. What the hell's wrong with you? You better get out, fast.

— But how will I know —?

— You'll get a notice. Now beat it.

Time after time Roberta would miss her train. Once she did get to the checking-out girl early. But she found she had lost her ticket. And she couldn't remember her number. Of course.

— What's your number, cucumber? Well, where's your ticket? Why the hell don't you keep it in your pocket? I can't bloody-well get your clothes if I don't know your number, can I? You'll have to wait till last and see what's left.

— There they are, those there.

Almost within arm's reach.

— Says you. Now get out of the way. Next!

She gave up. Bolting for the train to find it just pulling out. Something always went wrong. She'd get caught up in the crowd. Or something. So she simply gave up. And went home on the next train.

In that half hour — she no longer even goes to the Station in the hope of getting the first train after work — she walks to the Gardens. Walking slowly, not minding anything, noticing everything. Red cannas; water lilies; the susurration of a hose left running in a bed of delphiniums.

Living in this now. Faint sounds of traffic: you could be miles away. The trees, the beautiful trees. Two students from the university, talking quietly. Their male voices at one with this calm world. A boy and a girl hand in hand by the lily pond.

SYLIVA ASHTON-WARNER

The writing road

Occasionally on a Friday night after shopping in Ruatoria other teachers' families might come back to our place to eat and drink and talk and generally get over the week and there's a scene here in our kitchen with the Shaw family and another family at our large scrubbed table and I'm at the stove browning the potatoes as Puppa used to do. The dialogue is lifting with the wine until John halts his knife and fork and says squarely, sanely, 'Sylvia, are you an artist?'

I go on browning and I think. A pseudo-artist would giggle, evade the point and play coy, but I've got to be true to myself. Cost what it may. 'Yes.'

It's the other family who giggle and smirk. Philistines. But not John and not Leslie either. Their knives and forks remain poised. 'How do you know?' from John.

'My mother told me.'

It's marvellous the thinking one can cover when looking the other way, like practising on the very good English piano in the infant room which has oversized acoustics with its echoes. Or with Keith helping me to put up a brush fence between the house and the plain on account of the unkind wind. He cut and brought the manuka while I stood it up and bound it. In our late thirties then, the terrible thirties, I looked the whole thing in the face and tried to work it out, for I wanted to be sure that life was worth living so that I could live it. At this intersection in the journey, detours lured all ways; art, music, writing or teaching and a big road sign with an arrow pointed to FEARFUL FORTIES AHEAD, and another read DECISIONS HERE. A road patrol on a horse advised briskly, And don't be too long about it. And get it right first time. You pass this way but once.

There were crowds of other young people in their thirties at the crossroads but they were less disposed to examine the road signs than to forge ahead along the highway nearest at hand. By the wayside was a long open shed with the words CHECK EQUIPMENT HERE so I went in. Any number of others sat thinking on the benches so I did too. I took things out of my haversack, a sugar bag with a strap like the one Keith had made on the river.

Any brains? Not a grain. Well, what did I have to replace it? Instinct. Right, so I'd cultivate this to serve as a compass. What next?

Art. Plenty there but functional only. Home-brewed. Music? Having met Lili Kraus face to face I'd soon learnt that an effective pianist is a transmitter really between the composer and the listener, like the seemingly cold piano star Solomon, whom I'd seen playing as though preoccupied with the veracity of his visa more than with the message of the music, or like the Austrian Artur Schnabel, delivering the composer intact through the keyboard in 'the way of most resistance' as even Madame had not wholly achieved, her woman's emotion having too much to say; whereas I was the most flagrant interceptor ever loosed on a piano, wearing the glory for my own adornment. All I had was the fever of the passion, unable to control the momentum of practice. Also, in the complete absence of any musical interchange I'd developed a personal interpretation and a rogue style that no professional would ever accept. 'I don't know,' from Sophie years later, 'that Sylvia has any technique, but it's very exciting when she plays.'

As for the poor old teaching, an excellent source of income no doubt but not my chosen work. On the other hand, it called on and mopped up everything I had: any art, music, writing, language, walking, dancing, study, responsibility, people, appearance, clothes and even falling in love. A marvellously comprehensive medium on an incomparable stage if only you had the aptitude and desire. Well, my record at the department supported what I'd always known myself, that I'd never be a good teacher, though you'd think I'd not been able to avoid picking up something about it after all these years of training and in classrooms, wouldn't you; but even though I'd thought I was doing well, after the inquisition with Bletcher and Flake, it was obvious that I wasn't. I was some kind of monstrosity that lost its way in schools. Temperament trouble.

Which left only writing, the last in the running, with its accompaniment, study. From Herbet Read I'd become acquainted with the nature of the mind of a child, any child, including me. True, I'd had but one short story actually published but I'd got the message. In my non-stop novel, unruly native imagery found a channel through which to surface, clearing out on its way the delirium of both music and paint to enrich the main stream. Writing siphoned off the effervescence of dreaming, the constant opposition party, and there was discipline required for that. You can't think at all with a heart in uproar over longing for Opal and Pan, neither of whom I'd heard from in years. You learnt what mail was when you knew what no mail was. When you're in love with life your vision becomes blurred with dreaming and the solutions were to be found right down in the lower caverns of the mind where emotion combusted. Coleridge: 'Touch the true voice of feeling and it will supply . . .' the answers.

Checking my equipment in the wayside depot I could at least see that for the journey not to be boring I myself had to be not bored, me the most profligate hedon who had ever squandered her inheritance. What was the operative condition then? 'And the greatest of these is charity.' Without that you'd be drier than the boulder beneath the soil of the plain. Juice had to rise like sap in the spring, the lubricant in making love. You'd have to be lightweight as the birds in the kowhai on the unreachable hills in order to lift up high in the sky above the white-lipped plain and to see like a morning skylark.

Replacing my gear in the haversack I returned to the crossroads. After all, one did have a choice and I'd take the writing road. The decision was no weight, it was water to drink for anyone going places.

Old age

DARA McNAUGHT

A Gift of Life

It was painful to breathe: that was the first thought. Her throat hurt all the way to her stomach, a harsh, raw hurt and her ribs were bruised and aching.

The second thought, struggling to form through the heaviness of confusion, was dismay that she had failed, and following them a rage that took her to the edge of consciousness. But her body betrayed her, as it did so often now, and she slid back into the darkness and slept.

When she woke again it was evening and she was alone. That was an illusion, in this place no-one would ever be alone. She must remember not to take it personally. Already the watchers had sensed she was awake and one of the young ones moved in swiftly, lifting her head to a cup of water. It hurt to swallow but her mouth was dry and the water cool and sweet.

'There now, Miss Williamson,' the nurse said, patting the pillow smooth. 'You just rest while I tell Sister that you're awake.'

She was surprised at the vehemence of her reaction to the girl's indulgent tone. I could be your grandmother, she protested silently, and looking at the young face wryly recalculated. She smiled weakly and watched the girl scurry away.

But the effort had been too much. She closed her eyes and rested, holding her breath against the pain in her ribs, hoping the Sister was busy and there was time to pull herself together. It was an abrupt leap from the secluded comfort of her own room and the drowsy anticipation of death, to the forced intimacy of a hospital ward. In another time she might have laughed at the mockery of her awaking, but now she had to quell the wash of self-pity.

Across the room, on another locker, a small cluster of candyfloss pink geraniums were bunched into a jar; as she looked a petal fell to the polished floor. Geraniums took a long time to die, even when they were cut they shed their delicate petals one by one and teased you with their fading colour. In this white-walled room they offered a hard reality and the reminder of another life.

Presently there were footsteps, soft and competent, and her head turned reluctantly to meet them. The flicker of relief must have been evident, for the nurse's watchful blue eyes shadowed a smile in return.

'I'm sorry to have you back with us, Miss Williamson.'
'So am I, Sister.'

The irony slid past them. Sister Pearce nodded, a crisp professionalism overlaying her sympathy.

'Doctor says you're to rest. Take as much fluid as you can. A stomach pump doesn't leave much.' Even less for a frail old lady like this one.

The nurse held her smile against the blurred scrutiny from the old woman, her mind shying away from the appeal she glimpsed behind the rheumy hazel eyes that were faded almost to grey. Grey with specks of yellow . . . Amy Williamson must have been fine-looking as a young woman, she thought, wondering what had been the twists and turns in a life that led it to such a bleak ending.

Remembering the fractured bone and the long months of rehabilitation, Sister Pearce said with more concern than she intended, 'Have you had much trouble with your hip?' 'No more than I could expect.' The grey eyes were watching her, without hope. 'Oh, it aches now and then and wakes me in the night, but I can live with that.'

So it was not the pain, nor the memory of it, that haunted those long hours of darkness.

'When am I to see the Doctor?'

'Doctor Fletcher? He has a Ward Round tomorrow morning, so I expect he'll see you then.' Sister Pearce nodded again, an oddly reassuring gesture, and returned to her office.

Miss Williamson slept fitfully, dreading the inevitable daybreak. Dr Fletcher came, mercifully, early, briefly and alone, an earnest young man only acquiring the sense of power he would hold all his life long. He smiled down into the grey eyes, hooded now, and was disconcerted by the suspicion that she was assessing him too.

'Miss Williamson? How are you feeling this morning?'

Anxiety tightened her face. He even smelled the healthy young animal he was, his cheerful curiosity thinly covered, his questions not yet entirely automatic. If I tell him the truth, she thought wearily, he'll want to know why.

He examined her carefully, his questions prodding, sharp reminders of her body's anguish. 'Just hold out your hands for me . . .' and noted their uncontrollable quivering that seemed an extension of her whole body. 'Just relax now. You live alone, I remember,' he said, folding away his stethoscope. 'How have you been managing?'

She smiled, wary, and somewhere an echo shrieked in silence and wept. 'A nurse calls each day, and a woman comes weekly to clean the flat. They bring me meals.' She said with quiet emphasis, 'It's my home. I am too old to change now.'

He nodded, careful to acknowledge only the words. 'We have been very concerned about you. You could have done yourself a lot of damage with those pills. We'll have to do something about you, Amy.'

For a moment he was startled as her eyes flared tawny with anger, then were veiled by the heavy lids with their sparse lashes. Then he stood, folding away his notes. 'Don't worry now, we'll take good care of you.'

She watched the young man retreat, sensing there was sympathy but not understanding. Her hands lay at rest on the bedcovers, their trembling stilled until she needed them to obey. The helpless suffocating frustration rose and died.

Shaken and alone, she stifled tears. Her ribs ached as her lungs moved, she was weaker than ever. She was also frightened, now there was time to think — lately there was too much time to think — and she had no illusions about what lay ahead. Dr Fletcher was not unkind, he was astute and firm, but he was not unkind. It was his sense of kindness that she dreaded most.

There would be no more chances.

Her mind closed down against the knowledge and she dozed, dreaming of summertime when she was young, long before her world became the stale perfumes of boarding houses and gasoline and the eternal clacking of typewriters, — dreamed of the river with its cold smooth pebbles and the willows' gentle shade against the staring sun, of the long dusty days when only the rata tree could offer unwithered its blood-red splashes, and of the evenings drowsy with warmth and the drifting fragrance of wild honeysuckle and trumpet lilies by the front porch. There were three voices then to share sadness and pride and secrets whispered with joy.

When the summer ended she was alone, as the chill of memory merged into winter, and in her dreams she shivered with the cold.

Miss Williamson woke again in the late afternoon, as Sister Pearce stood by her bed. Her anger had burned out, leaving only an infinite despair that would be read as acceptance.

Sister Pearce thought, watching, 'It's the same with the dying, they always know.'

The tired grey eyes studied her face and the wrinkled mouth tightened as the last hope flickered. She said, wanting to offer comfort and unknowingly confirming an execution, 'Is there something we can do for you, Miss Williamson? Something we can bring from your flat, perhaps?'

'No. Thank you.' The old woman's voice rasped against the effort, but the words carried the finality of absolute courtesy.

Sister Pearce turned to go. She paused by the glass of geraniums that were beginning to look scruffy, a sparse ring of fallen petals lay around it. With a small impatient gesture she brushed them aside into the rubbish bag and lifted the bunch from the glass, then slowly, almost reluctantly, settled them back.

She glanced back once at the still figure in the bed and was surprised at the intentness of the gaze. She nodded in her reassuring way.

'Don't worry,' she said. 'You won't be disturbed for a while. We'll take good care of you.'

She smiled again and left, and her footsteps sounded, soft and competent, long after she was gone.

JULIA MILLEN
Mother moves in

I picked Mum up from the airport late one Saturday afternoon, but nearly didn't make it home. At the bottom of our hill I misjudged a hairpin bend and bumped into another car. It was the first time I had ever done such a thing — a sure sign of the jittery state I was in. Eventually I got Mum settled into our spare bedroom with her pictures, books, and colour TV, which I hoped would provide her with some entertainment. Surprisingly, she made little comment about the new arrangement. Perhaps she was too tired and jet-lagged.

Faced with the necessity of living with Mother, knowing there was no alternative, I managed better than I could have imagined. Since there did not seem to be any drugs that would help her condition, and I had not heard of any psychiatric therapy for the over-70s, I determined on my own therapeutic programme. This was where the diary came in handy. In it I made general observations about daily events, frustrations, successes, and failures. It was therapy for me and also helped to show if there were any patterns in my mother's behaviour and any improvement or deterioration.

14 May 1981
Such an extraordinary thing senility is. Mum has absolutely no concentration for stories, doesn't read except for headlines, the odd phrases, but can concentrate to the exclusion of everything else on a few things — washing her clothes, her hair . . . She loves the outside balcony — pops in and out all day with her washing. I watch the concentration on her face as she does crosswords, or eats a boiled egg, and she seems quite unaware that I am looking. Her face and features are so little changed, it's sad to realise that she's almost in another world.

One of the first problems I tackled was the question of diet. My mother had not been eating regularly and this could have contributed to her mental breakdown. Marion, who is a lecturer in women's studies, had done some research on the dietary needs of elderly women, and had established that older people do not need less food than the young, as is commonly suggested. They need plenty of food and certain nutrients, particularly protein, calcium, and vitamins. Many old people have poor teeth and as a result tend to cut down on eating meat; they also reduce their intake of roughage, depriving themselves of important minerals and vitamins. Mum was a case in point.

She had poor teeth and disliked eating wholewheat bread, or anything that she described as 'scratchy'. It was very likely that she had been missing out on B-vitamins. To counteract this, my sister recommended that she have a daily quantity of brewer's yeast. The problem was how to administer the dose. Marion suggested that we mix it into a glass of fruit juice, that way ensuring that Mum also got her quota of vitamin C.

My contribution to my mother's dietary improvement was more basic. I tried to ensure that she ate plenty of good, ordinary food at regular intervals, but most particularly first thing in the morning. By bitter experience we had found she had a good appetite at that time and, if she did not eat then, she suffered (and we suffered) from her paranoia and agitation. Frank would take Mum a cup of tea in bed first thing — at about quarter to seven. That was supposed to keep her in bed and relatively content until I got her breakfast. I trained myself to get up early, no matter how I felt, rush into the kitchen and start boiling eggs and making toast. I found that Mum could quite happily eat an egg — even two eggs — and two pieces of toast thickly sliced and spread with butter and honey. This seemed to add up to a lot of carbohydrate, but I thought she needed it. She was very thin; in the last few years her clothes had gone down from size 16 to size 12.

The room my mother was occupying had a pleasant outlook; as she sat up in bed eating breakfast, she could look out at the fountain playing in Oriental Bay, or watch the planes flying to and from the airport. Sometimes she would do a crossword, although as time went on she found these more difficult. I often started them off for her by getting the first few clues.

Problems arose in the weekend when Frank and I wanted to sleep in. We soon got into the habit of locking our bedroom door, apart from anything else to keep her away from the telephone. Fortunately the telephone was in the hallway, just outside our bedroom door, with a connecting cord just long enough to pull the phone into our room. Several times I was glad we took this precaution. Diary entries for July of that year tell the story.

Saturday, 4 July
Woken from a deep sleep at 8.30 a.m. 'I must ring fraud,' she says through the door. Groan. 'No you can't,' I shout at her. Hassle, hassle. We told her to go and make us a cup of tea. Frank really annoyed at being woken, having been out to a late movie. So that was the morning shot . . .

Saturday, 25 July
Woken early again. Still dark. 'Must get in. Use the telephone.' 'Go back to bed, Mum,' I kept shouting. Only about 6.30 a.m. Three weeks since this last happened. Must try and see a pattern in this. Strain on us. Mum keeps going on about the gang of thieves . . .

Sunday morning
Woken again. 'Why is this door locked?' To keep you out, I felt like saying, but didn't. This time she was going to town. Frank got up and told her not to be silly — it's Sunday etc. Gave her a good talking to . . . Part of the problem is that she goes to bed so early — at about 8 p.m. on the nights when we go out. Then of course she wakes even earlier.

Sunday afternoon we went for a long walk up Hawkins Hill with some others. Took Mum and she walked all the way — though it's a good ten to twelve kilometres there and back from here, uphill too.

In those first few weeks, when not at work, I tried to spend a great deal of time with my mother. Fortunately my part-time job was in the afternoon, so I could spend most mornings at home. That way I could keep her occupied and try to divert her from disturbing thoughts and fears. Sometimes I sent her to the local dairy with a list of groceries to buy. We lived half way up a steep hill and always walked everywhere. This ensured my mother got plenty of exercise, which seemed to clear her brain. After a walk she seemed calmer and less agitated. Exercise, I have read, also helps old people to sleep better. That term I was giving music classes at the WEA, and would often take Mum with me, as well as to the library to collect records and books.

If I was not going out anywhere, I made sure that Mum had a good breakfast, then left her to do dishes and tidy the kitchen while I got on with my writing. Although my mother had never been particularly fussy about tidiness, she suddenly seemed to have developed an obsession about clearing things away. No sooner had Frank or I put down a cup and saucer than she whisked it away and began washing up. During the year Mum was with us, I hardly did any dishes and always came home to a clean and tidy kitchen. Well, I certainly wasn't going to dissuade her from that activity. Sometimes she also cleaned the sink and the basin and, very occasionally, the bath. But her cleaning efforts never extended much beyond that. I encouraged Mum to do all her own washing, except for sheets, and always got her to help me hang the washing on the line. Keeping an eye on washing hanging outside — getting it in if it looked like rain — was another thing she was good at.

My major concern at this time was what my mother would or would not do in the afternoons when I was at work. I soon discovered that when I was not there she did not eat. Only a couple of days after she moved in with us, I left to go to work at about 12.30 p.m.

'Now, make sure you have a good lunch,' I said. I got out a loaf of fresh bread, some butter, honey, cheese, and some lettuce.

'Yes, of course,' she said. 'I'll be all right.'

When I got home I found the kitchen tidy, everything put away, and not a single slice taken off the loaf. It seemed that she could not remember whether she'd eaten lunch or not. I suspected also that she did not even make herself a cup of tea. The teapot was always stone cold when I got home; if it had been used it would have still been slightly warm even a couple of hours later. This eternal vigilance was beginning to be a normal part of my life. Sometimes I would ring from work and remind Mum to have a cup of tea. But it made little difference. The moment she put down the phone, it seemed, her mind would go blank. Not always. A couple of times I rang and asked her to put the roast in the oven, and she managed that.

Eventually I managed to solve the eating problem with a bit of ingenuity. I noticed that Mum ate a lot of fruit from a bowl on top of the fridge. It annoyed me that she kept eating fruit all the time — especially when it was expensive — but would not eat bread and cheese. Once she ate nothing all day except five bananas! She seemed to eat only what she could see. So I devised a system to extend this habit to better purpose. If I had to leave home earlier than usual, I would make some sandwiches and leave them with a few biscuits or a slice of nut loaf on a plate, covered with a piece of clear plastic. I also bought some dishes with clear plastic lids, and in these I put a mixture of raisins, dried pineapple, ginger, and other dried fruit. By this means I not only made sure Mum was eating — something in addition to bananas — I could also monitor her intake. The system worked well — too well sometimes. Occasionally she would be starting in on the sandwiches as I left the house as half past eleven.

As well as worrying about what Mum didn't do while I was at work, I worried about what she *did*. Within a few days of her return from Adelaide she went to see her flat. I wondered if the visit would upset her; but no, my mother returned from the visit quite happy and reassured. 'It was all just as I left it — very neat and tidy.' I thought she might have been worried in case someone else had moved in. Perhaps she was afraid of losing her property, in the same way that she thought she had lost her money. But this didn't seem to be causing her concern.

'And do you still feel happy about selling the place?' I asked.

'Yes, I've seen a real-estate agent and asked them to put it on the market.'

'Good on you,' I said. 'That's positive thinking.'

Sometimes in the afternoon Mum went downtown. Although her bank was at the opposite end of town — a good three kilometres walk from where we lived — she did go there a few times, but nothing disastrous happened.

15 July 1981

Mum a bit jittery this morning. Ate two eggs, but couldn't raise the concentration for the crossword. Off to town to — guess where — the bank at about 11. I refused to get her a taxi, so she walked. Was back by midday. She often gets a bus from Willis Street. Apart from insisting on going to the bank, she was all right.

Although I kept hoping for signs of improvement, I couldn't help noticing Mum was still very muddly and forgetful about bills and documents. One diary entry, for July 1981, shows me once more engaged in trying to sort out her income tax.

> What a morning! Started trying to sort out bits and pieces of Mum's for tax. Discovered in the process that she had lost??? her post office passbook. Great to-do. I sent her down to the post office. She got a form and tried to fill it in. I went back with her and we did our best. I went crook at her — felt guilty afterwards. In some ways it is fortunate I have the job — takes my mind off things at home.

A week later:

> Thought for a few ghastly minutes today that she'd lost her cheque book, but no — thank God. Started to give her a lecture about losing things and poor old Mum said, 'I'm worried I'm losing my mind'. Sad really.

In between her moments of madness were patches of sanity. My mother was quite practical and had always been a resourceful type of person. I was surprised and delighted when I came home one day to find she had been exercising another skill. As I made my way up the hill towards the house, I noticed smoke coming from the chimney and assumed that Frank must have come home early. But when I got inside I found that it was Mum who had got the fire going. It was lovely coming home to a cheerful fire burning in the grate, and I said so. I took care to notice if she was safety-conscious and was soon in no doubt of that. She would go outside and use a small tomahawk to chop up kindling, then set the fire — as though it were a work of art. While it was burning she fussed around the fire, making sure that logs did not fall out. She was more careful about it than we were.

Recognising this practical bent, and working on my theory 'play on your strengths', I tried her out on another skill. I asked Mum if she could mend a fuse that had blown on our switchboard. 'Of course I can.' I found her glasses, some fuse-wire, and a pair of pliers. Within about ten minutes she had mended the fuse.

People often warned me about security and safety problems with old people — their tendency to leave doors unlocked, heaters burning, or the gas on. I never found it a great problem. Mum, herself, always double-checked that doors were locked. The only trouble we had was with the electric-jug elements; she burned out two in the time she was with us, but we could have alleviated that problem by buying a safety element.

There was another angle to the problem of leaving my mother on her own in the afternoons: she often got herself into a dreadfully anxious state. This happened particularly in the winter, when it got dark early. A familiar greeting on my return home from work was: 'Oh, thank goodness you're here.'

'Why, what's happened?' At first I feared the worst.

'I thought I'd been left here all on my own.'

'Don't be silly, Mum. You know I always come home at this time.'

But in fact she didn't know. A person with severe memory loss has no past and no future; nor can they think and reason in the way most people do. Unlike a normal person who would have looked at the time and thought, 'Now it's half past three, my daughter should be home in two hours,' my mother, with her impaired brain function, could not reason in that way. Not fully understanding or accepting this fact, I was often impatient with her. But I did make some allowances.

While she was living with us, I tried to get home regularly at 5.30 p.m; I no longer went out with friends after work. Knowing that it was important, I did not mind very much — it didn't seem too great a sacrifice. I really did want my mother to be as happy and secure as possible. Occasionally I found that she had given me up for lost and cooked herself an egg and a few potatoes. Usually, in this case, I just gave her another meal, or added what she'd cooked to ours. But it was becoming obvious that five hours was far too long for my mother to be left on her own; she could not be sure in her own mind when I would be home.

What were the possible solutions, I wondered? Perhaps in a village or small town community, people would arrange for a neighbour to pop in during the afternoon to make a cup of tea and sit down with a lonely old person for half an hour or so. All our neighbours worked during the day; in any case, there was no one around whom Mum knew. Only later did I discover that the social work department at the hospital could arrange for a regular visitor — someone who could have handled any difficult situation that may have arisen. In time Mum might have got used to those visits; she might even have welcomed them. But at the time I didn't even consider such a possibility. It seemed to me unlikely that Mum would adapt to a stranger coming into the house. At times she did not even recognise me.

One evening when Frank had got in early and was cooking dinner, I decided to have a bath and wash my hair. As often seemed to happen — a source of increasing irritation — while I was in the bath, Mum came in. Next morning she said to me with a little laugh, 'I keep thinking about the girl who came in last night and had a bath.'

'That was me, Mum.'

'Really?'

'Who did you think it was?'

Poor Mum. Later she told Frank about it with a laugh at herself. She still had moments of lucidity.

One project Mum and I worked on together had been started by Marion when Mum was with her in Australia. Mum was to knit herself a cardigan to replace the shabby, old one she wore all the time. My sister was a good knitter and had got the project under way. Unfortunately I was not as good at knitting as Marion was, but every evening I would get out the half-finished cardigan. 'Okay, Mum, you knit a couple of rows and then I'll knit a few.' She could still knit, and would start willingly, but keeping her at it was another matter. I often had to pick up dropped stitches for her and would sometimes carry on the knitting myself. I'm not sure which of us knitted the most, but after several weeks it was nearly finished. Mum speeded up remarkably when she saw we were nearing completion. I got her to sew the pieces together, then I had to do some — for me — difficult things, like picking up stitches for the neck-band and making buttonholes. One morning, before I had even got up, Mum finished the work off and sewed on the buttons. The result was a creditable slate-blue cardigan — an achievement for one rather senile woman and her daughter, a hopeless knitter.

This occupational therapy provided a useful addition to my mother's wardrobe. Perhaps because of her deteriorating mental state, she had bought no new clothes for a long time. Everything was old, worn out, or far too big for her now she had lost so much weight. I wanted to improve her wardrobe, to make her feel and look better, but it was hard work trying to persuade her to buy anything new. I found such shopping expeditions frustrating, especially when my precious writing time was being taken up.

'Why don't you buy it, Mum? It looks lovely on you.'

'Well — it is very expensive.'

'Not really. Not for a good dressing-gown.'

'Well — I'll think about it. Come back tomorrow.'

'But we're here now. I haven't got time to come to town every morning.'

In one instance the saleswoman — a kindly middle-aged person — sized up the situation and succeeded where I was failing.

After that I seldom took Mum shopping with me, but instead got the money from her and bought the necessary garment myself. To make sure that she would accept new clothes, I usually bought something similar to what she already had. I discovered that, if she was given anything too different, she could not accept it as hers and would never wear it. Or — as happened a couple of times — if I lent her something of mine, she would lose it; presumably, having taken the garment off, she failed to recognise it again. That way I lost a cardigan and a headscarf. It was best to stick to the familiar.

15 July 1981

Nipped into town and bought Mum a jersey. So far this year I have bought, or got her to buy: 1 dressing gown, 1 nightie, underwear, sheepskin slippers, 2 jerseys (white and blue), and skirt (grey woollen). All essential as old ones completely worn out or — in the case of the only two skirts left — miles too big. What an effort it is to even get that much organised. Sad, as she used to care so much about her clothes.

Gradually I replaced the worn-out or too large garments and made sure the old ones were thrown out. I think Mum felt better with some fresh new clothes; I certainly felt better seeing her well dressed. And still I was optimistic that all these things — diet, exercise, occupation, company, new clothes — would somehow restore my mother to health and sanity.

MATARENA RENETI
(As told to Stanley Roche)

Of Love and Death: Matarena's Story

I am an old lady of sixty-seven and I still want food for knowledge. This little knowledge I have, this biblical knowledge in the Ringatu faith, this is giving me the courage to speak into this machine for the young people of the country to hear.

I remember my life as a very hazardous one. Poverty, poverty. A family so numerous living in one little wee room, a one-roomed shanty made of whatever was handy, mere coverings on the sides of the old corrugated iron roof. No floor in the shanty, an earthen floor and sacking at the window. But the cooking compartment is separate from this. That is the rule! You never sleep where the cooking is being done.

I remember then there was a number of us and though we are poor there was always laughter and joy amongst our family. Sometimes we laugh so much that people going along the road turn to look. They think we are laughing at them. But we are not, we are only young and laughing.

I was the baby, the youngest. I lost my mother when I was born. My father he was a very loving person I was told — kindly. Everyone speaks well of him. I think I just remember him and then he died too. I was brought up by the older girls and boys that was in the family. They fostered me from one to another till they all died too.

As time grew on I came to know the story behind my childhood. I knew then there was twenty-six in our family from one mother and father. And now today out of that twenty-six I am the sole survivor.

My very eldest sister, the eldest of the lot, is Merepeka. She is mother to us and father and grandmother and everything. She lives away from us with her husband at Whakatane. Living in the house at Te Teko with us is another sister, Amati. At the beginning of my memory Amati is taking care of us.

There is a swampy place near where we live with flax galore. My sister takes the young shoot of the flax and makes a boat of it for me. She puts sails on it and it drifts away down the stream. It makes a pretty toy. My brothers and sisters make whips and piu-piu.

I remember one brother, a big strong, hefty boy. He is full of fun. Then the sickness came and it just played on him. He got weaker and weaker and weaker. My sister used to carry him on her back. His legs hung down almost to touch the floor. I don't know whether they stuck then to the Maori way of thinking. The things they were doing on him I don't know. Before I was old enough to know how anything was, that boy was dead.

There was another one, another brother. He was near me in the family, two years older. He was the very clever one, then the sickness comes on him too. By this time my sister was beginning to come round to a different way of thinking. The doctor told her, 'That boy is too clever.' He has brain trouble, brain fever and that is what he died of.

Death never ceases for me. The grief, the sadness are very strong. Each new death brings back all the previous ones, and I get overcome by it. When it is bad, really bad, I sit on my own and close the door and pray a prayer. After a while strength comes to me and I feel better.

Here where we lived at Te Teko there was a sprinkling of families, not many, not very many, but all related. Ours was the biggest family of all. There may be families of eight, nine children but to the number of ours — no.

The faith and knowledge of the Church, Te Kooti's Church, is always with us. I think it is inborn in the child of a Ringatu-born child. We learn the words of the service, the Karakia, through being with it all the days of our life. There are no papers, no books; we learn by ear as the generations have done before us. The service speaks to our deep-down feelings, the waybackness of our true Maoritanga.

I was a girl of seven when I started school at the Te Teko school. My sister Amati had a tubercular back. I have to dress her back before I go to school in the morning. When I come home for lunch, dress her back again, and again when I come home at night before going to bed. I wasn't told to do these things but I knew what was to be done and that I must do it.

School. There is a beautiful old gentleman with a white flowing beard. I love that old gentleman. He tries to speak Maori for our benefit, to help us, to cross the meaning over to us so that we understand. I hardly know a word of English but I catch on quick. He teaches us the easy way.

I jump classes from one to the next. It is so easy, easy for me to catch up to what the teacher is telling us. It is just like as though I am given this knowledge. And I want it! I want so much to learn. If there is something we are learning one day and we don't finish it I cannot wait to get to school the next day to see how it ended. I want to know all about it, no matter what it is. I never miss a day. When the year is over I get a certificate for no absences. Every year at school I am getting that certificate. I keep on jumping classes. Sometimes twice in one year I jump. Girls that have been at school before me I have left far behind.

There are Pakehas in my class. I see them all with nice things. Nice clothes, nice pencil cases, nice playlunch. Sometimes I am sent to the teachers' houses or other Pakeha houses to fetch things. I see what they have in their houses and I am embarrassed and ashamed for our poverty. What have we in our home? Nothing but cobwebs! Such a state, I knew it wasn't right! The others in our family they never felt it as I felt it. I was very young and very foolish. I was whakama of the Pakeha. As I grew older I got wiser.

The teachers at school, they are sometimes very offensive to those Pakeha boys and girls. The teacher even holds my work up for being a Maori girl and the English I was having on my paper had no mistakes. The Pakeha with their own language had all the mistakes, 'Why are you not doing it right?' she says, 'And this Maori girl is doing exactly what you should be doing.'

Then my feeling of inferiority began to fly away. In my little brain I see the way to stand even with the Pakeha. I have my Pakeha mates in the class and we all play together. Rugby, I play rugby with the boys, and tennis and hockey and tug-of-war. Whatever is played, I played. I loved sport and I was good at it. And playing with the Pakeha boys and girls the shyness is knocked away from me.

The gentleman with the white beard, he was in his retiring age and it was not very long after I started school that I missed him. He had gone away and new teachers had come in.

That was when the caning started. In the classroom we speak in English, in the playground we speak our Maori tongue. But now — no! No! We are not to speak our Maori at all, not in the classroom, not in the playground, and we are being caned because in the playground we use our mother tongue.

I couldn't leave my Maori! I couldn't! No, no man on earth can take that away from me! They caned me, they caned me, time and time again. But it never stopped me. When the teacher hit me I swore back at him in Maori.

'What are you saying? What is that you are saying?' I wouldn't tell him. I couldn't swear at him in English; I couldn't embarrass him that way. Oh, but if I had been older, if I had been then as I am now! It was wicked, wicked! A shameful thing to beat their language out of little children, to try and take our language away from us!

And today they pay people to teach us back again the language they stole.

I was about ten years old and in Standard 4 when my sister Amati died. Now all my brothers and sisters had gone except only Merepeka and me, the eldest and the youngest. So she fosters me and I go to live with her at Whakatane. Merepeka. She is thirty — forty — years older than me. She is stone deaf. When I speak she reads my lips. She is mother to me, a good mother, but life is not easy. There are hardships.

I must help her on the farm, digging potatoes, doing land work. Before I go to school in the morning I have to milk the cows, clean up, take the cream to the gate, and then walk four, five, miles to the Maori school at Paroa. But a walk like that is nothing to children then. It was lovely. There were quite a few of us and you catch up with your friends and you play along the road and before you know where you are, you are at school. Oh, it's nice! And school, I am happy at school always.

It is at home there are hard things. There is my brother-in-law and I must fit in with his ways. But his ways are not all good. There are some bad ways. He said to me things he shouldn't have said. What was I to do? He was so much older than me, a man to be respected. It was very nasty.

In the end I had to tell my sister. I had to say it to her in front of him, out loud, for her to read my lips.

She wouldn't believe me! She hardly ever believes anything against her husband. I said, 'That's all right. If you don't believe me there is One that will. I am telling the truth.' Then my brother-in-law had to stop because I told it in his face in front of her.

Merepeka tries to teach me to make a kit or a hat. But I have no patience with it. The patience I have I took up in education. My sister was so disgusted with what I was doing she just grabbed it out of my hands and chucked it in the rubbish-hole. I was fifty years old before I learned to do those things. But now I am so thankful that I can honestly say I can do something Maori with my Maori fingers.

My sister is a good mother to me, a strict mother and I had to go along with her. If I disobey her, I did have her lashings. Whew!

The one thing I don't like is to miss school. One day she tells me not to go. I am to stay home and look after someone else's child that day. You know, I disobey her. I go to school. I leave that kid at home by itself. You know those leather stockwhips, long thick stockwhips? She hits me on the face and round the body and on my feet till I was bleeding all over. My brother-in-law, he had to come and take the whip off her. She was that mad at me for disobeying her. Well, she was quite right. Today I wouldn't blame her for doing it. I'd do the same as she did to me. I deserved it. I loved that education so much I didn't care if I was on the receiving end of that whip. Because I wanted education more than anything else in the world.

It was at Paroa school that the inspectors came and examined me. Then the teachers went to my sister and they asked her could I go to the Victoria College in Auckland. That is the Maori college for girls. There is nothing to pay — clothing, education, food — it will all be paid for me. I have won a bursary for three years. Whew! All my hunger for knowledge to be satisfied. That's what I wanted, that school! *I wanted it!*

The tohungas, the priests of the Church, discuss it and the elders. And soon Merepeka tells the teachers I am not to go.

'But there is nothing to pay,' they say again and again. 'Nothing to worry about.' They think she doesn't understand that and she is refusing because of poverty. But it is not that at all. It is the family thing we had, one dying after the other, mother, father, all the brothers and sisters. Just the two of us alive, Merepeka and me. Merepeka has no children. She is barren.

To save the two of us and to give issues from the youngest, me, she had to keep faith in having me in her hands until the day I marry. To keep me within the Church, never to let me out. I was to be the secluded one. I had to have a sheltered life. Just within the circle of the Church. Only never out of their hands, never out of their ways, out of their hands, away to school, away to anywhere else but her and the Church. So there will be issues from me, from the family of my father and my mother.

Whew! I cried and cried and cried. I cried till I have no more tears. But there it was! There it was!

Slowly, slowly, as I grew older my thoughts changed. No, I think, it must have been His will. His way too. He wanted me that way, as I am without learning. He wanted for me the hard life I have led. Ae!

When I left school we stayed on for a long while working the farm which was my brother-in-law's land. And then my sister began to want to come back to our forebears' land, and that is in Te Teko here. So we up and packed everything and with my horse and my dog, I drove the cows back home.

It was lovely in those days. I can remember it. Me and my horse and my dog driving all those cows. I was fifteen then, it was 1928. I used to work like a boy in those days and my companions were boys. They see me driving the cows those boys, and they ride up and watch me. And when they see I am all right they just let me go by.

When the cows are here, I ride back and bring all our gears and stuff over. See those trees back where the orchard is, that's where the old home used to stand. We farmed fifty, sixty acres here — just me and my sister. We had other properties too. We were quite well off in that respect, in land. But of anything else — nothing!

People from the county council and the government offices, they tell us, 'Get this, get that. Do this, do that.' But I didn't know what they were talking about. Oh, it was a job, a struggle, because of our ignorance. We know how to milk our cows and send our milk to the factory and how the cheques come in return. But the rest! The income tax returns! The rebates you could claim! The tax concessions, the bank statements, the advances! How on earth could a Maori understand these things without any knowledge of Pakeha things at all!

The Maori Affairs, they had officers there that were supposed to help us and educate us. Well, there were some good ones and plenty of no-good ones and some of those boys were doing nothing but educate their own pockets. A lot of farmers right along this road lost thousands and thousands of pounds. Everywhere Maori famers were going down the drain paying what they shouldn't have paid at all. And where was the Maori Affairs that should have told them and helped them?

How was I to survive, to not go broke? The only support I had was this thing on my face of being with people, of being friendly. Luckily for me I knew this lovely man that was very neighbourly. Not a Maori, not a Pakeha either. He was from somewhere else, some other country. I had befriended his family and this was the good return I got.

'You save those statements from the factory,' he told me. 'You file them, no matter what. They don't send you them for nothing. They are important in days to come.' So he told me how not to be caught, to be aware of those things. And so we survived because of that kindly man. But even so I never knew about the petrol rebate and I was one that was using hundreds of gallons for the truck and the tractor and the car.

When I was old enough, eighteen or twenty, they chose a husband for me. It was a match-marriage. Their choice, not mine. The elders, the tohungas, they just told you and you have to go along with what they think. No choice at all, never if you want to or not. If they say it, that's it.

So I married him and soon there is a baby coming and when she is born I am like a wild animal so fierce, so protecting. No one can come near her, no one is to touch her. For always with my babies I have the feeling I might lose them. I cannot forget the loss of my own brothers and sisters, my own mother and father. I had that fear at the back of my mind at all times, always. So I hold her close and guard her.

But that man, the match-marriage man, I don't like him at all. And after the baby has come I get sick of putting up with him. I said to my sister,' 'I'm not having HIM anymore. Anyone can have him! You can have him! But I'M not having him.' So I kicked him out, got rid of him, dissolved the marriage.

Then I made a promise to that baby. I will never look at another man, never! Never will I make a rift between that baby and myself. Never will I take another man to make a third party of one of them.

But after all my good care the baby is sick. There is this beautiful doctor, this old Doctor Appleby, every day he comes to see my baby. Even at night he comes out to look at her. One night he comes to see if I care enough for that baby to let him take her away from me to the hospital. He was thinking he might have to. I tell him I will do anything he says for that baby.

But he looks at me and he says, 'No, it's all right. The baby will have better care here.' He trusts me better than he trusts the hospital. With his care and my care that baby has a better chance. So she was left with me — and she was getting better, she was recovering, she was going to be well.

Then suddenly she develops an abscess. The doctor comes and looks at her and he must take her away from me. That was when I lost her. *I lost her.* My baby died in hospital.

That was a bad time. That was the worst time of all. Then I wanted to die. I wanted to go with my baby, be with my baby. I blamed myself for her death. Because I had done wrong. I had gone against what the old people wanted. I had broken the match-marriage, the marriage they made. I was punished for it. Everything was gone, everything. I wanted to die.

Luckily for me I still had my sister-mother, my Merepeka. She told me, 'No!' She was very religious and she had taught me to be religious too. 'It is no use crying over that baby,' she said. 'He has given you that but it is something He is taking away again. That is not supposed to be for you. That is how He wants it. So just stop being like that.'

She was a good mother and a strict one and I knew all the things she was saying were right. I had to go along with her. She got me out of that wish to die. She talked me out of a lot of things.

A year passed, two, and the darkness began to go away from me.

There had always been this other man. He was a relation of mine. I had known him all my life, never not known him. He used to live with my sister and brother-in-law and me when I was a child. I knew him, he was two, three, times my age. My brother-in-law and he used to go out sometimes and they would be hourangi. Hourangi is drunk. Late at night they'd come back and I am fast asleep. Then he would come and kiss me on the cheek and I didn't feel him. I am still asleep. All the time he has been doing that without me knowing.

I had always liked him, but not enough to marry him. But now I know he is the man I want. I felt rotten because I had promised I will never look at a man again. And I felt rotten because I wanted myself to be fresh for the man I want. But I loved that man so much I got this pain. I got this pain.

I said to my sister's husband, 'I want him. Go and get him. *I want him!*' Just like that — '*I want him!*'

Soon as I said it, my sister's husband went to him and he knew, he knew. All along he had felt like that for me. But he was thinking of his age — that I wouldn't have him. That I'd kick him out. Naa, he wouldn't come to me like that! But when my brother-in-law said, 'She wants you,' he knew and he came. And he knew how I felt for he felt that way too. And he had wanted me all the time.

The wedding was here — right here in the old house that used to stand by those trees. We just had what these young people call 'the holy tin-can'. The tin-cans going and the beer running. Then when that part is over we go to Paroa to have a service at our wharenui there — the meeting house — which is always for us the Church too.

They just married us as we were, in the blankets, sitting round the wharenui. We had a service, all the priests and all the visitors sitting round together and every one had each to say their prayers for us. Ae, it was lovely! I'd rather that than those big white weddings. His family, my family, everyone is there, so close and intimate. There is nothing can make you closer than the words of God. Nothing. No matter how good or rich you are, that won't make you any closer. In fact it will make you go wider apart. Money is the worst thing for putting people apart. But the words of God will draw you closer to people, to Church, to unity in all.

Well, after Bill and I got married we had these children one after the other. Year after year. In one year we had two, two in one year. One was only eleven months old and we had another one. Everyone used to laugh about it. That's the limit, eh? Two babies in one year.

But they are delicate. They are all delicate. Oh dear, you don't know what I had to put up with! Miscarriages sometimes. Sometimes they are born — big beautiful babies. One day beautiful, healthy — the next day very unhealthy, dying! I think if only I can get them to a year old they have a chance. But even after that it is always a case of careful nursing. There was all sorts of complications. Everything goes wrong for them. They have no resistance.

One day my cousin, the eldest daughter of our Koro, our chief, she offered to adopt one of my babies. She thought maybe having one of them might relieve me of having too much to do.

'No, no,' I say, 'it's all right. I can manage. It's just a natural happening to me.' Because I was hapu again.

But she said, 'No, I would like to have your baby.' She asked for the one that was still in my puku. So I said all right.

Time went on and it came nearer my time to have the baby. Then she came to me. Her father, the Koro, had told her not to take the baby. My babies were no good, he said. It might die on her hands. They are sickly children.

It was true. No matter how much doctoring or care I took after them it was always the same. I thought, 'I am not to be blessed with children at all. Never.'

But that baby, that one that was in my puku then, he did survive. Once I almost lost him. Two of them were *very* sick one night. Then there is one dead and the other about dying. But he pulled through, he lived. He was the first of my children to live to be a man.

My husband worked for the Ministry of Works. Every morning early he used to ride away on his horse. Later he was promoted onto machineries. Then we have to move to distances with our family and live in the public works huts.

Another time we live in a little house of our own, a one-bedroomed house across the river. My brothers and sisters, my family, are all dead, all gone, but Bill was the eldest of his and kept watch over them, looking after them. Often one lot or another comes and lives with us. Sometimes we used to have two, three families under our one roof.

We are lucky in having implements and tools to make our own gardens. An acre of kumara patch, an acre of potato patch and the rest under pumpkin, water-melon and whatever. Mothering, nursing my children, cooking, washing and the gardens to tend as well. Under rough conditions. It is hard. You have to be up with the birds.

There was only one tank. Before sunset you have to carry the water up from the drain in four-gallon kerosene tins, till you have filled the copper. You boil it up to have water to give the children. Then right up to the middle of the night I'm still doing my washing and hanging it on the line. People say, 'How early you've got your washing on the line!' But that's the midnight's wash that's hanging there.

No electricity of course — candles and kerosene lamps. We had a car but it was a working car, never there for me to drive around in. There was a horse. I used to catch it and harness it to the spring cart to go out and get our stores. Our young children, they loved that driving out in the spring cart.

Apart from that I hardly ever went beyond the gate. All that old inferiority complex came back on me because of the house, because it can never, never compare with a Pakeha's house. Then, in those days, you go in any Pakeha's house and it is always different to a Maori house. It was only much later that I got all this that you see around me now.

They were hard years, hard for me anyway. Sometimes I think I will never live through them. Yet I was not unhappy. I didn't know any other way. I had been brought up the hard way and so secluded. I had to be happy with what I had. I had no other choice. I did not know there was another choice.

I had fourteen children and four of them lived to grow up. Now there are only three. But I am always thanking Him for giving me that much. For giving me these three. And out of them I have got — how many? — twelve grandchildren.

For these grandchildren I am crying out for what I missed out on. For knowledge and education. That is what they are going to need in the life they have to fight.

Twelve grandchildren. Ae! And I thought I was one never to be blessed with children.

I think I've done marvellous.

MORE ABOUT PENGUINS

For further information about books available from Penguin please write to the following:

In New Zealand: For a complete list of books available from Penguin in New Zealand write to the Marketing Department, Penguin Books (N.Z.) Ltd, Private Bag, Takapuna, Auckland.

In Australia: For a complete list of books available from Penguin in Australia write to the Marketing Department, Penguin Books Australia Ltd, P.O. Box 257, Ringwood, Victoria 3134.

In Britain: For a complete list of books available from Penguin in Britain write to Dept EP, Penguin Books Ltd, Harmondsworth, Middlesex UB7 0DA.

In the U.S.A.: For a complete list of books available from Penguin in the United States write to Dept DG, Penguin Books, 299 Murray Hill Parkway, East Rutherford, New Jersey 07073.

In Canada: For a complete list of books available from Penguin in Canada write to Penguin Books Canada Ltd, 2801 John Street, Markham, Ontario L3R 1B4.